Palgrave Explorations in Workplace Stigma

Series Editor
Julie Gedro
Empire State College
Rochester, NY, USA

This series is a call to action for organizations to not only recognize but include, support, and value employees of all walks of life, regardless of the social stigmas that might create material, affective, or psychological divisions between them and their ostensibly "normal" counterparts. It fills the gap in scholarship surrounding the difficult issues employees or job seekers might face based on their demographics, life events, or other factors. The series explores issues such as mental illness and wellness; and alcohol and drug addiction and recovery. It explores the complex and often times nuanced issues that face sexual minorities, or those who are formerly incarcerated, or military veterans in the context of employment or career decision making.

Through rigorous research and contributions from the foremost scholars in human resources, books in the series will provide an in-depth exploration of each population and challenge HR scholars and practitioners to effectively consider and embrace these explorations. and consider expanding their own awareness. The series speaks on behalf of anyone who has ever been affected–directly or indirectly–by discrimination or exclusion in the context of work, and promotes a positive, productive, and purposeful working environment for employees at all levels.

More information about this series at
http://www.palgrave.com/gp/series/15458

Stefanos Nachmias • Valerie Caven
Editors

Inequality and Organizational Practice

Volume II: Employment Relations

Editors
Stefanos Nachmias
Nottingham Business School
Nottingham Trent University
Nottingham, UK

Valerie Caven
Nottingham Business School
Nottingham Trent University
Nottingham, UK

Palgrave Explorations in Workplace Stigma
ISBN 978-3-030-11646-0   ISBN 978-3-030-11647-7   (eBook)
https://doi.org/10.1007/978-3-030-11647-7

Library of Congress Control Number: 2019934470

Cover illustration: imagedepotpro

This Palgrave Macmillan imprint is published by the registered company Springer Nature Switzerland AG.
The registered company address is: Gewerbestrasse 11, 6330 Cham, Switzerland

Preface

Managing diversity and equality has generated an enormous amount of tools and frameworks advising organisations as to how key issues could be effectively addressed; however, there is still no agreement as to how we need to recast organisational attitudes and make real and sustained progress towards addressing discrimination in the workplace. Professional and academic literature is too complex to the point that it is difficult to recognise how organisations could positively address workplace inequalities. We know that a highly diverse organisation that is free from discriminatory behaviours and with appropriate levels of good human resource practices promotes inclusion, and eventually leads to performance gain. However, we need to acknowledge that changes in employment relations, social stigmas, cultural differences, organisational realities and demographic changes put pressure on organisations across the globe to not just consider these challenges, but to make significant changes in the way they manage and treat people. It is essential for everyone to be treated equally in the workplace with access to appropriate levels of support and resources. Of course, 'reality is a lot messier than that' (Burrell 2016), but our goal is to stimulate a positive debate around key diversity issues related to work and welfare. As the Chartered Institute of Personnel and Development (CIPD) (2018) argued, business leaders have now the opportunity to champion diversity away from easy financial returns by focusing on the numerous benefits that diversity and inclusion can bring to organisations. This is the leitmotif of this volume, aiming to provide insightful knowledge on how we can further promote visible and non-visible difference in modern organisations.

Our intention in assembling this volume has been to assess how organisations manage or generate hidden inequalities and question whether the current legislative framework offers adequate solutions to contemporary organisational issues. Various laws and legislations offer some support to promote equality in the workplace. However, many areas of organisational and individual activities are not covered by the existing legal framework, thus serving as an exclusionary mechanism upon individuals' dignity and ability to complete work-related tasks. This shows the need to accept and support employees who are experiencing any form of unseen social stigmas and inequalities in the workplace. Hence, we have specifically used the term *hidden* in our volume title to provide an explicit label and assess how organisational practice and purpose reinforce readily unseen potential differences amongst individuals. This volume acts as a critical platform to unveil hidden inequalities with employment practices. Our emphasis was to produce a new volume that offers practical and strategic insights for practitioners', managers', students' and policymakers' thought-provoking positive dialogue. This has been achieved through the selection of a unique blend of contributors across the globe. Their experience and understanding of hidden inequalities have enabled us to produce this volume, but most importantly to put at the forefront anyone who has been affected by social stigmas and discrimination. Raising awareness around hidden inequalities is a great achievement as new knowledge can contribute to remove hurtful, offensive and unacceptable discriminatory behaviours and practices from the workplace. This is the ideal outcome; however, we still have a long way to go to ensure equality for everyone.

We hope that readers will enjoy reading the content of this volume and appreciate the inclusive positive arguments expressed in this volume. Hopefully, the numerous case studies, examples and insightful stories can support organisational change in the future.

Nottingham, UK   Stefanos Nachmias
                                                                  Valerie Caven

References

Burrell, L. 2016. We just can't handle diversity. https://hbr.org/2016/07/we-just-cant-handle-diversity. Accessed 9 Sept 2018.

CIPD. 2018. Diversity and inclusion at work. Facing up to the business case. https://www.cipd.co.uk/Images/diversity-and-inclusion-at-work_2018-summary_tcm18-44150.pdf. Accessed 21 Aug 2018.

Acknowledgements

The authors wish to thank all contributors for taking part in this book and sharing their personal stories, expertise and knowledge. We also wish to thank the team at Palgrave Publication for giving us the space to produce this new volume. The reviewers are also thanked for their feedback and comments on making this volume a good piece of reading. Finally, we would like to give our gratitude to our colleagues at Nottingham Trent University for their continued support throughout the journey of producing the book.

Contents

Notes on Contributors

Eleni Aravopoulou is a senior lecturer at St Mary's University, Twickenham, London. She is an academic member of the Chartered Institute of Personnel and Development (CIPD) and a member of the Chartered Management Institute (CMI) and the British Academy of Management (BAM). Her research interests lie in the fields of human resource management and organisational behaviour, and in partnership with several organisations she has been involved in consultancy projects.

Serena Bradshaw is a founding member of Goddard Consultants and has a wide and varied background in senior management, training and coaching. Following her degree in French and Mediaeval History at Lancaster University and Université de Grenoble III, respectively, she began her career in tourism, working in and Egypt and Europe. She worked in European institutions and the private sector in Brussels for five years and completed an MBA before returning to England. Here her experience includes senior posts in higher education and the NHS in communications, public relations, marketing and public involvement. Bradshaw has also served as a non-executive director in an NHS mental health trust and in the voluntary sector as a trustee and treasurer for Community Voluntary Partners in Bolsover.

Chris Brewster has substantial industrial experience and got his doctorate from the London School of Economics before becoming an academic. He is now a part-time Professor of International Human Resource Management at Vaasa University in Finland; Henley Business School, University of Reading in the UK; Radboud University in the Netherlands; and Instituto Universitário de Lisboa in Portugal. He has been author or editor in the publication of more than 30 books, more than 100 chapters in other books and well over 200 articles.

Valerie Caven is a senior lecturer at Nottingham Business School, Nottingham Trent University, and Academic Fellow of the CIPD with research interests in the transmission of diversity policy into practice, specifically, how policy becomes ignored or corrupted during the transfer. She has authored extensively in the area of gender inequality in particular, including several cross-national studies.

Ian Clark is a professor in the Human Resource Management (HRM) Department at Nottingham Business School, Nottingham Trent University. He works on various projects including an assessment of the implications of businesses which use informal business and employment practices. Ian previously worked at Birmingham Business School and at the Centre for Sustainable Work and Employment Futures (CSWEF) at the University of Leicester. At Birmingham, Ian was part of the teams which secured CIPD accreditation for the MSc HRM programme and the EFMD Quality Improvement System (EQUIS) accreditation and re-accreditation and led the organisation, work and employment group.

Washika Haak-Saheem holds a PhD in International Business Management from Leuphana University in Lueneburg, Germany. Prior to her appointment at Henley Business School, University of Reading in the UK, she worked for more than nine years at Dubai Business School in the United Arab Emirates. Washika has rich industrial experiences in the aviation industry where she served in diverse roles and geographic locations. Her recent research has encompassed international human resource management, international business management, talent management, knowledge management and comparative and international employment relations. She has published many articles in highly reputable international peer-reviewed journals.

Evanthia Kalpazidou Schmidt is an associate professor and research director at the Department of Political Science, Aarhus University, Denmark. Kalpazidou Schmidt's research interests include gender in science and organisations, European science policy and evaluation, science and society studies and higher education studies. She has been involved in a number of European Union-funded projects and has frequently been engaged as expert in the evaluations of projects funded by the European Union. She was member of the European Union group of experts working on the ex-ante impact assessment of Horizon 2020 in the area of environment and climate change and on the ex-post evaluation of the 7th Framework Programme for Research and Development, in the area of international cooperation. Kalpazidou Schmidt is expert member of the European RTD Evaluation Network and of the Horizon 2020 Advisory Group for Gender, established by the European Commission.

Konstantina Kougiannou is Senior Lecturer in HRM at Nottingham Business School, Nottingham Trent University, UK. Konstantina has published in *Human Resource Management Journal* and is an academic associate of the CIPD. Research projects include investigating the impact trust and justice on the efficacy of Information and Consultation (I&C) bodies, the effect of organisational decisions on community trust perceptions and the role of line managers in the implementation of employee engagement.

Yvonne McNulty (PhD, Monash University, Australia) is a senior lecturer, SR Nathan School of Human Development at Singapore University of Social Sciences, Singapore. She has published over 100 academic articles, book chapters and conference papers on expatriates and expatriation, including *Management International Review, Journal of World Business, International Journal of Intercultural Relations* and *The International Journal of Human Resource Management*, and his research has been extensively cited in the *New York Times, Wall Street Journal, Financial Times*, BBC Radio and Economist Intelligence Unit. Yvonne serves on the editorial board of *Global Business and Organisational Excellence* and is associate editor at *the Journal of Global Mobility* and *The International Journal of Human Resource Management*. Yvonne is lead author of *Managing Expatriates: A Return on Investment Approach* (2013), co-editor (with Jan Selmer) of the *Research Handbook of Expatriates* (2017), editor of the *Research Handbook of Global Families* (2018) and editor of the *Research Handbook on Cross Cultural Childhoods* (2019). She is co-author (with Chris Brewster) of the forthcoming *Expatriate Management: Teaching Labour Mobility in the New Global World of Work* (Edward Elgar 2019).

Fotios Mitsakis is Lecturer in Human Resource Management at Nottingham Business School, Nottingham Trent University, UK, and an academic associate member of the CIPD. His research interests lie within the field of human resource development (HRD), strategic HRD (SHRD), training and development (T&D), diversity training and so on, mostly by undertaking qualitative research through a multi-constituent research perspective.

Christine Mortimer is an international senior teaching associate at Lancaster University Management School. Before academia, Christine spent 14 years working in manufacturing across the UK, with particular involvement in cultural change management and the implementation of continuous improvement. Her specialist teaching areas are leadership and management development and practice, operations management, project management, strategy, and supporting entrepreneurial businesses and community interest companies. Her research interests include the interface between business leadership, organisational behaviour and society, with particular emphasis on Principles for Responsible Management Education (PRME), business curriculum design and challenges linked to employability.

Stefanos Nachmias is a principal lecturer at Nottingham Business School, Nottingham Trent University, and academic member of the CIPD with research interests in employability and diversity issues, especially in relation to the business case for diversity and diversity education. He is experienced in developing and running diversity awareness events and conducting research studies around the areas of diversity management, training and management awareness.

Louise Oldridge is a lecturer at Nottingham Trent University and a chartered member of the CIPD. Her research interests focus on women's careers, concepts of work, the intersection of work and care, equality, diversity and inclusion. With a generalist HR background in industry prior to joining higher education, Louise works closely with practitioners and policymakers in the public sector.

Gaye Özçelik (PhD, Işık University, İstanbul) is an assistant professor, Faculty of Communication at İstanbul Bilgi University, İstanbul, Turkey. Gaye had seven years of industrial experience before becoming an academic. She worked for Arthur Andersen, in İstanbul, as a senior human resource consultant. Gaye has also worked for Danone, İstanbul, as HR development executive, being responsible from performance and career management processes. After becoming an academic, she has published academic articles, conference papers on human resource management at the organisational and societal levels and selected topics on organisational behaviour in journals such as *Human Resource Development Review, Procedia – Social and Behavioural Sciences, European Management Review* and *International Journal of Business and Management.* She teaches various topics including HRM, management and organisation, organisational behaviour, entrepreneurship and innovation management at the undergraduate and postgraduate levels. Gaye serves as the research partner of the Academy of Management Ambassadors Global Work Design Project.

Maranda Ridgway is a senior lecturer in the Human Resource Management Division, Nottingham Business School, Nottingham Trent University, having gained extensive strategic and operational HR experience from a range of diverse industries including aviation, engineering consultancy, FMCG, financial services, hospitality and retail. As a commercially focused HR practitioner, Maranda has offered expertise encompassing human resource management, project management and support of the entire employee life cycle. She spent five years in Abu Dhabi, United Arab Emirates (UAE), and during this time she had management responsibility for HR activity in the Gulf Cooperation Council (GCC) region. Maranda also has led numerous projects including acquisitions, new business creation, programme implementation, service centralisa-

xxii   Notes on Contributors

tion and organisation restructures. Finally, she has represented HR at board-level meetings, coached and influenced senior executives, and led multicultural and disciplinary teams based in different countries.

Amanda Thompson is a member of the leadership team at Nottingham Business School, Nottingham Trent University. Her subject specialism is HRM, and as an academic in this field, she has researched and written on a number of HRM/Employment Relations (ER) themes including employee reward, employment relations in small and medium-sized enterprises (SMEs) and the changing role of healthcare assistants in the National Health Service (NHS). She is co-editor of the 7th and 8th editions of *HRM: A Contemporary Approach*, published by Pearson. Amanda is undertaking a doctorate, exploring how men working part-time in managerial and professional occupations construct and reconstruct masculinity.

Daniel Wheatley is a senior lecturer in the Department of Management at Birmingham Business School, University of Birmingham. His research interests are subjective well-being, time-use, quality of work, work-life balance, flexible working arrangements, work-related travel (commuting, mobile working and business travel) and the household division of labour. He is author of *Time Well Spent: Subjective Well-being and the Organisation of Time*. His work has appeared in a number of edited volumes and in peer-reviewed journals including the *Cambridge Journal of Economics*; *Industrial Relations Journal*; *New Technology, Work and Employment*; *Work and Occupations* and *Work, Employment and Society*.

Ning Wu is Senior Lecturer in Human Resource Management at Brunel University London, London. Having been developing research interests in high performance work systems, employee well-being and work-life balance practice with a special focus on the setting of the private sector, Ning has published in academic journals such as *International Journal of Human Resource Management* and *Human Resource Management Journal*.

List of Figures

List of Tables

1

Inequality and Organisational Practice: Employment Relations

Stefanos Nachmias, Valerie Caven, and Serena Bradshaw

1.1 Background and Introduction to Key Issues

The purpose of this chapter is to introduce the reader to the main themes of the first volume entitled: *Inequality and Organizational Practice: Employment Relations*. It seeks to outline the key context and concepts explored across the chapters and enable the reader to examine the importance of understanding hidden inequalities in the workplace.

Changes in employment relations and working conditions underscore the increase in thinking around diversity and equality issues in the workplace. There is a paradigm shift in thinking around organisations'

S. Nachmias (✉) • V. Caven
Nottingham Business School, Nottingham Trent University, Nottingham, UK
e-mail: stefanos.nachmias@ntu.ac.uk; valerie.caven@ntu.ac.uk

S. Bradshaw
Goddard Consultants, Manchester, UK
e-mail: Serena@goddardconsultants.onmicrosoft.com

© The Author(s) 2019
S. Nachmias, V. Caven (eds.), *Inequality and Organizational Practice*, Palgrave
Explorations in Workplace Stigma, https://doi.org/10.1007/978-3-030-11647-7_1

responsibility in recognising and valuing diversity and equality in the workplace. Literature reinforces the argument that organisations place less strategic emphasis in managing those hidden inequalities due to poor leadership commitment (Tomlinson and Schwabenland 2010) and limited allocation of budget and resources for addressing diversity issues in the work (CIPD 2012). Policy makers have been actively addressing a number of equality and diversity problems that arise with the implementation of national, industry and organisational policy initiatives against discriminative practices. Nevertheless, there is still informal discrimination in organisations as the legal framework did not provide effective guidance to address all aspects of unfairness and discrimination in the workplace. As Klarsfeld et al. (2012, p. 312) assert, current approaches are not effective, in that 'control rules are not as binding as they appear … [and] voluntary practices are not as deliberate as they seem'. This shows the need for organisations to take actions to provide feasible solutions to diversity needs in modern organisations (Greene and Kirton 2011). For example, current employment practices fail to address long-standing employment issues including training, work design and flexibility. According to Charted Institute for Personnel and Development - CIPD (2018) report, there is a lack of appropriate use of job design and flexible practices leading to unfavourable management actions. Further to that, Ballard (2017) provides a critical perspective around organisational capacity to develop effective and fair developmental opportunities. The report argues that managers fail to provide sufficient opportunities to train employees for the future and encourage organisations to use emerging technologies to and raise the quality of life for the employees.

As educators, we felt the need to have some contribution in this area and provide insightful findings to support changes on how hidden inequality is addressed. After we published our first book,[1] we received a high number of messages from the academic and professional community. This was a positive outcome given that the book challenges traditional ways of understanding diversity in the workplace. Comments highlighted the need to make radical changes on diversity

---

[1] Caven V. and Nachmias S. (2018) 'Hidden inequalities in the workplace: A guide to the current challenges, issues and business solutions.'

and equality by producing relevant knowledge (at both individual and organisational levels) and undertake an appropriate assessment of the wider business practices in diversity. We noted that individuals were keen to discuss their concerns about hidden inequality due to high level of 'frustration' as to how organisations address work and welfare issues. We have to admit the realisation that individuals shared similar concerns about the way organisational practices create hidden inequalities boosted our confidence to carry on our work and produce this new volume. What is more positive is the fact that many individuals were eager to gain more knowledge regarding this topic. Our first book shows that theory and practice could generate positive outcome by enabling individuals to challenge current thinking and raise awareness (Caven and Nachmias 2018). In fact, individual awareness is an important first step in enabling change to happen at both an individual and organisational level, with Celik et al. (2012) suggesting that establishment of awareness is followed by acceptance, adoption and adherence. Management of hidden inequalities should be seen as a necessity, where individuals should be involved in a process of examining the operational and behavioural realities leading to durable and relevant diversity work-based solutions (Caven and Nachmias 2018). Therefore, we have to move away from the 'force-feeding' attitude towards satisfying legal expectations, enabling individuals to have a key part in tackling inequality, encouraging diversity and creating an inclusive workplace culture (CIPD 2018).

1.2   Aims and Objectives

The scope of this volume is to provide further practical and strategic insight with the scope to support practitioners, managers and policy makers' needs with UK, European and International perspectives. It seeks to address the following areas that generate hidden inequality:

- Academic evaluation of the meaning of diversity management, and diversity training needs for modern organisations.

- Managerial and organisational practices that perpetuate social exclusion, cross-cultural discrimination and management/employee trust withdrawal.
- Diversity management, training and learning contribution towards addressing 'hidden' inequalities and workplace stigmas.
- Voluntary and involuntary disclosure of difference in relation to organisational realities and employment practices.

Through our work as educators and researchers, we have become very aware that there exists a strong legislative framework. There are fracture points where the transfer of policy to practice (from macro-level to industry level, then again from industry to organisational level) fails or becomes corrupted (Ackrill et al. 2017). Our students researching for their dissertations on the topic of equality also provided us with further evidence about the theme, with Human Resource (HR) managers quoted as saying "of course we have an equality policy, it's in that drawer there"—in other words, the organisation could show it was complying with the legislation but was clearly not prepared to put it into practice. This saddened us and has led us to develop our ideas further with this and other volumes in the series showing the many and varied areas of hidden inequalities in the workplace. While we are keen not to lay blame on the part of the legislation, we are eager to identify why the take up of diversity practices and policies other than merely complying with legislation remains to be low on the organisational agenda. Thus, the central aim of this specific volume is to introduce solutions and suggestions for the eradication of hidden inequalities in employment practices. This is stimulated by a recent CIPD report (2017) on Work, Health and Disability produced as a response to consultation on a Government Work, Health and Disability Green Paper which identifies barriers to greater employment opportunities for the disabled which we feel are readily transferable to the areas of hidden inequality covered within this series of books. It identifies several areas of weakness which are summarised below:

- There is a lack of awareness, knowledge and understanding on the part of managers and employers about different forms of disability and health conditions particularly regarding reasonable adjustments.

- Misconceptions and unconscious bias on the part of employers and managers exist concerning recruitment of those with a disability and/or health condition with many (particularly small) employers and line managers having no previous experience of this.
- Lack of training for line managers with just 22% of organisations training managers to more effectively manage and support people with mental health problems.
- Lack of open and inclusive working environments to encourage the effective disclosure of a disability and/or health condition.
- Inadequate use of job design and flexible working patterns.

The report goes on to discuss areas of good practice already put in place by some organisations in terms of designing good employment practices which is the subject of the chapters within this volume. A key finding from the report was that the emphasis should be on developing supportive good practice and moving away from a compliance-based approach as this is counter to creating an inclusive culture where diversity is embraced and encouraged. There are areas of the legal framework that are not covered which creates a complex challenge for organisations to reduce effects of social exclusion and discrimination and achieve greater inclusion which promotes visible and non-visible differences. This supports our scope to explore how employment practices generate hidden inequalities and the need for organisations to take some responsibility for the lack of progress in promoting diversity and equality (Caven and Nachmias 2018).

Perspective Analysis by Serena Bradshaw, Goddard Consultants Coaching Practice
In the last 12 months we've delivered well over 1000 coaching sessions for individuals with mental health conditions—and during this time we've encountered countless adults who are still suffering from the long-term impact of child abuse. Managers report that they don't have confidence to manage employees with mental health problems—the likelihood of being confident to support Survivors of childhood trauma seems small. Yet, when managers have the skills and knowledge to support Survivors, they will also feel empowered

to support all employees with mental illness. That's because the impact of childhood trauma includes and goes beyond mental health.

Why does this matter?

People are astonished when that conservative estimates suggest that one in five adults have experienced sexual abuse in childhood. This means that, in a team of five, it's quite possible that one individual is affected. In an organisation of 500 staff, it could be 100 individuals. And these figures only relate to sexual abuse. Other forms of child abuse—for example, neglect, physical abuse, emotional abuse, are not included in these figures. Mental illness is described as a taboo subject in the workplace—and understandably employees will only be encouraged to speak out if they believe they will be heard, understood and helped. Stigma, shame, myths and misunderstanding still abound. But I believe we're making significant progress at least in terms of Having That Conversation. Lloyds bank is raising awareness in its advertising, Mental Health First Aid is taking off and high-profile figures from business, sports and entertainment are talking openly about mental health. I'm heartened to see and hear about all initiatives that tackle stigma.

Yet, stigma and shame are frequently life-long companions of the adult Survivor of childhood abuse. Indeed, many Survivors will hide behind a mental health label because this may appear more palatable than the real reasons they are seeking support in the workplace. This is wrong on so many levels—not least because children are abused in silence. And silence in later life reinforces stigma and shame. Of course, some Survivors may never wish to disclose their past. However, when they do come forward, it's important that Managers and HR professionals feel confident to provide the right support and to speak openly. This should be no different from learning to talk about common mental illnesses or the support needs of Veterans. When we gathered personal accounts of Survivor experiences in the workplace, we were saddened, though not surprised, that 80% said that their childhood abuse has had a negative impact on their career.

What are the issues?

The support needs for each Survivor are different, in the same way that two individuals with a diagnosis of depression are different—but it's not surprising to see common themes emerge. Managers need to understand that there are links between adult survivors of childhood trauma and other areas of an employee's life. For example, there are well-documented links with re-victimisation in *adulthood—for example in the form of domestic violence. There are also links with substance misuse and alcohol dependency. Add into the mix as well the fact that Survivors can also present with long-term physical health conditions.*

Most HR Directors I speak to agree that their line managers simply do not have the confidence or knowledge to handle these situations. Managers need the confidence to navigate complex (or scary) diagnoses for example complex post-traumatic stress, personality disorders. And it's useful also to know what to do when a traumatic childhood is disclosed, how to support someone through a court case or how to handle workplace behaviours such as apparent hypersensitivity or interpersonal difficulties.

Savvy managers know that the potential cost of mental ill health in the workplace—and the significant return on investment in proactive solutions, such as training, the unique Thrive Portal, solution-focused coaching or counselling. It's important that we don't work in silos: I've seen excellent programmes to maximise the potential of all employees—for example, training and policies about domestic violence, diversity and inclusion, mental health, wellbeing and so on. But we must remember that the whole person turns up to work and we need to join the dots: An employee with a long-term physical health condition may well have mental health conditions; a black senior manager may have a mental illness; a white male may still be experiencing the impact of child abuse or sexual assault; an apprentice may be experiencing domestic violence. Survivors of childhood abuse who work in any organisation have, by definition, an unusual depth of resilience and "stickability" which, with understanding, can be very useful in the workplace. They should not suffer this hidden inequality in silence. There's a sound business case for action—and I'd suggest also that it's simply the "right thing to do".

1.3   Volume Content

Reflecting the issues briefly outlined above, the volume is structured into 12 insightful chapters considering various aspects of employment practices. Contributors have used a number of different tools to assess key issues through primary research, experiential assessment and case studies. Maintaining respondent confidentiality while protecting the identities of the individuals who participated in the first volume is critical. Hence, we have used pseudonyms for any individual names across all chapters.

This chapter provides an introductory assessment of the volume's key dimensions and offers an insight into the key themes on 'hidden' inequality in the workplace. The chapter allows the reader to get an overview of the context and access the key objectives of this second volume emphasising issues around employment practices.

Chapter 2 provides a critical evaluation of the key issues in diversity and equality through the exploration of the historical developments in the subject. It attempts to assess the current issues that modern organisations face in relation to managing a diverse workforce. To achieve that the chapter offers a critical discussion on how the concept of equal opportunities have evolved at social and organisational levels and evaluate the role of diversity management in addressing contemporary issues related to managing differences in the workplace. The scope is to enable the reader to assess key academic and professional developments in the field and provide useful critical insights as to whether current philosophical arguments could generate any sources of hidden inequalities. Finally, the chapter offers useful operational and strategic recommendations to organisations, academics and individuals.

Chapter 3 provides a discussion of key theoretical contributions on diversity training and assesses the role of learning in changing individual attitudes. It offers a critical insight into the current literature on diversity training and learning and examines how organisations respond to addressing discriminatory behaviours and attitudes in the workplace. The scope of the chapter is to evaluate the discourse on diversity training and assess the extent to which diversity-training interventions could generate 'hidden' inequalities towards individual attitudes.

Chapter 4 examines age discrimination which is multi-faceted and complex, and policy interventions have only partial effects. In contrast to an accelerating rise in studies into unfavourable treatment experienced by older employees in a wake of tackling an ageing society, in particular among the developed world, there is a limited number of studies investigating younger workers. Since age discrimination can happen to any age group, this chapter sets out to review the literature of ageism particularly engaging with young and old workers and to discuss the hidden inequalities associated with age at work. Findings from the literature review of age discrimination will inform management practice and feed into policy development in relation to both developing new talent pool and retaining valued and experienced workers of various ages.

Chapter 5 examines ageing populations; people are not only living longer but doing so with health problems and reduced investment in adult social care. This has resulted in an ever-increasing, and unrecognised, reliance on care provided on an informal basis, by friends and family. The highest provision of this care is provided by mid-life women, the majority of whom combine work and care. This chapter offers an examination of existing legislation and literature on supporting working carers and is relevant to both academic and practitioner audiences and concludes that current practices provide insufficient support and contribute to the ongoing factor of caring being a 'hidden' inequality in workplaces. As a result, it closes with recommendations for employers and policy makers.

Chapter 6 advances understanding of men's use of part-time work, and the quality of the part-time work they encounter. Using UK data from wave 4 (2012–13) of Understanding Society, plus extracts from WERS 2011, analysis is conducted to consider the association between part-time work and job quality measures, and wider measures of subjective well-being, notably men's satisfaction with leisure time and life overall. The findings demonstrate that men work part-time for a variety of both voluntary and involuntary reasons, not restricted to the career-start and career-end strategies most commonly depicted. The insight the chapter offers is likely to be of interest to organisations seeking to recruit and retain part-time workers, especially those operating in sectors where part-time working is an embedded work pattern or a growing phenomenon. The findings support calls for improved quality of part-time jobs for both men and women.

Chapter 7 examines how recent studies in science and technology organisations reveal how a complex set of hidden factors of different nature and depth interact in the workplace, producing negative effects on gender equality, and underline the complexity in addressing hidden gender inequality in the workplace of research organisations. However, effectively addressing hidden, deeply rooted structural and cultural gender inequalities in scientific organisations remains an understudied area. Insights into concrete actions aimed at successfully addressing hidden structural barriers are highly necessary to avoid marginalising inequality issues. The chapter contributes to the limited literature on cultural and structural challenges in the workplace by mapping the currently known hidden, deeply rooted systematic inequalities and suggesting how to address them in complex organisations. It offers insights into structural change practices for policy makers, practitioners and researchers. Several recommendations are presented in broad strategic areas, namely in the fields of (1) organisational management and communication, (2) culture and environment and (3) visibility, networking and women's empowerment.

Chapter 8 explores the role of employee silence and voice in addressing hidden inequalities at work. In this chapter, we examine the following: When and how employees in organisational settings exercise voice and when and how they opt for silence; under what conditions would employees articulate voice, revealing issues of hidden inequalities at work; and under what conditions would they opt for silence? Why would employees make the decision to be silent, and what types of issues would they be most likely to be silent about? How could organisations overcome this problem? Management, through practices and institutional structures, can perpetuate silence over a range of issues, thereby organising employees out of the voice process. Any inequality in the workplace can lead to separation and isolation from the mainstream workforce, and this can influence affected employees' voice and silence in the workplace. On the other hand, opportunities to exercise voice, with transparent and fair mechanisms, can reveal a range of issues at work, from sexual harassment to any non-declared physical or psychological condition that otherwise can remain hidden. This can be a first step in addressing inequality in the workplace. Implications for theory and practice are discussed in this chapter.

Chapter 9 argues that professionalised Human Resource Management (HRM) research ignores hidden inequalities such as work that is non-compliant with prevailing employment regulation; accordingly, it is necessary to extend the reach of HRM research to recognise this omission. Firstly, both compliant informalisation, frequently referred to as casualisation, and non-compliant informalisation centre on in-work exploitation, precariousness and vulnerability. Secondly, these hidden inequalities enable a re-skilled human resource function to deliver value to business owners and investors. These arguments on hidden inequalities are important to HRM research because the socio-economic origins of informal work practices and associated hidden inequalities lie in formalised practice often under the label of best way strategic HRM.

Chapter 10 focuses on low-status expatriates who have been largely hidden from managerial scholarship. They are hidden because they are ignored by the migrant literature which looks at people trying to remain in their new society and gain citizenship; they are ignored by the expatriation literature which is mainly concerned with high-status 'top' talent. These hidden expatriates are typically maids, drivers, security guards and construction workers—low status and low paid, unable to obtain citizenship and liable to be sent home, unemployed, at the whim of their employer. If we, as scholars, are to contribute to the betterment of society by elevating the health and well-being of those who live in it, then we must recognise the existence of and address the management issues and concerns of those at the 'bottom of the pyramid'. We use Organisational Justice theory and draw on examples from Turkey, Singapore and the Middle East to examine the position, the concerns and the issues of such workers and their often-unequal place in the workforce.

Chapter 11 explores the topic of international migration which has gained increasing importance for organisations as they expand internationally. At the organisational level, skilled migrants are considered an important part of the global talent pool, contributing to the competitive advantage of global multi-national organisations. Despite the importance of international migrants for organisations and the host countries, the challenges of inequality, both visible and hidden, that this group of individuals might face could affect their employment and development, which remains under-researched. Research has examined inequality of working conditions to the benefit of expatriates (in comparison to host country nationals' working conditions); however, an examination of inequalities faced by expatriates is rarer, with some exceptions. This chapter discusses how culture and trust can influence perceptions of inequality as experienced by expatriates. Notions of culture and the nature of exchange relationships are used to explore the potential effects of trust perceptions on expatriates' attitudes and behaviours. We argue that organisations, in order to appear trustworthy, should evaluate whether equal opportunities and diversity management practices effectively address social exclusion and cultural discrimination in the host country, thus enhancing (or hindering) expatriates' successful employment. Implications for future research are also discussed.

Chapter 12 examines how the ability of UK-based academics to function within collaborative partnerships is becoming an important part of the UK universities' internationalisation agenda. This chapter offers an auto-ethnographical academic expatriate experience detailing some of the challenges faced when moving to work in a 'UK environment positioned abroad', specifically in China. It will provide HR personnel with alternative understandings of possible support strategies that could assist individuals in dealing with a variety of hidden inequalities that surface. These hidden inequalities can contribute to a possible shortening of the assignment due to cultural contexts in which they are operating.

1.4   Concluding Remarks

The aim of this volume is to draw attention to hidden inequalities within employment practices and to examine how their existence and perpetuation serves to hinder the development of true and sustained actions to address issues of diversity and equality within organisations. The overarching benefit of this volume is to continue to expand and stimulate academic and professional scholarship with a British, European and International perspective. We hope that our work highlights a number of current issues in the workplace with the scope to challenge traditional thinking and mobilise individual action towards developing inclusive working environments. Issues with expatriate employment (Ridgway 2018), quality of older workers' employment (Lawton and Wheatley 2018), disengagement in employment relations (Pass 2018) and treatment between paid and unpaid work (Wheatley et al. 2018) produce sources of inequality in the workplace. In many cases, organisational and employment practices create hidden inequality which reinforces the need to explore how people and systems might reinforce workplace hidden inequalities and undervalue a diverse workforce. The uniqueness of this volume lies within its scope and context as it encourages positive thinking by providing an evaluation of hidden inequalities in the workplace. Organisations, policy makers and practitioners can inform future thinking and actions in promoting effective employment and organisational practices.

Given the rise of diversity management, this volume offers an appropriate learning context for higher education institutions to enhance awareness amongst students as to how workplace hidden inequality can be addressed. More specifically, it provides a critical reflection of current academic debates on diversity management needed to advance higher education students' knowledge and provide useful learning resources to enrich their understanding of diversity and equality in business. Higher education plays a vital role in changing individual attitude and thinking. Therefore, it offers useful resources (case studies, practical research and theoretical contributions) to support academic modules on diversity and contemporary management issues.

We hope that the many and varied debates in the chapters will provide an opportunity for educators, students and practitioners to examine their practice in order to facilitate real change for the betterment of future generations of workers. It is important to generate positive action enabling managers to understand and support employees who are experiencing any form of unseen social stigmas and inequalities in the workplace. Building management commitment and accountability is key in any successful diversity policy implementation. After all, we have to attempt to fully address the CIPD's argument to look beyond 'fads or fashions' around the future of work and ensure employees' voices are heard in a world of increased uncertainty and volatility (Caven and Nachmias 2018, p. 336). These voices represent part of our society that has suffered from discrimination and social stigma. The aim is to give these individuals the space to place their voice in a constructive and effective way.

References

Ackrill, R.V., V. Caven, and J. Alaktif. 2017. The regulation of gender equality in the UK and France: A cross-national perspective. *The International Journal of Human Resource Management* 28: 3027–3046.

Ballard D.W. 2017. Managers aren't doing enough to train employees for the future. https://hbr.org/2017/11/managers-arent-doing-enough-to-train-employees-for-the-future. Accessed 21 Aug 2018.

Caven, V., and S. Nachmias. 2018. *Hidden inequalities in the workplace: A guide to the current challenges, issues and business solutions.* London: Palgrave.

Celik, H., T. Abma, I. Klinge, and A. Widder. 2012. Process evaluation of a diversity training program: The method strategy. *Evaluation and Program Planning* 35: 54–65.

CIPD. 2012. *Managing diversity: Linking theory and practice to business performance.* London: Chartered Institute of Personnel and Development.

———. 2017. *Work, health and disability: Response to consultation on the work, health and disability green paper.* London: Chartered Institute of Personnel and Development.

———. 2018. Diversity and inclusion at work. Facing up to the business case. https://www.cipd.co.uk/Images/diversity-and-inclusion-at-work_2018-summary_tcm18-44150.pdf. Accessed 21 Aug 2018.

Greene, A.-M., and G. Kirton. 2011. *The dynamics of managing diversity.* 3rd ed. London: Routledge.

Klarsfeld, A., E. Ng, and A. Tatli. 2012. Social regulation and diversity management: A comparative study of France, Canada and the UK. *European Journal of Industrial Relations* 18: 309–327.

Lawton, Ch., and D. Wheatley. 2018. The quality of work among older workers. In *Hidden inequalities in the workplace: A guide to the current challenges, issues and business solutions,* ed. V. Caven and S. Nachmias, 91–126. London: Palgrave.

Pass, S. 2018. Examining the relationship between discrimination and disengagement. In *Hidden inequalities in the workplace: A guide to the current challenges, issues and business solutions,* ed. V. Caven and S. Nachmias, 279–301. London: Palgrave.

Ridgway, M. 2018. Hidden inequalities of the expatriate workforce. In *Hidden inequalities in the workplace: A guide to the current challenges, issues and business solutions,* ed. V. Caven and S. Nachmias, 303–329. London: Palgrave.

Tomlinson, F., and C. Schwabenland. 2010. Reconciling competing discourses of diversity? The UK non-profit sector between social justice and the business case. *Organization* 17: 101–121.

Wheatley, D., Ch. Lawton, and I. Hardill. 2018. Gender differences in paid and unpaid work. In *Hidden inequalities in the workplace: A guide to the current challenges, issues and business solutions,* ed. V. Caven and S. Nachmias, 181–214. London: Palgrave.

2

Diversity and Equality Issues in Modern Organisations

Stefanos Nachmias, Eleni Aravopoulou, and Valerie Caven

2.1 Introduction and Background

Undoubtedly, the current social and economic challenging conditions provide a great opportunity to assess the wider developments on equality and diversity in the workplace.[1] Over the past 30 years, there is a dramatic change as to how individuals, policy makers and organisations perceive the meaning and purpose of diversity and equality. The question that has dominated professional and academic communities for years is related to how we can ensure appropriate level of equality and diversity in

---

[1] No real names used in this chapter. They have been replaced with pseudonyms.

S. Nachmias (✉) • V. Caven
Nottingham Business School, Nottingham Trent University, Nottingham, UK
e-mail: stefanos.nachmias@ntu.ac.uk; valerie.caven@ntu.ac.uk

E. Aravopoulou
Business Management, St Mary's University, Twickenham, London, UK
e-mail: eleni.aravopoulou@stmarys.ac.uk

© The Author(s) 2019
S. Nachmias, V. Caven (eds.), *Inequality and Organizational Practice*, Palgrave Explorations in Workplace Stigma, https://doi.org/10.1007/978-3-030-11647-7_2

the society. Social injustice, discriminatory behaviours, poor access to work opportunities and unfair organisational practices are just few dimensions that have reinforced the discussion around equality and diversity. Currently, there is a growing concern about social cohesion, racial and ethnic discrimination and the role of mass immigration to social and economic prosperity. Organisations must develop strategies to address any challenges and prepare themselves for the future. The terms equal and diverse are often used interchangeably; however, they reflect different concepts and discourse. They are complementary in terms of addressing organisational, social and individual needs; however, the notion of equality and diversity somehow demonstrates different philosophical approaches as to how social inequality and lack of diversity could be addressed at different levels (Kumra and Manfredi 2012). This has generated an extensive set of academic arguments demonstrating the importance of understanding and assessing equality and diversity issues. There are a number of competing options as to how organisations should address inequality in the workplace and the role of the society to support disadvantaged individuals. The current macro-economic, generational trends and labour market changes have generated a high level of traction and momentum to explore different ways to address discrimination issues and establish effective working environment.

Nevertheless, the purpose of this chapter is simply not to debate the meaning of these terms, but to demonstrate the shift in thinking and enable the reader to assess how a range of key concepts and theories could be used to address equality and diversity issues. Most importantly, we seek to explore any sources of hidden inequalities generated by the diverse, and in many cases complex, philosophical debates. To achieve that, this chapter aims to explain the differences between equal opportunities and diversity management, evaluate the various academic arguments on equality and diversity, analyse key theoretical developments and examine the role of diversity in enhancing performance. Finally, we seek to explore current and future implementation issues and identify any sources of hidden inequality.

The chapter is structured as follows: firstly, there is a discussion on equal opportunities and diversity philosophies followed by an evaluation of key weaknesses and strengths. Secondly, there is an evaluation of key theoretical models on diversity management. Thirdly, the chapter provides an analysis of the key factors influencing individual workplace attitude and the extent to which diversity management strategies could enhance individual performance. Finally, the chapter concludes with a number of key recommendations and implications to organisations, academics and policy makers.

2.2 From Equal Opportunities to Diversity Management: A Battle of Two Philosophies

2.2.1 The Concept of Equality in the Workplace

From a historical perspective, the concept of equal opportunities stems from the liberal conceptualisation of society, of the individual and of the role of the state (Jewson and Mason 1986). It is based on the social justice belief that everyone should have a right to equal access to employment and training, and development based solely on merit (CIPD 2018). According to Ross and Schneider (1992), equality is concerned with fair and equal treatment for all employees which means consistently recognising and responding to their individuals' needs (Armstrong 2002). It means providing equality of opportunity to eliminate workplace discrimination. In Western societies, equal opportunities are rooted in theories of classical liberalism and liberal democracy (Arblaster 1984).

Thus, to ensure individuals can compete equally, freely and fairly for social rewards, legislation on the equal opportunities legal framework has been introduced (mainly established over 1970s and 1980s due to the unprecedented global trend in the development of anti-discrimination and equal opportunities legislation), including, in the case of the UK, the Equality Act 2010.[2] Policy makers act as a catalyst to set up rules and

---

[2] The Equality Act 2010 legally protects people from discrimination in the workplace and in wider society basis by protecting individuals and their rights from unfair treatment, and advance equality of opportunity for all. Equal opportunities in the workplace we inevitably come into contact with the relevant legal framework. The most recent is the Equality Act 2010 that merges nine previous Acts [Equal Pay Act 1970, Sex Discrimination Act 1975, Race Relations Act 1976, Disability

procedures to ensure equal opportunities for all individuals. This is based on the principal of fairness and justice as policy makers provide the framework to appropriate level of social mechanisms with the scope to remove social barriers (Jewson and Mason 1986). Government intervention to address social inequality is translated into the major regulatory frameworks aiming to bridge the gap between equality of citizens (constitutional right) and the unequal treatment of employees in the workplace.

In practice, organisations have a responsibility to ensure that all policies and procedures provide equal opportunities and access to all regardless their social background (Liff 1996). This demonstrates the rational-legality and bureaucratic impartiality of this philosophy as organisations have been heavily scrutinised based on how well they address key requirements. Therefore, equality is related to the application of a symmetrical approach to the principle of equal treatment by considering dignity and inclusion (Vickers 2011). This has been mainly addressed through the equal employment opportunity model where affirmative action manifested any decisions in relation to employment. This model is not equality of outcomes; it is equality of opportunities.

Absence of unfair discrimination in employment is a key dimension in the equal employment opportunities perspective. It is important to highlight that the level of inequality of employment opportunities is related to society characteristics. Pluralistic societies have more potentials for individuals to seek fair and equal employment opportunities compared with monolithic societies. A rich basis for unequal treatment in the society is related to the demographic and social characteristics of the country. Gender, ethnicity, age, race, religion, social stratification and disability are some of the common bases for unequal treatment. The concept of equal employment opportunities aims to remove artificial barriers in employment and eradicate (or minimise) the occurrence of unfair treatment of employees. Hence, many countries have instituted regulations or

---

Discrimination Act 1995, Employment Equality (Religion or Belief) Regulations 2003, Employment Equality (Sexual Orientation) Regulations 2003, Employment Equality (Age) Regulations 2006, Equality Act 2006, (Religion or Belief) and Equality Act (Sexual Orientation) Regulations 2007].

laws to enhance equal employment opportunity amongst their citizens (Orife and Chaubey 2001).

2.2.2 The Myth of Equality

Whilst the existence of the above legal framework has been aiming to eliminate any type of direct discrimination against gender, age, disability, race, religion and sexual orientation, however, there is irrefutable evidence that in practice we are far from equality in employment. For instance, in relation to gender, although the latest statistics show that progress has been made, the gender pay gap remains a key issue for many countries. According to the Global Gender Gap Report (2017), almost half of the countries covered by the Index (82 out of 142) have increased their overall gender gap score in 2017 compared to 2016. In addition, the glass ceiling has not been broken for females aspiring to reach top corporate jobs, as they are still under-represented even in major economies such as the USA. As shown in Fig. 2.1, Standard & Poor's index on 500 American large companies having common stock listed on the NYSE or NASDAQ indicates that only 21.2% are women who possess positions as board of directors, whilst only 4.6% are CEOs (Catalyst 2018). It is also noteworthy that a positive relationship between women's representation in leadership positions and gender pay gap exist. Cohen and Huffman (2007) found that businesses with fewer women in top corporate positions have a greater gender wage gap. This clearly creates a vicious circle that takes organisations further away from achieving equality goals in the workplace.

Moreover, in the UK, in terms of race and ethnicity, ethnic minorities are under-represented in the highest positions and over-represented in the lowest ones (Bratton 2015) and pay gaps exist for the main ethnic minorities compared with White British employees (Equality and Human Rights Commission 2017). For instance, evidence on pay gaps of ethnic minority men relative to White British men shows that the latter earned more than all ethnic minority men groups in all three periods except for Indians and Chinese in the middle period where the differences were not statistically significant (Equality and Human Rights Commission 2017).

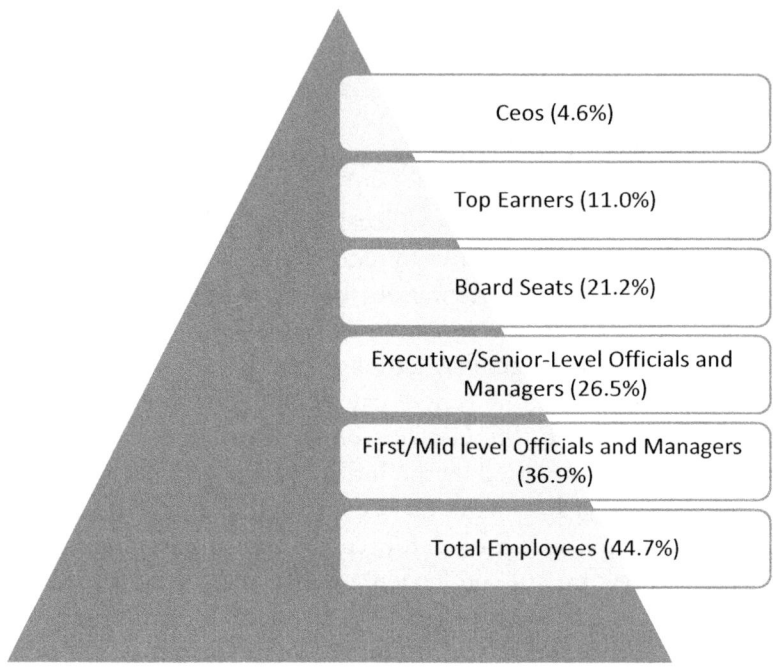

Fig. 2.1 Women in Standard and Poor's Index on 500 Companies

Apart from the abovementioned data, there are also a number of hidden inequalities ranging from assumptions about what men and women can and cannot do (e.g. women cannot make tough decisions) to informal ways of excluding individuals or groups (e.g. humour) that are inseparably linked to indirect discrimination and conscious as well as unconscious bias—which often result from prejudices or stereotypes—that do not allow all employees to be treated equally and fairly. For instance, in their study on peer sexual harassment, Mitchell et al. (2004) found that males who strongly perceive women as opponents tell more sexist jokes to female co-workers.

In addition, some characteristic examples are during the recruitment and selection process where, for instance, questions asked may be discriminatory—for example, by asking a candidate if he/she plans to have a family—or there may be a gap between the formal procedures and the informal evaluation of candidates. Salvaggio et al. (2009) conducted a study investigating sexism and its impact on applicants' evaluations. Their findings suggest that individuals with high hostile sexism evaluated candidates who are believed to be females more negatively and they were less likely to recommend women for employment, compared to those that believed to be males. Similarly, Masser and Abrams (2004) found that participants who evaluated a woman candidate for a management post, and had higher hostile sexism, were less likely to give her high employment recommendations.

Hidden inequities arise from organisational structure too. For example, in relation to gender, due to the fact that females tend to be associated with lower-status positions, contrary to men, they experience adverse reaction/ response for pursuing high-status positions (such as managerial and leadership roles). In their study, Rudman et al. (2012) found that agentic female leaders who are competitive and confident in their role are rated as less likeable and hireable, and more socially deficient, compared to male leaders who act the same way. Contrary and interestingly at the same time, Eagly and Karau (2002) found that if females pursue positions that are matching with traditional gender expectations, they evoke positive responses and reactions.

Therefore, the relevant legislation aims to eliminate it in any form— prejudice is an attitude whilst stereotyping is a belief, we believe the need for finding effective ways to address the aforementioned hidden inequalities is imperative; otherwise, we cannot claim that equality in employment exists and is a reality.

2.2.3 Diversity Management Perspective

Diversity management highlights the need to move away from the 'social justice' to equality arguments for diversity. It should have become apparent by now that the concept of equal opportunities relates to legislation against any type of direct discrimination aiming to achieve equality of opportunity in employment. However, although the concept of workplace diversity is associated with treating all employees equally, it goes beyond legal requirements and further develops initiatives on equal opportunities (Mullins 2016). Diversity originates from the idea of treating all employees fairly by creating a climate, which is based on recognising valuing and harnessing individuals' differences (Kim 2006). Managing diversity is concerned with the systematic commitment of businesses to recruit, select, retain and develop individuals not only with diverse backgrounds but also with diverse abilities (Bassett-Jones 2005), because as Leonard and Swap (1999) very aptly argue it takes more than demographic or racial diversity to lead to creativity and give business the competitive edge. This point highlights the radical approach to diversity, which stresses the importance of establishing interventions at the level of the workplace rather than at state level (Kumra and Manfredi 2012). The concept of equal opportunities has been adopted by individuals who held strong political and ethical values and recognised the historical disadvantage that certain groups, such as women, ethnic minorities and disabled persons, experienced in employment (Jewson and Mason 1986). It is shaped by the demographic and socio-economic realities in the Western world (Syed and Özbilgin 2009; Liff 1997).

Therefore, the radical approach focuses on developing strategies that go beyond legal compliance and expectations in an attempt to address issues associated with equality, talent and organisational capabilities. This perspective dismisses the argument of sameness, as it approaches equality from a diverse perspective. As Kumra and Manfredi (2012, p. 57) argued, 'the radical approach focuses on the outcome of the contest, rather than the rules of the game; fairness of distribution of rewards rather than fairness of the application of process'. This supports the anti-racism and anti-discrimination groups' argument that equality issues should be addressed as integral parts of an organisation strategy to promote diversity and equality (Wrench 2005). However, this is a source of hidden inequality as organisations might have poor knowledge or skill-set to develop appropriate strategies promoting diversity and equality. Diversity management relies on trust and proactive action generated by organisations.

It is simply defined as the process of creating and maintaining a positive work environment where individual similarities and differences are valued. The radical approach is framed around the principles of acceptance and response where individuals are treated as unique entities regardless of their background and personal characteristics. It is about recognising individual differences including race, religion, ethnicity, sexual orientation, age, physical abilities, religious beliefs, political beliefs or any other aspect of human life (Wrench 2005). Jewson and Mason (1986) added to the debate that unfair distribution of rewards from all groups across the various occupations is de facto evidence of inequality in the society. This highlights the argument that state and wider social interventions are ineffective until the distribution of rewards is equally dispersed across the society as a whole.

This is related to the concept of managing diversity and the need to achieve diversity within organisations. It is argued that diversity highlights the need to establish a safe working environment that foster a diverse workforce and move away from tolerance to celebrate the organisational rich dimensions of diversity (CIPD 2018). Further to that, there is a need to set a number of conscious practices to enable employees understand and appreciate interdependence of individual behaviour, culture and, most importantly, the natural environment. This is critical as organisations have to develop key practices that encourage way of knowing, recognising and supporting difference in the workplace. Therefore, the scope of workplace diversity is to encompass differences between people in terms of their social, educational and cultural background (Kumra and Manfredi 2012). There is now the expectation that individuals assess how they perceive themselves, but most importantly, how they perceive others in the wider working environment. We have to recognise that personal, cultural and institutional realities create and sustain discriminatory behaviour where the less privileged are not recognised (Patrick and Kumar 2012). Therefore, it is important to highlight the need to foster effective interactions amongst these groups with the scope to build alliances and avoid hidden discriminatory practices in the workplace.

Literature also highlights the need for recognising diversity in an attempt to maximise organisational and individual potentials. This is partly because diversity management is a management strategy (top-down approach) aiming to ensure that organisations develop their workforce by representing the multitude of differences between individuals in the organisation (Fischer 2008). By utilising these differences,

Table 2.1 From equal opportunities to leveraging differences

Equal opportunities	Diversity management
Issues (problem) focused	Opportunity focused
Tactical emphasis	Strategic emphasis
Focused on a small number of defined groups	Aimed at everyone in a wider range of groups
An HR issue	Issues owned by everyone
Hard targets (get the numbers)	Changing thinking and behaviours to change the culture
About enforcing the distribution of power, privilege and advantage	About increasing collaborative endeavour and sharing
Driven by legislation	Driven by organisational need

organisations would be able to enhance personal effectiveness, respond more effectively to social and demographic changes and provide greater level of fairness and equality in the workplace. Table 2.1 illustrates the differences between the two philosophies.

The shift in agenda is highlighted by the desire to move beyond redressing disadvantage to leveraging differences. This is because the concept of equality highlights the reality that 'we all have different characteristics and different needs [...] therefore, we need to take a symmetrical approach to equal treatment' (Kumra and Manfredi 2012, p. 5). However, the issue highlighted in the literature related to the need to have a 'comparator' to measure equal treatment (Vickers 2011). This raises a fundamental question as to 'who should be compared against whom' (Kumra and Manfredi 2012, p. 5) and what are the main criteria to assess individual differences. Fredman (2001) does not dismiss the idea of a comparator based on the premises of 'universal individual'; however, she highlights the issue of attractive construct as those universal criteria will be highly influenced by the dominate culture, religion, ethnicity and social behaviour. This does not leave any room for accommodating individual differences as well as to challenge individuals thinking outside the 'norm'. Therefore, the idea of 'sameness' and setting up comparators for equal treatment has been criticised as a highly deceptive philosophy arguing the need to recognise and understand people's different characteristics (Vickers 2011). Bleijenbergh et al.'s (2010) view of diversity management supports social justice as the scope is to advance individual development and inclusion across individuals, therefore promoting equal opportunities.

2.2.4 Diversity Management, Performance and Its Dark Side

A key dimension of diversity management is the emphasis on the business case and its role to support organisational performance. As Kumra and Manfredi (2012, p. 61) state 'it is primarily applied in a top-down manner and the aim is to enhance the productivity'. This highlights the managerialist dimension of this approach as a large body of research has demonstrated the positive effects that diversity can have on an organisation's performance (Richard et al. 2013; Soni 2000; Thomas and Ely 1996). Specifically, high levels of diversity have been linked to increased organisational commitment (Giffords 2009) and performance (Sacco and Schmitt 2005). There is also a consensus that promoting diversity in the workplace can bring many benefits to organisations (which indirectly promotes performance) including:

- Increased customer base: a diverse workforce that reflects the organisations' diverse customer base is likely to attract a wider range of customers. A very recent example is that of Vogue which has its first hijab-wearing model on its front cover (Pithers 2018).
- Enhanced innovation, creativity and problem-solving: a heterogeneous workforce is more likely to come up with creative and innovative ideas and challenge team members' perceptions, values and approaches that allow them to reach better-justified decisions (Cox 1994; Galinsky et al. 2015; Leonard et al. 2004; McLeod et al. 1996; Schwenk 1984).
- Increased organisational effectiveness: a well-managed diverse workforce can increase the effectiveness of an organisation and experience growth by combining individual talents, maximising individuals' potential and increasing productivity, as well as enhancing an organisation's flexibility to any changes in the market place (Ely and Thomas 2001; Kochan et al. 2003; Zanoni et al. 2010).
- Bigger talent pool: an organisation that embraces diversity will attract a diverse group of candidates enabling them, for example, to fill skills gaps (Mullins 2016).

Despite the positives, empirical research that investigates the link between diversity and performance has produced conflicting results (Choi and Rainey 2010; Groeneveld 2011; McKay and Avery 2015) with limited empirical assessment (Pitts 2006). Nevertheless, some studies found that the lack of a diversity management policy could lead to high labour turnover, loss of talented employees, employment tribunals and the associated bad publicity (Özbilgin and Tatli 2011). They argue that alternative work arrangements (Choi and Rainey 2010), targeted recruitment practices (hire a diverse workforce) (Sabattini and Crosby 2008) and inclusive organisational climate (Choi and Rainey 2010; Pitts 2009) generate positive organisational and individual outcomes. A number of other research studies have identified that diversity can contribute towards role stress (Findler et al. 2007), organisational commitment (Cho and Mor Barak 2008) and innovation (Richard et al. 2013).

However, there are several contextual factors that contribute towards the overall impact of any diversity initiatives to performance. These factors demonstrate the highly individualistic approach to managing diversity within organisations as well as the need for management involvement. There is no a single approach that all businesses can adopt to promote equality and diversity in the workplace. These factors are as follows:

- The firm's economic and organisational context is crucial in determining how diversity brings about business benefits.
- The business case is likely to depend on the markets a firm operates in, its labour market, organisational and other strategies and the actions of managers and leaders.
- The way that diversity is managed is a crucial part of the relationship between diversity management and performance; if managed appropriately, it can bring benefits to business, and if managed poorly, it can increase costs.
- Diversity leads to counterproductive work behaviours such as derogation, ostracism and discrimination (Roberge and van Dick 2010); therefore, there is a need for continuous training and learning for employees. Failure to address lack of acceptance and prejudice feelings causes negative dynamics such as ethnocentrism, stereotyping and culture clashes (White 1999).

- Management style and level of involvement are critical as failure to take strategic actions to address any 'superior' feelings and behaviours, and eventually organisational performance, would suffer losses. Those employers who work harder are able to gain acceptance by creating a solution (White 1999).

Although there is consensus of the undeniable benefits of workplace diversity, there are a number of negative effects that diversity can bring to an organisation and these need to be discussed. There are some criticisms around the over emphasis on performance outcomes. At group level, diversity lowers performance due to the nature of heterogeneous groups as these groups require extra time and effort to come together (Foldy 2004). Diverse groups may be dysfunctional due to their heterogeneity as it may be challenging for them to incorporate their diverse backgrounds, values, perceptions and approaches and manage effectively to collaborate (Jehn et al. 1999), leading to ineffective communication (Polzer 2008). Hence, these differences consequently result in a number of high-profile issues impacting on performance and how diversity is managed. Choi and Rainey (2010) also suggested that membership to diverse groups limits access to important network and decision-making processes due to the nature of how individuals perceive diversity.

At an organisational level, there are studies that have found that diversity reduces the speed of a business to respond and act to competitive threats. There is evidence of decreased group and social cohesion and interpersonal conflict that may arise due to employees' perceived dissimilarity, bias and stereotyping (Thomas et al. 2004). For instance, an employee with a different nationality is more likely to remain social distant at work (Parrillo and Donoghue 2005) by showing less willingness to interact with the rest of the team (Chan and Goto 2003). This is explained by the fact that people tend to like and feel more comfortable to interact with those whom they feel that they are similar to them. Further, this social distance, and generally the existence of subgroups, often results in team polarity and conflict (Ayub and Jehn 2006).

It is obvious that academic literature fails to reach an agreement on the business case of diversity management. Organisations need to promote participation across all individuals regardless their social and demographic differences. This ambiguity also shows that diversity management in practice can generate some undesirable outcomes creating sources of hidden inequality that hijack the benefits of having a diverse workforce. Given this challenge, organisations should be more proactive in dealing with equality and diversity in the workplace.

2.2.5   Key Models and Theories

Diversity management has been researched and evaluated by several different theoretical approaches and tools. This is because diversity management has been seen as an alternative approach to managing equality as the equal opportunities approach has failed to achieve greater organisational inclusion and reduce discrimination. For some, diversity management is a tool to re-energising management interest and manage strategically key changes in the labour market including demographic and educational shift (Bleijenbergh et al. 2010; Wrench 2005). This is supported by the argument that successful organisations know that diversity is more than just a tick box exercise, but instead a reality that enhances their competitiveness and effectiveness (Karsten 2006).

The most common approach to the management of diversity is based on individual contribution. Liff (1999) argues that there is a need to differentiate how differences are approached. The individualism approach is based on *dissolving differences* where differences are not seen as being distributed systematically according to membership of a social group, but rather as random differences. In contrast, *valuing differences* is based on the membership of different social groups by offering effective training to groups who may be disadvantaged and lack self-confidence. She also emphasises two further approaches: *accommodating and utilising differences*. These are highly related with equal opportunities approach where specific initiatives are available to aid identified groups, and also other members of the organisation. In both cases, talent is recognised and utilised regardless social differences by recognising different patterns of qualifications and organisational roles (Liff 1999).

Furthermore, there is also an emphasis on developing a relational framework. Syed and Özbilgin (2009) provide an interesting framework on diversity management through understanding the relational concerns. Due to the complexity of the legal, organisational and social context, diversity management should be developed around the following points:

- *Macro-national level analysis* takes into consideration the significance of national structures and institutions including the legislation, religion strictures, gender and race.
- *Meso-organisational level analysis* considers organisational processes, rituals and routinised behaviours at work as well as rules around gender and race relations.
- *Micro-individual level analysis* considers issues related to individual power, motivation and agency to affect change.

Syed and Özbilgin demonstrate the need to multilevel assess factors responsible for individual and group differences in the workplace. This is because diversity management strategies are shaped by the history of the local context as well as the context of social policy. This is not limited to the legal framework, but also limited to cultural implications for individuals' workplace experiences and perspectives on equality and diversity. For example, cognitive differences are shaped by socio-cultural contexts (Syed et al. 2005). The scope is to bring together the subjective and objective issues highlighted in managing inequality and enable organisations to assess these issues across multiple levels of social reality (Syed and Özbilgin 2009). Finally, a more contextual approach to diversity management should be encouraged by the current changes in work and life as well as variations in social and economic conditions across groups and countries. This lends support from the social identity theory. Social identity theory categorises individuals into social groups and assesses how they interact with others in their own groups as well as those in other groups (Stahl et al. 2010). This is important tool as any diversity strategy should be able to explore how individuals perceive others within their groups, as this perception determines team cohesion and organisational linking.

Jackson's (1992) framework on organisational culture to achieve diversity outcomes provides support to Syed and Özbilgin's argument that a macro- or micro-level analysis is needed. Their findings demonstrate that culturally diverse groups outperform homogeneous groups on different tasks. This is because social categorisation is required as a basis for diverse employees to find a common ground in organisational membership as well as to develop mutual trust and respect (Chatman et al. 1998). Hence, they proposed that organisational culture should be developed from 'exclusionary' organisations (organisational culture that with limited diverse and dominance of specific groups) to a 'multicultural' organisation (fully diverse and equal organisation for all). This approach is clearly based on the idea of cultural change and learning to ensure that organisations are evolving throughout the time. Kandola and Fullerton (1994) support the argument on cultural change to ensure that all individuals within the organisation are able to contribute and reach their potential.

It is also clear that leadership (top-down) has the responsibility for creating the space for those individuals to achieve their potential through learning and development. Organisations have to respond to diversity management issues through proactive learning. Thomas and Ely (1996) distinguished three different perspectives as to how organisations approach diversity: the discrimination and fairness paradigm, the access and legitimacy paradigm, and the learning and effectiveness of diverse workforce. These key dimensions demonstrate the organisations' normative beliefs and expectations about the reason to diversify, why diversity can generate value and most importantly to address individual needs. Dass and Parker (1999) extended the model by adding a fourth perceptive. Resistance demonstrates the increased external demand for organisations to address diversity. However, this need is perceived as a threat to the organisation to generate positive action and dialogue in the workplace. These demonstrate different reactions to diversity including exclusion, denial, assimilation, isolation or/and fear (Roosevelt 1995).

Positive learning actions and development of appropriate policies are essential to promoting diversity management. Failure to promote cultural diversity will result in interpersonal disputes characterised by anger, frustration and other negative feelings. Cultural diversity is positively associated with high levels of emotional conflict (Pelled et al. 1999). As Cox (1994) suggested, emotional conflict might negatively impact upon organisational diversity progress as there are misunderstandings and misinterpretations among culturally diverse individuals. This is manifested in a variety of ways, including leadership style and organsiational reality. Leaders can ensure that the corporate values, culture and practices do not isolate "diverse" individuals, so that such losses to the organisation are minimised, thus 'The presentation of a robust business case increases the likehood of obtaining the leadership commitment and resources needed to successfully implement diversity initiatives' (Robionson and Dechant 1997, p. 21). Cox and Blake (1991) identified six areas where organisations can create a competitive advantage through diversity. Figure 2.2 illustrates the key dimensions related to positive management of diversity in the workplace.

The above figure illustrates the key advantages related to positive diversity culture in the workplace. Cox and Blake (1991) summarised the key advantages into six categories: cost (lack of attention to diversity and equality issues increase work costs and result is less productivity); resource acquisition (positive publicity enables the attraction of top-quality employees); marketing and creativity (satisfy diverse market demands based on their own cultural preferences and sensitivities) and problem-solving and system flexibility (individuals exposure to culture and individual differences encourages positive exchange information and fosters flexibility). This illustrates the advantages of organisational intervention in addressing diversity and equality issues, and the main positive gained in adopting a more proactive approach to diversity.

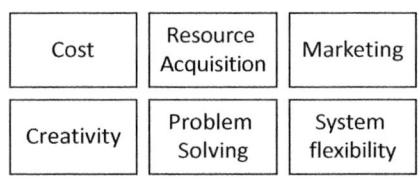

Fig. 2.2   Advantages of diversity management

2.3   Conclusion and Implications

Despite the benefits that diversity brings to an organisation, our evaluation has revealed a number of challenges and problematic areas that make the management and implementation of diversity a complex task. Effectively implementing and managing diversity currently is not and definitely will not be an easy task to do, even in the future. Nevertheless, organisations need to ensure that they maintain HR practices such as their policies and strategies, for example, on recruitment and selection, reward systems and training and development that are fair, promote equity (Thomas 2005) and meet individual's needs. The current socio-political environment demonstrates the need for organisations to ensure effective management of diversity and equality to avoid public exposure. A major area of debate regarding equality and diversity in the workplace revolves around the fact that many organisations address these two issues mostly from the standpoint of legal compliance. They begin to realise that "just complying" not only does not help them to achieve their objectives, as for example staff retention and performance issues, but also hinder organisational effectiveness. A good example to illustrate this is the failure of many diversity programmes that according to Peña et al. (2017, p. 1) is attributed to the fact that 'from entry-level through the development of top talent, the established system favors a narrow range of individuals who have fewer barriers to opportunity'. This is how the issue of hidden inequality arises and which lies within the way managers and HR departments fail to actually address real problems. Therefore, instead of creating diversity programmes, they must take effective actions to reduce/eliminate these barriers in practice.

Mini Case Study 1: Diversity and Knowledge Sharing
Mark is an officer in a large organisation dealing with HR matters including diversity. The organisation has a set of distinctive policies on discrimination, equality and diversity. Despite that, Mark feels that his views and ideas have not been recognised by the management. As he said, 'It is extremely important to be able to share your ideas without thinking about being politically correct and being cautious about your manager's views. I have so many good, and most importantly, cost-effective solutions; however, I don't feel able to

share this with the management. I just do my job and take part in the ticking box exercises which does not offer anything to the organisation, but this is how it is'.

Another case of hidden inequality is that the more homogeneous a group is in an organisation, the more chances that it will develop its own subculture by excluding, marginalising or exhibiting a critical attitude towards individuals outside this team. Creating an inclusive work environment will allow more individuals flourish and allow their talents to thrive. 'Inclusion puts the concept and practice of diversity into action by creating an environment of involvement, respect, and connection—where the richness of ideas, backgrounds, and perspectives are harnessed to create business value' (Hudson 2011). That is why we strongly believe that the shift that currently takes place from diversity to inclusion will rapidly continue to grow. An inclusive culture that values individual differences and does not require extensive adjustments to fit in can only assist organisations in several aspects.

Mini Case Study 2: Bringing Together the New and the Old

Louise was asked to bring together two teams after a major acquisition of a medium-sized family business. The company was characterised for its traditional management values and lack of diverse workforce. The challenge for Louise was to ensure that everyone had the same opportunities in the newly formed organisation. However, this was not an easy task for her. As she said, 'The level of resistance was enormous. It was obvious that the level of heterogeneity in the groups did affect my ability to put in practice by addressing plans on team work and values. Every attempt to bring them together failed as people were trying to protect the status quo and their deeply rooted values. Of course, people prefer to spend time and work with people that they agree/ like, but this was not an option. In many cases, I felt like a negotiator rather than a liaison officer with a clear remit to ensure that strategic goals would be addressed in the future. However, I soon realised that forming homogenous groups requires management support, clarity and ensure that all levels of performance are recognised. I was getting the sense that fear of the unknown in terms of new personalities, pressure to proof themselves, dynamics in politics and resources were the key reasons for their reactions. After all, I believe that diversity in the workplace is often seen as a good way to inject fresh ideas into an otherwise stagnant environment, and incorporating new perspectives; however, this should be done methodologically with clear strategy'.

Given the competition and the need for immediate results (e.g. productivity, profits), managers expect from their diverse teams to be fully functional as soon as possible. However, this is very difficult as they need to allow enough time for teams to develop and understand and recognise how their different values and approaches can assist achieve their common mission as a group. The members of a diverse team need time to learn to trust each other and how to work together (Knouse 2006). In a very interesting study conducted by Watson et al. (1993), it was found that whilst at the first stages of group development homogenous teams were more effective compared to diverse groups; after some weeks, the latter became more effective.

Another challenge organisations have to face is to maintain cohesion among team members. In the past, when the workforce was more homogenous, aiming to achieve cohesion among groups to collaborate well and become functional, organisations focused on team development exercises so as to build interpersonal closeness and liking among their workforce (Lu et al. 2017). However, this is difficult to achieve within a diverse workforce. Thus, as several researchers suggest, there should be a shift from social/interpersonal cohesion to task cohesion (Ahronson and Cameron 2007; Knouse 2006). Their rationale derives from the fact that all group members—regardless of the type of diversity that exists at work, for example, cultural and racial—share a common group mission.

Moreover, organisations should be able to address key current and future challenges by establishing and maintaining a culture of diversity by showing commitment to it through continuous support from top management and leadership that is direct and overt, a well-articulated statement of the business case for diversity that fits for that business, and line managers' accountability on employees' financial rewards, for example, bonuses and performance evaluations (Slater et al. 2008). In order to prove the deficiencies of 'conventional equality measures', Liff and Cameron (1997), by using women as an example, state that by treating them as employees who require special treatment, this leads to management's dissatisfaction and adoption of defensive attitudes. Therefore, as they suggest, one of the major steps organisations need to make in order to enact change is to reflect on their organisational culture and climate and think how it could shift to an equality culture.

Finally, there is a need to enhance knowledge base and undertake research with practical implications. The current theoretical debate creates hidden issues as to what is the best approach for organisations to deal with diversity and equality challenge. There is no denial that a new approach is needed to speak out the benefits of organisations valuing diversity through understanding employees' needs and requirements. Of course, identification of generic processes and boundary conditions provides support for organisations; however, these policies should be combined with appropriate level of knowledge, resources and personalised approach to implementation. Last but not least, organisations and policy makers should access the impact of the current socio-economic changes towards employees' perception of diversity, work and employment relations.

References

Ahronson, A., and J.E. Cameron. 2007. The nature and consequences of group cohesion in a military sample‖. *Military Psychology* 19: 9–25.

Arblaster, A. 1984. *The rise and fall of western liberalism*. Oxford: Blackwell.

Armstrong, C. 2002. Complex equality: Beyond equality and difference. *Feminist Theory* 3: 67–82.

Ayub, N., and A. Karen Jehn. 2006. National diversity and conflict in multinational workgroups: The moderating effect of nationalism. *International Journal of Conflict Management* 17: 181–202.

Bassett-Jones, N. 2005. The paradox of diversity management, creativity and innovation. *Creativity and Innovation Management* 14: 169–175.

Bleijenbergh, I., P. Peters, and E. Poutsma. 2010. Diversity management beyond the business case. *Equality, Diversity and Inclusion: An International Journal* 29: 413–421.

Bratton, J. 2015. *Introduction to work and organizational behaviour*. Basingstoke: Palgrave Macmillan.

Catalyst. 2018. Pyramid: Women in S&P 500 companies. http://www.catalyst. org/knowledge/women-sp-500-companies. Accessed 17 May 2018.

Chan, D., and S.G. Goto. 2003. Conflict resolution in the culturally diverse workplace: Some data from Hong Kong employees. *Applied Psychology* 52: 441–460.

Chartered Institute of Personnel and Development (CIPD). 2018. Diversity and inclusion in the workplace. https://www.cipd.co.uk/knowledge/fundamentals/relations/diversity/factsheet. Accessed 12 Mar 2018.

Chatman, J.A., J. Polzer, S. Barsade, and M. Neale. 1998. Being different yet feeling similar: The influence of demographic composition and organizational culture on work processes and outcomes. *Administrative Science Quarterly* 43: 749–780.

Cho, S., and E. Mor Barak. 2008. Understanding of diversity and inclusion in a perceived homogeneous culture: A study of organizational commitment and job performance among Korean employees. *Administration in Social Work* 32: 100–126.

Choi, S., and H.G. Rainey. 2010. Managing diversity in US federal agencies: Effects of diversity and diversity management on employee perceptions of organizational performance. *Public Administration Review* 70: 109–121.

Cohen, Ph.N., and M.L. Huffman. 2007. Working for the woman? Female managers and the gender wage gap. *American Sociological Review* 72: 681–704.

Cox, Taylor. 1994. *Cultural diversity in organizations: Theory, research, and practice*. San Francisco: Berret-Koehler Publishers.

Cox, T.H., and S. Blake. 1991. Managing cultural diversity: Implications for organizational competitiveness. *The Executive* 5: 45–56.

Dass, P., and B. Parker. 1999. Strategies for managing human resource diversity: From resistance to learning. *The Academy of Management Executive* 13: 68–80.

Eagly, A.H., and S.J. Karau. 2002. Role congruity theory of prejudice toward female leaders. *Psychological Review* 109: 573–598.

Ely, R.J., and D. Thomas. 2001. Cultural diversity at work: The effects of diversity perspectives on work group processes and outcomes. *Administrative Science Quarterly* 46: 229–273.

Equality and Human Rights Commission. 2017. The ethnicity pay gap. https://www.equalityhumanrights.com/sites/default/files/research-report-108-the-ethnicity-pay-gap.pdf. Accessed 18 May 2018.

Findler, L., L.H. Wind, and M.E. Mor Barak. 2007. The challenge of workforce management in a global society: Modeling the relationship between diversity, inclusion, organizational culture, and employee well-being, job satisfaction and organizational commitment. *Administration in Social Work* 31: 63–94.

Fischer, M.D. 2008. Cultural dynamics: Formal descriptions of cultural processes. Structure and Dynamics. http://www.escholarship.org/uc/item/557126nz. Accessed 18 May 2018.

Foldy, E.G. 2004. Learning from diversity: A theoretical exploration. *Public Administration Review* 64: 529–538.

Fredman, S. 2001. Equality: A new generation? *Industrial Law Journal* 30: 145–168.

Galinsky, A.D., A.R. Todd, A.C. Homan, K. Phillips, E. Apfelbaum, S. Sasaki, J. Richeson, J.B. Olayon, and W. Maddux. 2015. Maximizing the gains and minimizing the pains of diversity: A policy perspective. *Perspectives on Psychological Science* 10: 742–748.

Giffords, E.D. 2009. An examination of organizational commitment and professional commitment and the relationship to work environment, demographic and organizational factors. *Journal of Social Work* 9: 386–404.

Global Gender Gap Report. 2017. Gender information. http://www3.weforum.org/docs/WEF_GGGR_2017.pdf. Accessed 18 May 2018.

Groeneveld, S. 2011. Diversity and employee turnover in the Dutch public sector: Does diversity management make a difference? *International Journal of Public Sector Management* 24: 594–612.

Hudson, J.T. 2011. Moving from diversity to inclusion. http://www.diversity-journal.com/1471-moving-from-diversity-to-inclusion/irreversibility. Accessed 18 May 2018.

Jackson, S.E. 1992. Team composition in organizational settings: Issues in managing an increasingly diverse work force. In *Symposium on group productivity and process*, ed. S. Worchel, W. Wood, and J.A. Simpson, 38–73. Newbury Park: Sage.

Jehn, K.A., G.B. Northcraft, and M. Neale. 1999. Why differences make a difference: A field study of diversity, conflict and performance in workgroups. *Administrative Science Quarterly* 44: 741–763.

Jewson, N., and D. Mason. 1986. The theory and practice of equal opportunities policies: Liberal and radical approaches. *The Sociological Review* 34: 307–334.

Kandola, R.S., and J. Fullerton. 1994. *Managing the mosaic*. Wiltshire: The Cromwell Press.

Karsten, M.F. 2006. *Management, gender, and race in the 21st century*. New York: University Press of America.

Kim, B.Y. 2006. Managing workforce diversity: Developing a learning organization. *Journal of Human Resources in Hospitality & Tourism* 5: 69–90.

Knouse, S.B. 2006. Task cohesion: A mechanism for bringing together diverse teams. *International Journal of Management* 23: 588–596.

Kochan, T., K. Bezrukova, R. Ely, S. Jackson, A. Joshi, K. Jehn, J. Leonard, D. Levine, and D. Thomas. 2003. The effects of diversity on business performance: Report of the diversity research network. *Human Resource Management* 42: 3–21.

Kumra, S., and S. Manfredi. 2012. *Managing equality and diversity: Theory and practice.* Oxford: Oxford University Press.

Leonard, J.S., D.I. Levine, and A. Joshi. 2004. Do birds of a feather shop together? The effects on performance of employees' similarity with one another and with customers. *Journal of Organizational Behavior* 25: 731–754.

Leonard-Barton, D., and W. Swap. 1999. *When sparks fly: Igniting creativity in groups.* Cambridge, MA: Harvard Business School Press.

Liff, S. 1996. *Managing diversity: New opportunities for women?' Warwick papers in industrial relations no. 57.* Coventry: IRU, Warwick University.

———. 1997. Two routes to managing diversity: Individual differences or social group characteristics. *Employee Relations* 19: 11–26.

———. 1999. Diversity and equal opportunities: Room for a constructive compromise? *Human Resource Management Journal* 9: 65–75.

Liff, S., and I. Cameron. 1997. Changing equality cultures to move beyond 'women's problems'. *Gender, Work and Organization* 4: 35–46.

Lu, L., F. Li, K. Leung, K. Savani, and M. Morris. 2017. When can culturally diverse teams be more creative? The role of leaders' benevolent paternalism. *Journal of Organizational Behavior* 39: 402–415.

Masser, B.M., and D. Abrams. 2004. Reinforcing the glass ceiling: The consequences of hostile sexism for female managerial candidates. *Sex Roles* 51: 609–615.

McKay, P.F., and D.R. Avery. 2015. Diversity climate in organizations: Current wisdom and domains of uncertainty. In *Research in personnel and human resources management,* ed. J.R. Buckley, B. Halbesleben, and A. Wheeler, 191–233. Bingley: Emerald Group Publishing Limited.

McLeod, P.L., S. Lobel, and T. Cox. 1996. Ethnic diversity and creativity in small groups. *Small Group Research* 27: 248–264.

Mitchell, D., R. Hirschman, and R.S. Lilly. 2004. A laboratory analogue for the study of peer sexual harassment. *Psychology of Women Quarterly* 28: 194–203.

Mullins, L.J. 2016. *Management and organisational behaviour*. Harlow: Pearson Education Limited.

Orife, J.N., and M.D. Chaubey. 2001. Models of equal employment opportunity: A three-nation comparison. *Journal of African Business* 2: 93–113.

Özbilgin, M., and A. Tatli. 2011. Mapping out the field of equality and diversity: Rise of individualism and voluntarism. *Human Relations* 64: 1229–1253.

Parrillo, V.N., and C. Donoghue. 2005. Updating the Bogardus social distance studies: A new national survey. *The Social Science Journal* 42: 257–271.

Patrick, H.A., and V.R. Kumar. 2012. *Managing workplace diversity: Issues and challenges*. London: SAGE Open.

Pelled, L.H., K.M. Eisenhardt, and K.R. Xin. 1999. Exploring the black box: An analysis of work group diversity, conflict, and performance. *Administrative Science Quarterly* 44: 1–28.

Peña, K., K. Hinsen, and M. Wilbur. 2017. Why diversity programs fail and how to fix them. In *SMPTE 2017 annual technical conference and exhibition*, 1–27. White Plains, New York: SMPTE.

Pithers, E. 2018. Meet Halima Aden, the first Hijabi model on the cover of Vogue.   http://www.vogue.co.uk/article/halima-aden-interview-2018. Accessed 18 May 2018.

Pitts, D.W. 2006. Modeling the impact of diversity management. *Review of Public Personnel Administration* 26: 245–268.

Pitts, D. 2009. Diversity management, job satisfaction, and performance: Evidence from US federal agencies. *Public Administration Review* 69: 328–338.

Polzer, J.T. 2008. Making diverse teams click. *Harvard Business Review* 34: 20–21.

Richard, O.C., H. Roh, and J. Pieper. 2013. The link between diversity and equality management practice bundles and racial diversity in the managerial ranks: Does firm size matter? *Human Resource Management* 52: 215–242.

Roberge, M.-É., and R. Van Dick. 2010. Recognizing the benefits of diversity: When and how does diversity increase group performance? *Human Resource Management Review* 20: 295–308.

Robinson, G., and K. Dechant. 1997. Building a business case for diversity. *The Academy of Management Executive* 11: 21–31.

Roosevelt, T.R. 1995. A diversity framework. In *Diversity in organizations. New perspectives for a changing workplace*, ed. M.M. Chemers, S. Oskamp, and M.A. Costanzo, 245–263. Thousand Oaks: Sage.

Ross, R., and R. Schneider. 1992. *From equality to diversity – A business case for equal opportunities*. London: Pitman.

Rudman, L.A., C. Moss-Racusin, J.E. Phelan, and S. Nauts. 2012. Status incongruity and backlash effects: Defending the gender hierarchy motivates prejudice against female leaders. *Journal of Experimental Social Psychology* 48: 165–179.

Sabattini, L., and F. Crosby. 2008. Overcoming resistance: Structures and attitudes. In *Diversity resistance in organizations*, ed. K.M. Thomas, 273–302. Mahwah: Erlbaum.

Sacco, J.M., and N. Schmitt. 2005. A dynamic multilevel model of demographic diversity and misfit effects. *Journal of Applied Psychology* 90: 203–231.

Salvaggio, A., M. Streich, and J.E. Hopper. 2009. Ambivalent sexism and applicant evaluations: Effects on ambiguous applicants. *Sex Roles* 61: 621–633.

Schwenk, C.R. 1984. Devil's advocacy in managerial decision-making. *Journal of Management Studies* 21: 153–168.

Slater, S.F., R.A. Weigand, and T. Zwirlein. 2008. The business case for commitment to diversity. *Business Horizons* 51: 201–209.

Soni, V. 2000. A twenty-first-century reception for diversity in the public sector: A case study. *Public Administration Review* 60: 395–408.

Stahl, G.K., K. Mäkelä, L. Zander, and M. Maznevski. 2010. A look at the bright side of multicultural team diversity. *Scandinavian Journal of Management* 26: 439–447.

Syed, J., and M. Özbilgin. 2009. A relational framework for international transfer of diversity management practices. *The International Journal of Human Resource Management* 20: 2435–2453.

Syed, J., F. Ali, and D. Winstanley. 2005. In pursuit of modesty: Contextual emotional labour and the dilemma for working women in Islamic societies. *International Journal of Work Organisation and Emotion* 1: 150–167.

Thomas, K.M. 2005. *Diversity dynamics in the workplace*. Belmont: Thomson Wadsworth.

Thomas, D.A., and R. Ely. 1996. Making differences matter. *Harvard Business Review* 74: 79–90.

Thomas, K.M., D.A. Mack, and A. Montagliani. 2004. The arguments against diversity: Are they valid? In *Psychology and management of workplace diversity*, ed. M.S. Stockdale and F.J. Crosby, 31–52. Malden: Blackwell.

Vickers, L. 2011. The expanded public sector duty: Age, religion and sexual orientation. *International Journal of Discrimination and the Law* 11: 43–58.

Watson, W.E., K. Kumar, and L. Michaelsen. 1993. Cultural diversity's impact on interaction process and performance: Comparing homogeneous and diverse task groups. *Academy of Management Journal* 36: 590–602.

White, R.D. 1999. Managing the diverse organization: The imperative for a new multicultural paradigm. www.pamij.com/99_4_4_white.htm. Accessed 14 Nov 2017.

Wrench, J. 2005. Diversity management can be bad for you. *Race and Class* 46: 73–84.

Zanoni, P., M. Janssens, Y. Benschop, and S. Nkomo. 2010. Guest editorial: Unpacking diversity, grasping inequality: Rethinking difference through critical perspectives. *Organization* 17: 9–29.

3

Diversity Training and Learning in Modern Organisations

Stefanos Nachmias, Fotios Mitsakis, and Valerie Caven

3.1 Introduction

Despite the rapidly changing workforce demographics that have led many organisations to take positive actions in promoting diversity, inclusion and equality, discrimination still represents a major issue in the workplace. Diversity training is viewed as an essential instrument in addressing this challenge (Pendry et al. 2007). There is a diverse collection of academic resources on the importance of diversity training (Bezrukova et al. 2012; Kulik and Roberson 2008; Ely 2004; Wentling 2001) and its short-term impact by focusing only on a specific aspect of

S. Nachmias (✉) • V. Caven
Nottingham Business School, Nottingham Trent University, Nottingham, UK
e-mail: stefanos.nachmias@ntu.ac.uk; valerie.caven@ntu.ac.uk

F. Mitsakis
Department of Human Resource Management, Nottingham Business School, Nottingham Trent University, Nottingham, UK
e-mail: fotis.mitsakis@ntu.ac.uk

© The Author(s) 2019
S. Nachmias, V. Caven (eds.), *Inequality and Organizational Practice*, Palgrave Explorations in Workplace Stigma, https://doi.org/10.1007/978-3-030-11647-7_3

45

diversity including gender or race (King et al. 2010; Curtis and Dreachslin 2008; Paluck 2006; Kalev et al. 2006; Kulik and Roberson 2008). However, evidence shows that diversity training fails to deliver the expected long-term changes in individual attitudes and organisational culture (Celik et al. 2012; CIPD 2012; Kumra and Manfredi 2012; Kochan et al. 2003).

This chapter aims to provide a critical evaluation of the mainstream literature on diversity training. Current practices outline a 'hidden' inequality element as to how organisations address individual assumptions and eliminate discriminatory practices. Constantly changing environments create a unique challenge for Human Resource Development (HRD) practitioners to provide training interventions that could diminish the effects of the changing workforce towards organisational success without relinquishing the benefits of diversity (Ely 2004). Therefore, this chapter aims to offer a critical understanding as to how an integrated diversity training programme could impact upon individual diversity attitude in response to addressing calls to create knowledge to 'the badly needed credibility and value of diversity training' (Combs and Luthans 2007b, p. 115). This is in line with the Chartered Institute of Personnel and Development's (CIPD) (2012) suggestion that new thinking concerning the implications of a person being different is needed. The following sections provide an evaluation of the current academic literature around diversity training and learning, explain key barriers to addressing diversity training needs and discuss the role of higher education and organisations (e.g. corporate universities) in delivering diversity training and learning. The chapter concludes with a number of operational and strategic recommendations on how organisations can address any 'hidden' inequality that arises while developing and delivering diversity training and learning.

3.2   Understanding Diversity Training

Since the 1990s, there has been a positive discourse around diversity training resulting in an increased number of organisations offering different types of training to individuals (Kochan et al. 2003). Diversity training is perceived as a knowledge enhancement tool to resolve workplace issues (Naff and Kellough 2003). It is frequently defined as any discrete programme aiming to create norms of behaviour, which can facilitate cooperation and motivation to problem-solving (CIPD 2012; King et al. 2010), facilitate positive intergroup interaction, reduce prejudice and discrimination and improve awareness within the workforce (Bezrukova et al. 2012; Pendry et al. 2007). Any leading diversity training and learning programme aims to provide employees with the tools to embrace inclusive attitudes into their daily work. A recent survey from PricewaterhouseCoopers (PwC) (2017a) highlighted the areas in which most diversity training and learning initiatives focus (Fig. 3.1), by identifying the primary objectives for diversity programmes (Fig. 3.2).

Yet, besides those objectives identified, diversity training further seeks to enhance individual skills and knowledge in avoiding potential failure of diversity initiatives (Pendry et al. 2007; Wentling 2001), as well as to enable individuals to become more satisfied due to positive work and social climates (Combs and Luthans 2007a). Organisations are increasingly offering diversity and cultural awareness training. For example, Galvin (2003) found that 72 of the responding companies in the USA offered some form of diversity training. CIPD (2012) also found an increasing number of employers identifying diversity training as an important element within their training and development agenda. Both practitioners and scholars introduced a number of training interventions to address diversity issues. Table 3.1 illustrates various types of diversity training that can be introduced in the workplace.

Non-discrimination and regulation compliance	38%
Embracing differences	48%
Overcoming unconscious bias	42%
Managing diverse populations	39%
Embedding inclusive behaviour in Job	34%

Fig. 3.1 Diversity training interventions

Achieve business results	17%
Respond to customer expectations	9%
Enhance external reputation	16%
Comply with legal requirements	21%
Attract and retain talent	38%

Fig. 3.2 Primary objectives for diversity programmes

Diversity training can be offered through instructional methods such as awareness-based training. As per its name, this approach aims to raise awareness to reveal unexamined assumptions, biases and tendencies to stereotypes (i.e. Roberson et al. 2001). Dovidio et al. (2004) found that awareness and enlightenment practices contribute towards encouraging individuals to challenge hidden and openly held assumptions in an attempt to create emotional empathy, and ultimately to reduce and remove entrenched stereotypical beliefs. This approach is considered the most popular one, with further aiming to foster group interaction and sharing, collective decision-making, as well as by outlining the associated benefits of a diverse workforce through presenting relevant demographic data (Schachner et al. 2016).

Experiential methods of diversity training are also used to educate participants as to how to take a personalised and participatory approach to diversity through the development of behavioural-based skills. In essence, skills-based training aims to move away from just raising awareness amongst the workforce to skill development and actual actions in addressing people's interaction and other diversity concerns (Appannah et al. 2017).

Integration-based practices refer to a combined version of diversity training that is informed from both awareness- and skills-based training initiatives, as well as being fully integrated with an organisation's diversity and inclusion strategy (Thurston et al. 2015). This approach requires for a coordinated effort on behalf of those being involved in the design and delivery of diversity training initiatives to ensure vertical integration with

Table 3.1 Types of diversity training

Type	Description
Instructional methods (Awareness-based training)	This form of training offers the learner the opportunity to raise awareness of key diversity issues and challenge existing assumptions. The primary objectives are to provide information about diversity in general, heighten awareness and sensitivity through uncovering hidden assumptions and biases, assess attitudes and values, correct myths and stereotypes, and foster individual and group sharing
Experiential methods (Skills-based training)	Learning by doing, this training approach is used to develop behavioural skills and physical abilities. The primary objective is to build new diversity-interaction skills, reinforce existing skills, and inventory skill-building methodologies
Integration-based training	A combined training intervention that focuses both on skills development and awareness enhancement. This is an extensive set of training intervention with the scope to remove any existing resistance based on personal biases or prior experiences
Mentoring for diversity	Mentoring for diversity is a comprehensive approach to help people from different backgrounds develop into a team and a community. The primary objective is to use this method aiming to establish a workplace that appreciates and embraces employee differences, spread knowledge and create an effective organisational culture
Diversity audits	It is a self-assessment process that enables organisation to assess current policies and procedures and examine whether equality and diversity is effectively practiced and discrimination eliminated in the organisations. The primary aim is for the organisation to gather information about current thinking and practices, and then design effective training and learning interventions related to the self-assessment needs

the business strategy and horizontal integration with the organisation's Human Resource (HR) approach (Dobbins et al. 2014). Given the dynamic nature of today's business landscapes, and the need to constantly revise business strategies and HR policies to address on-going change, globalisation, workforce's changing nature and so on, an integration-based training can increase the volume of the diversity and inclusion offerings (ibid).

Mentoring for diversity could also prove an effective tool at the hands of the HR professionals in maintaining a collaborative environment in organisations through raising awareness of the workforce on issues relating to diversity and inclusion (Garvey et al. 2017). As to that, mentoring for diversity could be implemented as an instructional training method (Dutton and Ragins 2017). Mentoring could further prove important to leadership in enhancing a diverse mind-set, as well as in supporting a diversity-focused and inclusive organisational culture, to ensure organisational success within the globalised labour markets (Chin et al. 2016).

Finally, a diversity audit refers to a thoughtful review of the existing organisational practices relating to diversity and inclusion concerns (Mujtaba et al. 2016). The practice itself does not represent a training practice, yet it is an important process in evaluating and ensuring that all the above practices are implemented in the right order (Cooke and Jacobs 2018). Such audits could also ensure an organisation's legitimacy to relevant legal diversity and inclusion frameworks, as well as to raise awareness amongst the workforce in relevant concerns within the business (ibid).

3.3 Evaluating the Discourse on Diversity Training

While there is a consensus on the importance of diversity training (Hite and McDonald 2006; CIPD 2012), research has shown that the context of some training interventions can be questioned due to the lack of understanding their possible outcomes and impact on individuals and organisations (Bezrukova et al. 2012; Paluck 2006; Hite and McDonald 2006). Some authors argued that an integrated approach to diversity training (combination of awareness and behavioural skills training) could be more effective in addressing workplace challenges (Naff and Kellough 2003). Indeed, that could be the case due to the horizontal and vertical integration of the diversity practices with the HR and organisational strategy, respectively. Kaplan (2006) further suggested that a behavioural change-awareness diversity training could be linked with increased commitment, as well as with a positive change on individuals' inner assumptions and belief system relating to diversity and inclusion in the workplace. With regards to the latter, a training context that focuses exclusively on a single aspect of diversity might not lead to positive behavioural change of individuals as differences should be validated and valued by the organisation (Zhu and Kleiner 2000; Holladay et al. 2003). In contrast, training interventions with a broader context could lead to greater training success (Rynes and Rosen 1995; Hayles and Russell 1997), as well as could increase an individual's awareness, critical attitude, knowledge and willingness to take action to address diversity and inclusion concerns (Ahonen et al. 2014; Celik et al. 2012).

Critical Point *One of the most common ways that companies attempt to address organisational diversity is through formal training. Yet, research on the effectiveness of such programmes has yielded mixed results: Some studies show that diversity training is effective, others highlight its ineffectiveness. Furthermore, there are others suggesting that it may actually lead to backlash. This has led to pessimism regarding diversity training, with some claiming it simply does not work.* (Lindsey et al. 2015)

Literature also highlights that diversity training is not effective in recognising individual attitudes and behaviours (Foster and Harris 2005). This lends further support for the individual psychological contract of employment: 'the subsequent undermining of collective bargaining, and therefore the power associated with managing diversity' (Mavin and Girling 2000, p. 422). Yet, this is set against Rossett and Bickham's (1994) contention that diversity training is all about harmony, inclusion, justice and transformation. The goal of diversity training is to enable individuals to become more satisfied due to positive work and social climates rather than compliance (Combs and Luthans 2007a). This echoes the views of Özbilgin and Tatli (2011) that a lack of an appropriate diversity training programme could increase labour turnover and dissatisfaction. Foster and Harris (2005) contend that diversity training is a key to changing attitudes and behaviours.

This type of training could enable individuals to understand the concepts of diversity and inclusion better, as well as to realise their profound societal impact, and therefore to comprehend the social and psychological contacts that could affect employees' relationships in the workplace (Kochan et al. 2003). However, such training usually fails to deliver long-term attitudinal and behavioural change outcomes (Celik et al. 2012). There is a tendency to ignore environment and trainees' personal characteristics regardless of their critical importance as transfer factors while implementing diversity knowledge obtained from the training initiative in the workplace (Colquitt et al. 2000). The management and understanding of diversity interventions are also considered crucial, associating with a wide range of benefits if appropriately addressed, and higher costs if not (Hopkins and Hopkins 2002).

The second approach aims to deliver diversity training initiatives that engage with cultural and attitudinal change. As Nemetz and Christensen (1996) suggested, some individuals are unwilling to challenge individual views and therefore the training would have little effect on them and their surroundings. There is a risk of exacerbating current issues (Paluck 2006) if the trainer does not have a full understanding of the organisational context and personnel, often resulting in leaving 'trainees confused, angry, or with more animosity toward differences' (Anand and Winters 2008, p. 361). This could further indicate an organisational inability to consider two fundamental issues: firstly, the implementation of effective knowledge transfer systems; secondly, the existence of practices and policies that may inhibit knowledge transfer (Holton et al. 2000). These challenges identified could lead to a conclusion that diversity training for individuals is often ineffective in producing attitudinal and behavioural change at individual and organisational levels due to the management's unwillingness to embrace change as well (Celik et al. 2012). Further to that, it may also have to do with other individual (e.g. resistance to change, unwillingness to receive training), group (e.g. social norms, limited group cohesiveness) or organisational (e.g. rigid organisational structures, lack of communication, unsuccessful design and delivery of training initiatives) constraints impeding possible change action (Waddell et al. 2017).

The critical issue here is that diversity management is still considered as less strategic with less implicit links to business strategy. The dominant discourse of legal compliance is seen as a key barrier to promote effective diversity training. Diversity trainers themselves have also observed that legal compliance mitigates the process as to how organisations deal with relational issues as they are generally too political and emotional to deal with as part of a training programme (Paluck 2006). The literature indicates that until diversity management is part of the strategic planning process, knowledge transfer routes will not be developed, nor will policies and practices change in order to facilitate awareness, acceptance, adoption and adherence of diversity and inclusion issues within the organisational settings. As Van Oers and Wardekker (1999) argued, learning can potentially relate with the process of personal learning whilst simultaneously developing subject-specific knowledge and understanding for individuals. The above argument reinforces the need to consider the 'dominant narratives' of knowledge development in the field of diversity training (Ahonen et al. 2014) and stimulate the 'sense of urgency' to overcome the barriers of lacking awareness and knowledge of diversity (Celik et al. 2012).

3.4 Potential Barriers to the Successful Implementation of Diversity Training

Many of the barriers associated with the design and implementation of diversity training in organisations do not specifically relate to diversity. Indeed, many of them represent generic challenges that organisations could face in relation to any of their training initiatives.

The most profound obstacles to diversity training are time and costs. From either an organisational or an individual point of view, when both are not ready to change, time and costs appear as being of greater importance than the associated benefits of a diversity training programme (Mor Barak 2017). To overcome time constraints, organisations should be proactive and strategic in nature to identify forthcoming challenges and the change actions required to address them (Paludi 2012). The easiest way to overcome such challenges is to implement effective communication processes to keep organisational members constantly informed on new business objectives. Having a diverse workforce results in the emergence of different interpretations. If employees feel unclear as to how diversity training would benefit themselves and the organisation, their lack of involvement and engagement will be strengthened. As to that, effective communication channels will ensure that everyone is up-to-date with the latest actions undertaken, and thus for smoother transitions to new realities to take place both for the individuals and for the organisation as a whole (Triana 2017).

Having time and cost challenges addressed, another possible barrier to diversity training relates with the lack of a strategic integration between the HR and the business strategy. As suggested within a recent report conducted by PwC (2017b), 'there is a tendency to see diversity and inclusion as the responsibility of HR or a specialist team, rather than integrating them into the wider business management' (p. 11). Indeed, there are many organisations, which do not successfully implement a vertical integration, as well as a horizontal one, between their HR and other business practices. That eventually results in designing and implementing training initiatives that do not match the respective business strategy and objectives. In that case, the failure of diversity training is certain, making diversity as an organisational reality unlikely to happen.

Critical Point *While many organisations can claim they put diversity and inclusion at the core of their people strategy by covering issues such as interviews and assessment methods, grievance procedures and training and development, many key activities that would help to create non-discriminatory and inclusive workplaces are less common.* (CIPD 2012, p. 6)

Employees' attitudes could also play an important role throughout the design and delivery of diversity training. Negative attitudes such as prejudice and stereotyping could impede any diversity management initiative and thus to inhibit the creation of a diverse workplace. Stereotyping could harm employees' relationships, as well as decrease their commitment, morale and productivity (Hays-Thomas 2016). In a similar vein, prejudices held by employees could prove detrimental to the successful creation of a diverse workplace. The creation of a cultural-sensitive business mentality could offer a possible solution in eliminating stereotyping and prejudice in organisations. As to that, awareness-based training, and mentoring, could challenge stereotypes and demonstrate the benefits associated with diversity and inclusion in the workplace (Syed and Özbilgin 2015).

Finally, yet importantly, a huge barrier to diversity training relates with the lack of the appropriate knowledge on behalf of the trainers themselves (Mattiske 2012). If trainers are not competent enough in designing and delivering diversity training programmes, failure is certain. Trainers and diversity management consultants could help organisations to attract, retain and create a diverse workforce. A relative lack of knowledge will lead to employees' misunderstanding of the associated benefits of diversity training; it will decrease their willingness levels to embrace a diverse mind-set, as well as it will impede the building of an inclusive organisational culture (ibid). In addition, relying too heavily on external consultants may lessen organisational commitment to diversity initiatives (Ravazzani 2016).

Successful diversity programmes should clearly demonstrate the business case of diversity training amongst all organisational members, and to communicate effectively how the training relates to the general diversity and inclusion business strategy. In addition to that, diversity training programmes should be tailored to specific organisational and individual needs rather than being offered in a more general manner. It should be made clear that relevant programmes are for everyone in an attempt to create a supportive learning infrastructure. Trainers should also be trained as to how they could address diversity concerns, with that further maximising the effectiveness of the design and delivery of diversity training. Senior management's involvement and engagement is also considered critical in demonstrating the benefits of such initiatives. Having all these elements secured, individual and organisational confidence and accountability could be built. Yet, considering the potential barriers to diversity training, and having them reinforced due to the constantly changing economic and business landscapes, other options should be examined; diversity learning could offer an alternative route to suit diverse learning styles.

Case Study 1: Diversity Training for Police Officers *Having communities which are more diverse nowadays, police officers have to deal with many discrimination cases on a regular basis. Respectively, the police force itself embraces equality, diversity and inclusion in relation to its workforce planning by welcoming applications from people with different cultural backgrounds so on. However, there are many reports indicating a power misuse on behalf of the police officers towards citizens of different race (in some cases) and/or lack of knowledge on how to deal with equality and diversity concerns successfully. The nature of work of the police force is also different to regular jobs, as well as it is changing (e.g. the type of crime is changing, police workforce is shrinking, and more qualifications are required).*

3.5   Exploring Diversity Learning

The demanding nature of today's business environments requires organisations to become knowledge-intensive repositories within which various forms of training and learning occur to ensure that the entire organisation, and its members, could adapt to constantly changing landscapes through creative and innovative solutions (Andresen 2007). Innovation and creativity could be fostered within a diverse business environment owing to the differences that could emerge amongst the organisational members in relation to their knowledge, skills, experience, abilities and so on. Diversity learning initiatives appear as knowledge-management approaches for organisations to advance and engender new knowledge, moving beyond knowledge sharing through diversity training. Diversity learning has been seen as an alternative approach, as well as an important dimension of diversity, to address relevant concerns and deliver real change to organisations (Andresen 2007). Learning interventions emphasise on learning that include the acquisition of knowledge, awareness and skills (King et al. 2010).

Constantly changing and turbulent business environments demand that organisations apply learning and training initiatives to ensure that individuals and the entire organisation as well could adapt easily to on-going change (Andresen and Lichtenberger 2007). Friday and Friday (2003) suggested that through a diverse work environment, creativity and innovation could be fostered due to the different perspectives different people could bring. As to that, raising awareness of the importance of diversity and inclusion through diversity training and learning is critical. It is important to offer unique learning opportunities by understanding the target audience needs and managing perceptions of preferential treatment to establish the appropriate organisational policies and procedures that could enable transfer of knowledge in the workplace.

The argument here is not to distinguish the difference between diversity training and learning. Yet, while the former deals with sharing existing knowledge amongst the organisational members, the latter takes a more strategic approach aiming to generate new knowledge and proposed actions to address diversity concerns more effectively (Sun et al. 2017; Scott and Sims 2016). Diversity learning is primarily focused on increasing individual and organisational inclusion through reinforcing knowledge. As to that, an important aspect of diversity learning is to utilise learners' existing knowledge and the workforce's diverse nature within the learning process. That could enable both the learners and those delivering diversity learning to engage into a knowledge-exchange session and thus to promote creative and innovative thinking (McIntyre and Harrison 2016). Therefore, diversity learning could lead to organisational competitive advantage through integrating existing knowledge, experience and employees' capabilities within the learning process (Andresen 2007).

Inclusion also plays a crucial role within the learning process. In the words of Andresen (2007, p. 746), 'inclusion, in the context of the learning process, describe the extent to which existing differences among knowledge bearers are consciously included, ranging from rejection to the awareness and understanding of differences to the profitable integration and use of knowledge diversity'. The author's suggestion actually argues that although existing knowledge might be at high levels amongst the workforce, it cannot be guaranteed that it will be used throughout a learning process (ibid). Eventually, there has to be an effective evaluation mechanism to ensure that knowledge-exchange interventions run under a high volume of inclusion.

There is no doubt that training employees is considered somehow a 'trendy frame' amongst organisations; however, the assumptions that only those things we see can make a difference in diversity are seen as inappropriate and ineffective (Hite and McDonald 2006). Invisible differences may lead to radically different workplace values and behaviours, as well as to improved awareness of diversity issues. The idea of awareness is an important first step in enabling change to happen at both individual and organisational levels. Celik et al. (2012) suggested that the establishment of awareness should be followed by acceptance, adoption and adherence. Therefore, diversity learning can be seen as a minded process, where managers and employees involve in a process of examining the operational and behavioural reality, which could lead to durable and relevant work-based solutions rather than to a policy implementation solution (Foster and Harris 2005). This shows the importance of developing diversity training and learning interventions that could enhance individual and organisational diversity awareness.

Changing individual capabilities is a key part of any diversity initiative. Nussbaum (1999) suggest that basic, internal and combined capabilities are fundamental to developing appropriate diversity training and learning interventions. Firstly, basic capabilities are defined as individual abilities, which form the basis of developing capabilities that are more advanced. Organisations should be able to foster an environment where employees could develop those capabilities through positive action. Secondly, internal capabilities are internal states of readiness to act or freedom which could be secured by education or training. It is essential to minimise internal resistance and address any individual discriminatory behaviours (ibid). In this case, diversity training and learning act as a tool to ensure that all employees have the opportunity to assess and develop internal capabilities regardless their diverse background. Thirdly, the combined capabilities work in conjunction with external structural conditions as individuals develop basic capabilities through improving internal capabilities of promoting diversity (Nussbaum 1999).

Critical Point *Level of awareness and knowledge of how culture and other aspects of one's group identity work are crucial to inform a professional understanding of human behaviour in and outside of work. Interpersonal skills are also essential to effectively work with and manage demographically diverse individuals, groups and organisations.* (Avery and Thomas 2004, p. 382)

3.6 The Role of Higher Education in Diversity Training and Learning

Higher education plays a critical role in developing appropriate set of skills and capabilities for the future. For example, Nelson (2011) and Nelson and Engberg (2011) argued that universities which wish to cultivate an equality, diversity and inclusion culture should design and implement relevant strategies, policies and plans that aim to foster a collaborative and safe environment for their staff and students based on mutual trust and respect. Further to that, they should recognise the unique characteristics of individuals and manage any potential differentials arising from their diverse environments (ibid). Also of importance is to promote an anti-racist, anti-sexist and anti-homophobic behaviour through avoiding stereotyping as well. Having these elements secured, both their staff's and their students' engagement and belonging will be enhanced, with this behaviour being transferred within their work settings upon graduation in most cases (Thomas 2015; Healey et al. 2014). Although there is mixed evidence on the impact of equality and diversity-based programmes offered by universities, a recent survey conducted by the Higher Education Academy (2016) suggests that the 'partnership ethos that could be fostered through relevant courses could prove crucial and effective in all spheres of learning and teaching activities' (p. 9).

Case Study 2: Diversity Awareness Amongst University Students *You are a research project supervisor of a mixed group of undergraduate students. Everything seems to work well for the group until one of its members raises a concern to you regarding a fellow student. A tension emerged within the group after getting out for drinks one day, and some of them noticed that one of their group members has a different sexual orientation to them (he is homosexual with them being heterosexual). Since then, they marginalised that student and refused to work with him, as they believe his case contrasts their beliefs. They have even requested you to transfer the "gay man" (as they have called him) to a different team.*

Thomas and May (2010) suggested a framework for universities to establish a conducive teaching environment and experience for their students which will not place them at a disadvantage based on their individual characteristics. The authors suggested the elements of a diverse and inclusive learning approach as presented in the following Fig. 3.3.

To ensure that this could happen, educational institutions need to design their curricula in such a way to incorporate equality, diversity and inclusion data within their study programmes. Students' demographic data and other statistics could offer important information relating to the structure of the cohorts to allow teaching staff to design and deliver those learning interventions that could address diverse learning styles and to foster engagement and participation (Hanesworth 2015). Course contexts should also be designed by incorporating the students' and the

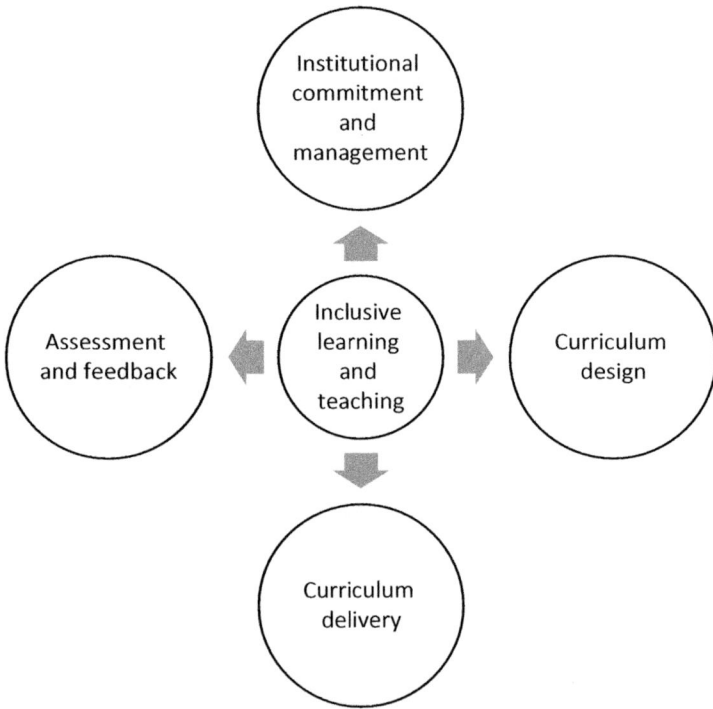

Fig. 3.3 Elements of diverse and inclusive curricula

teaching staff's multi-cultural contributions (ibid). Lee et al. (2012) also suggested that by integrating relevant diversity themes/concerns into teaching and learning contexts (e.g. material, activities etc.), it could offer the path to constructive dialogues through sharing diverse interpretations and viewpoints.

Morgan (2013) further argued that universities should provide students the opportunity to engage in a range of activities within mixed/diverse groups to allow them to offer their diverse perspectives (curriculum delivery). Educational institutions should develop an effective class climate through addressing the social dynamics of students' interaction (Thomas and May 2010). Having secured fair and inclusive class conditions would lead to positive behaviours towards diversity concerns, as well as it is expected to enhance all participants' motivation and intellectual capacity through engaging and interactive sessions.

The assessment and feedback processes should also embrace an inclusive approach to allow students to demonstrate their knowledge and understating of the topics taught, as well as allowing them to involve actively throughout their development and alteration (Sadler 2009). There are authors suggesting that a gender bias can be identified amongst students' assessment in many universities (Hartley et al. 2007; Read et al. 2005), as well as amongst students coming from disadvantaged social, economic and cultural backgrounds (Ertl et al. 2009; Richardson 2008). As to that, these should be designed in such a way to ensure fairness and benefits for all with a degree of flexible arrangements as well for individuals under particular or exceptional circumstances (Fuller and Healey 2009).

All educational institutions further need to take a strategic approach towards addressing equality, diversity and inclusion concerns through their curricula. The commitment of their managerial and academic staff is important to ensure that everyone works towards the same objectives relating to the creation of an equal, diverse and inclusive environment (May and Bridger 2010). As to that, their vision, mission, policies and structures should reflect their overall commitment in incorporating the notion of equality, diversity and inclusion both within their teaching and learning practices and within their daily business conduct (ibid).

Further to educational institutions, corporate universities (universities established by firms to offer training interventions to their workforce, Schultz 2015) also play a crucial role nowadays in raising people's awareness of equality, diversity and inclusion in the workplace. Corporate universities can be viewed as repositories of knowledge within which both knowledge sharing and new knowledge could be generated. Organisations could achieve competitive advantage through the introduction of a corporate university as they could integrate, utilise and coordinate their workforce's skills, capabilities, knowledge and experience within. To talk about a successful corporate university, all suggestions made above could apply here as well. Andresen (2007) used a metaphor to exemplify the importance of corporate universities by suggesting that 'competitiveness at the national and especially at the international level does not primarily depend on which way the wind is blowing, but rather on how you set the sails' (p. 747). Therefore, it is of the captain's and his/her crew experience, knowledge and qualifications to sail their boat, regardless of the direction and the power of the wind. Implicitly, the metaphor suggests that organisations should be engaged in a continuous process of identifying the learning needs of their workforce, assess all internal and external environmental factors, and finally design and deliver the appropriate training and learning interventions to ensure that their employees possess the right skills and attitude to move forward the business. In that case, a corporate university could set the right conditions (like conventional universities, Rheaume and Gardoni 2015; Thornton 2014; Baporikar 2014).

All the aforementioned approaches to teaching and learning within the conventional university settings could develop students' equality, diversity and inclusion awareness and competences, and thus to largely inform their approach within their workplaces in the future. Entering employment, it is the role of corporate universities to ensure a continuum of these successful practices through quite similar settings. For both cases though, self-reflection of diversity awareness is important, on behalf of all participants within the learning process, to ensure that all share the same understanding of the purpose and the significance of embedding equality, diversity and inclusion into curricula and business processes.

3.7   Concluding Remarks

Diversity in the workplace continues to pose challenges in today's organisations due to the complexity of human relations. However, our evaluation on diversity training and learning literature reveals a very vague picture as to how individuals challenge assumptions, biases and prejudice in the workplace. The issue of 'hidden' inequality emerges from the fact that current diversity training practices do not promote and support the development of a positive culture that allows individuals to take a proactive role in understanding diversity through generating new knowledge (diversity learning). This 'hidden' aspect needs to be addressed as organisations are now encouraged to develop social relations at both individual and organisational levels to challenge held assumptions that are culturally and socially driven. As Argote et al. (2001) argued, social interaction could produce new insights into organisational culture and develop diverse skills and knowledge. It is necessary to provide equal opportunities to enable individuals to change permanently their attitude and behaviours. We recognise that this can be seen as an overly simplified statement as organisational reality (i.e. resources, management styles, working conditions) might not encourage the opportunity to acquire skills and knowledge. Nevertheless, we are unable to address long-standing concerns about the appropriateness of diversity training and provide effective solutions to diversity needs. Legal compliance training failed to recognise individual attitudes and behaviours. This has resulted in an unrealistic view of how diversity management contributes to the organisational success (Bezrukova et al. 2012) and enables organisations to develop appropriate skills-set by recognising individual differences (CIPD 2012).

Analysis also highlights a submerged discourse arguing that moral obligations, accountability and pluralistic perspectives to diversity issues should be an integral part of the relationship between training development (participants' needs) and organisational strategy. As De Meuse and Hostager (2001) suggested, for diversity training and learning to be effective, participants must perceive themselves as being accountable for their actions, motivated to choose to perform, willing to exert the necessary effort and be persistent in that effort over time. Of course, we can debate the differences between training and learning; however, we argue that this level of debate is ineffective to support current organisational needs. Individuals who are offered an inducement to behave in a certain way are less likely to carry on with that behaviour than those who are simply asked to behave in that way (Kohn 1993). Our analysis shows that organisations need support to re-consider how they design and deliver diversity training and learning. This 'hidden' source of inequality on diversity training development should be addressed by increasing awareness, critical attitude, knowledge and willingness to take actions. To achieve that, we argue that positive management actions are required to deliver desired diversity training results. This is in line with the CIPD's (2012) suggestion that new thinking is required to address the implications of a person being different.

Evaluation also shows that learners' personal characteristics could not be considered as being able to deliver attitudinal and behavioural change. Diversity factors such as the workforce's professional experience, the work itself, as well as other diversity aspects such as age, gender and culture, could directly affect the design and provision of diversity learning, furthering to their impact on the existing knowledge repository. As Nemetz and Christensen (1996) suggest, some individuals are unwilling to challenge individual views and therefore the training would have little effect on them. Therefore, organisations should address this 'hidden' inequality by investing in instilling knowledge to promote positive work climates.

It is evident that diversity training should be evolved from concentrating on legal regulatory compliance to recognition of the performance impact through challenging individual differences and perception; thus, moving to diversity learning. This chapter confirms previously highlighted arguments that there is a need to provide diversity training programmes that will have the potential to stimulate the 'sense of urgency', and to overcome the barrier of lacking awareness and knowledge of diversity (Celik et al. 2012). Of course, there is no single answer to this, but we need to address long-standing issues in diversity training provision. There is a need to initiating and supporting a range of activities as a way of furthering diversity and inclusion. Almost invariably, these initiatives should be supported through effective management skills and should be able to deliver appropriate behavioural, attitudinal and skills changes that assimilates the complex nature of the current workforce.

References

Ahonen, P., J. Tienari, S. Merilanlnen, and A. Pullen. 2014. Hidden contexts and invisible power relations: A Foucauldian reading of diversity research. *Human Relations* 67: 263–286.

Anand, R., and M. Winters. 2008. A retrospective view of corporate diversity training from 1964 to the present. *The Academy of Management Learning and Education* 7: 356–372.

Andresen, M. 2007. Diversity learning, knowledge diversity and inclusion. Theory and practice as exemplified by corporate universities. *Equal Opportunities International* 26: 743–760.

Andresen, M., and B. Lichtenberger. 2007. The corporate university landscape in Germany. *Journal of Workplace Learning* 19: 109–123.

Appannah, A., C. Mayer, R. Ogrin, S. McMillan, E. Barrett, and C. Browing. 2017. Diversity training for the community aged care workers: A conceptual framework for evaluation. *Evaluation and Program Planning* 63: 74–81.

Argote, L., D. Gruenfeld, and C. Naquin. 2001. Group learning in organisations. In *Groups at work: Theory and research*, ed. P. Turner, 369–411. New York: Erlbaum.

Avery, D.R., and K.M. Thomas. 2004. Blending content and contact: The roles of diversity curriculum and campus heterogeneity in fostering diversity management competency. *Academy of Management Learning & Education* 3: 380–396.

Baporikar, N. 2014. Corporate university edification in knowledge society. *International Journal of Strategic Change Management* 5: 125–139.

Bezrukova, K., K. Jehn, and C. Spell. 2012. Reviewing diversity training: Where we have been and where we should go. *The Academy of Management Learning and Education* 11: 207–227.

Celik, H., T. Abma, I. Klinge, and A. Widder. 2012. Process evaluation of a diversity training program: The method strategy. *Evaluation and Program Planning* 35: 54–65.

Chin, J.L., L. Desormeaux, and K. Sawyer. 2016. Making way for paradigms of diversity leadership. *Consulting Psychology Journal: Practice and Research* 68: 49–71.

CIPD. 2012. Diversity and inclusion – Fringe or fundamental? https://www.cipd.co.uk/knowledge/fundamentals/relations/diversity/inclusion-report. Accessed 15 May 2018.

Colquitt, J., J. LePine, and R. Noe. 2000. Towards an integrative theory of training motivation: A meta-analytic path analysis of 20 years of research. *Journal of Applied Psychology* 85: 678–707.

Combs, G.M., and F. Luthans. 2007a. Diversity training: Analysis of the impact of self-efficacy. *Human Resource Development Quarterly* 18: 91–120.

———. 2007b. Diversity education: Analysis of the impact of self-efficacy. *Human Resource Development Quarterly* 18: 91–120.

Cooke, N.A., and J.A. Jacobs. 2018. Diversity and cultural competence in the LIS classroom: A curriculum audit. *Urban Library Journal* 24: 1–21.

Curtis, E.F., and J.L. Dreachslin. 2008. Integrative literature review: Diversity management interventions and organizational performance: A synthesis of current literature. *Human Resource Development Review* 7: 107–134.

De Meuse, K., and T. Hostager. 2001. Developing an instrument for measuring attitudes toward and perceptions of workplace diversity: An initial report. *Human Resource Development Quarterly* 12: 33–51.

Dobbins, J.E., B. Beale, A. Thornton, and T.G. Porter. 2014. Exploring the intersection of parenting, ethnicity, race, and gender in the deconstruction of the nuclear family archetype. In *Handbook of race-ethnicity and gender in psychology*, ed. M.L. Miville and A.D. Ferguson, 131–149. New York: Springer.

Dovidio, J.F., M. ten Vergert, T. Stewart, S.L. Gaertner, J. Johnson, V. Esses, B.M. Riek, and A.R. Pearson. 2004. Perspective and prejudice: Antecedents and mediating mechanisms. *Personality and Social Psychology Bulletin* 30: 1537–1549.

Dutton, J.E., and B.R. Ragins. 2017. *Exploring positive relationships at work: Building a theoretical and research foundation.* New York: Psychology Press.

Ely, R. 2004. A field study of group diversity, participation in diversity education programs, and performance. *Journal of Organisational Behaviour* 25: 755–780.

Ertl, H., G. Hayward, and M. Hoelscher. 2009. Learners' transition from vocational education and training to higher education. In *Improving learning by widening participation*, ed. M. David, 27–45. London: Routledge.

Foster, C., and L. Harris. 2005. Easy to say, difficult to do: Diversity management in retail. *Human Resource Management Journal* 15: 4–17.

Friday, E., and S. Friday. 2003. Managing diversity using a strategic planned change approach. *Journal of Management Development* 22: 863–880.

Fuller, M., and M. Healey. 2009. Assessing disabled students: Student and staff experiences of reasonable adjustments. In *Improving disabled students' learning*, ed. M. Fuller, J. Georgeson, M. Healey, A. Hurst, K. Kelly, S. Riddell, H. Roberts, and E. Weedon, 60–77. New York: Routledge.

Galvin, T. 2003. Industry report. *Training* 40: 21–36.

Garvey, B., P. Stokes, and D. Megginson. 2017. *Coaching and mentoring: Theory and practice*. London: Sage Publishing.

Hanesworth, P. 2015. Embedding equality and diversity in the curriculum: A model for learning and teaching practitioners. https://www.heacademy. ac.uk/knowledge-hub/embedding-equality-and-diversity-curriculum-model-learning-and-teaching-0. Accessed 17 May 2018.

Hartley, J., L. Betts, and W. Murray. 2007. Gender and assessment: Differences, similarities and implications. *Psychology Teaching Review* 13: 34–43.

Hayles, V.W., and A.M. Russell. 1997. *The diversity directive: Why some initiatives fail and what to do about it*. New York: McGraw-Hill.

Hays-Thomas, R. 2016. *Managing workplace diversity and inclusion: A psychological perspective*. New York: Routledge.

Healey, M., A. Flint, and K. Harrington 2014. Engagement through partnership: Students as partners in learning and teaching in higher education. https://www.heacademy.ac.uk/system/files/resources/engagement_through_partnership.pdf. Accessed 14 May 2018.

Higher Education Academy (HEA). 2016. Equality and diversity in learning and teaching in higher education. A series of papers from Equality Challenge Unit and Higher Education Academy joint conferences. http://www.ecu. ac.uk/wp-content/uploads/2016/03/Equality-and-diversity-in-learning-and-teaching-Summary-report.pdf. Accessed 15 May 2018.

Hite, L., and K. McDonald. 2006. Diversity training pitfalls and possibilities: An exploration of small and mid-size US organisations. *Human Resource Development International* 9: 365–377.

Holladay, C.L., J. Knight, D. Paige, and M. Quiñones. 2003. The influence of framing on attitudes toward diversity training. *Human Resource Development Quarterly* 14: 245–263.

Holton, E., R. Bates, and W. Ruona. 2000. Development of a generalized learning transfer system inventory. *Human Resource Development Quarterly* 11: 333–360.

Hopkins, W., and S. Hopkins. 2002. Effects of cultural recomposition on group interaction processes. *Academy of Management Review* 27: 541–553.

Kalev, A., F. Dobbin, and E. Kelly. 2006. Best practices or best guesses? Assessing the efficacy of corporate affirmative action and diversity policies. *American Sociological Review* 71: 589–617.

Kaplan, D.M. 2006. Can diversity training discriminate? Backlash to lesbian, gay, and bisexual diversity initiatives. *Employee Responsibilities and Rights Journal* 18: 61–72.

King, E.B., L.M. Gulick, and D. Avery. 2010. The divide between diversity training and diversity education: Integrating best practices. *Journal of Management Education* 34: 891–906.

Kochan, A., K. Bezrukova, R. Ely, L. Jackson, A. Joshi, K. Jehn, L. Leonard, D. Levine, and D. Thomas. 2003. The effect of diversity on business performance: Report of the diversity research network. *Human Resource Management* 42: 3–21.

Kohn, A. 1993. *Punished by rewards: The trouble with gold stars, incentive plans, A's, praise and other bribes.* New York: Plenum Press.

Kulik, C., and L. Roberson. 2008. Common goals and golden opportunities: Evaluations of diversity education in academic and organizational settings. *The Academy of Management Learning and Education* 7: 309–331.

Kumra, S., and S. Manfredi. 2012. *Managing equality and diversity: Theory and practice.* Oxford: Oxford University Press.

Lee, A., R. Williams, and R. Kilaberia. 2012. Engaging diversity in first year college classrooms. *Innovative Higher Education* 37: 199–213.

Lindsey, A., E. King, M. Hebl, and N. Levine. 2015. The impact of method, motivation, and empathy on diversity training effectiveness. *Journal of Business and Psychology* 30 (3): 605–617.

Mattiske, C. 2012. *Understanding and managing diversity: Manager and employee toolkit for an inclusive workplace.* Sydney: The Performance Company Pty.

Mavin, S., and G. Girling. 2000. What is managing diversity and why does it matter? *Human Resource Development International* 3: 419–433.

May, H., and K. Bridger. 2010. *Developing and embedding inclusive policy and practice in higher education.* York: The Higher Education Academy.

McIntyre, L.J., and I.R. Harrison. 2016. Knowledge exchange methods in practice: Knowing how to design for older adults. *Architectural Research Quarterly* 20: 271–280.

Mor Barak, M.E. 2017. *Managing diversity: Toward a globally inclusive workplace.* 4th ed. Singapore: Sage Publications Ltd.

Morgan, M. 2013. *Supporting student diversity in higher education: A practical guide.* Abingdon: Routledge.

Mujtaba, B.G., F.J. Cavico, and T. Seanatip. 2016. Managing stereotypes toward American Muslims in the modern workplace through legal training, diversity assessments and audits. *Journal of Human Resources Management and Labor Studies* 4: 1–45.

Naff, K., and E. Kellough. 2003. Ensuring employment equity: Are federal diversity programs making a difference? *International Journal of Public Administration* 26: 1307–1336.

Nelson, L.T. 2011. Measuring the diversity inclusivity of college courses. *Research in Higher Education* 52: 572–588.

Nelson, L.T., and M.E. Engberg. 2011. Establishing differences between diversity requirements and other courses with varying degrees of diversity inclusivity. *The Journal of General Education* 60: 117–137.

Nemetz, P., and S. Christensen. 1996. Cultural diversity: Harnessing a diversity of views to understand multiculturalism. *Academy of Management Review* 21: 434–462.

Nussbaum, M. 1999. Women and equality: The capabilities approach. *International Labour Review* 138: 227–245.

Özbilgin, M., and A. Tatli. 2011. An emic approach to intersectional study of diversity at work: A Bourdieuan framing. *International Journal of Management Reviews* 14: 180–200.

Paluck, E.L. 2006. Diversity training and intergroup contact: A call for action research. *Journal of Social Issues* 62 (3): 577–595.

Paludi, M.A. 2012. *Managing diversity in today's workplace: Strategies for employees and employers*, Women and careers in management series, volume 1: Gender, race, sexual orientation, ethnicity, and power. Santa Barbara: Praeger.

Pendry, L., F. Driscoll, and S. Field. 2007. Diversity training: Putting theory into practice. *Journal of Occupational and Organizational Psychology* 80: 27–50.

PricewaterhouseCoopers (PWC). 2017a. Diversity and inclusion benchmarking survey. A global data sheet. https://www.pwc.com/gx/en/services/people-organisation/global-diversity-and-inclusion-survey/global-report.pdf. Accessed 15 May 2018.

———. 2017b. No holding back: Breaking down the barriers to diversity. A real diversity report. https://www.pwc.co.uk/human-resource-services/assets/documents/real-diversity-2017-no-holding-back.pdf. Accessed 11 May 2018.

Ravazzani, S. 2016. Understanding approaches to managing diversity in the workplace: An empirical investigation in Italy. *Equality, Diversity and Inclusion: An International Journal* 35: 154–168.

Read, B., B. Francis, and J. Robson. 2005. Gender 'bias', assessment and feedback: Analysing the written assessment of undergraduate history essays. *Assessment and Evaluation in Higher Education* 30: 241–260.

Rheaume, L., and M. Gardoni. 2015. The challenges facing corporate universities in dealing with open innovation. *Journal of Workplace Learning* 27: 315–328.

Richardson, J.T. 2008. The attainment of ethnic minority students in UK higher education. *Studies in Higher Education* 33: 33–48.

Roberson, L., C. Kulik, and M. Pepper. 2001. Designing effective diversity training: Influence of group composition and trainee experience. *Journal of Organizational Behavior* 22: 871–885.

Rossett, A., and T. Bickham. 1994. Diversity training: Hope, faith and cynicism. *Training* 31: 40–46.

Rynes, S., and B. Rosen. 1995. A field survey of factors affecting the adoption and perceived success of diversity training. *Personnel Psychology* 48: 247–270.

Sadler, D. 2009. Indeterminacy in the use of pre-set criteria for assessment and grading. *Assessment and Evaluation in Higher Education* 34: 159–179.

Schachner, M.K., P. Noack, F. Van de Vijver, and K. Eckstein. 2016. Cultural diversity climate and psychological adjustment at school equality and inclusion versus cultural pluralism. *Child Development* 87: 1175–1191.

Schultz, D. 2015. The rise and coming demise of the corporate university. *Academe* 101: 21–23.

Scott, C., and J. Sims. 2016. *Developing workforce diversity programs, curriculum, and degrees in Higher Education*. Hersey: IGI Global.

Sun, H., P. Teh, K. Ho, and B. Lin. 2017. Team diversity, learning, and innovation: A mediation model. *Journal of Computer Information Systems* 57: 22–30.

Syed, J., and M. Özbilgin. 2015. *Managing diversity and inclusion: An international perspective*. London: Sage Publications.

Thomas, K. 2015. Rethinking belonging through Bourdieu, diaspora and the spatial. *Widening Participation and Lifelong Learning* 17: 37–49.

Thomas, K., and H. May. 2010. Inclusive learning and teaching in higher education. https://www.heacademy.ac.uk/system/files/inclusivelearningandteaching_finalreport.pdf. Accessed 20 May 2018.

Thornton, M. 2014. Legal education in the corporate university. *Annual Review of Law and Social Science* 10: 19–35.

Thurston, I., W. Gray, and E. Pulgaron. 2015. Going above and beyond: Exemplar diversity training in pediatric psychology. *Clinical Practice in Pediatric Psychology* 3: 241–248.

Triana, M. 2017. *Managing diversity in organisations: A global perspective*. New York: Routledge.

Van Oers, B., and W. Wardekker. 1999. On becoming an authentic learner: Semiotic activity in the early grades. *Journal of Curriculum Studies* 16: 62–72.

Waddell, D., A. Creed, T. Cummings, and C. Worley. 2017. *Organisational change, development and transformation*. 6th ed. South Melbourne: Cengage Learning.

Wentling, R. 2001. Evaluating of diversity initiatives in multinational corporations. *Human Resource Development International* 3: 435–450.

Zhu, J., and B. Kleiner. 2000. The failure of diversity training. *Nonprofit World* 18: 12–14.

4

Silenced Inequalities: Too Young or Too Old?

Ning Wu

4.1 Introduction

Age discrimination is interpreted differently between countries, especially when it comes to which age group or groups are more likely to be disadvantaged and need protection than the other. Ageism, conceptualised as a third great 'ism' alongside racism and sexism (Palmore 1990) in the US, is defined as 'a process of systematic stereotyping and discrimination against people because they are old' (Butler 1995, pp. 38–39). Contrasting to the Age Discrimination in Employment Act 1967 in the US, where only older people (over 40) are protected, EU member countries passed and adopted the Employment Equality Framework Directive in 2000 to ensure all ages are protected from unfair treatment on the grounds of their age (Council Directive 2000/78/EC). In Britain, the Equality Act 2010 includes provisions that ban age discrimination against

N. Wu (✉)
Brunel University London, London, UK
e-mail: ning.wu@brunel.ac.uk

© The Author(s) 2019
S. Nachmias, V. Caven (eds.), *Inequality and Organizational Practice*, Palgrave
Explorations in Workplace Stigma, https://doi.org/10.1007/978-3-030-11647-7_4

adults in the provision of services and public functions, because they are either 'younger' or 'older' than a relevant and comparable employee. The ban came into force on 1 October 2012, and it is now unlawful to discriminate any individual on the basis of age unless there is an objective justification for the differential treatment or the practice is covered by an exception from the ban. This Act concerns all age groups: any prejudice or discrimination against or in favour of any specific age group is prohibited (Acas 2014; Palmore 1999). In practice, nonetheless, two groups appear to be more likely discriminated against than the other: those who are deemed 'younger' or 'older' than the middle-aged (Acas 2017; Sargeant 2006).

While prominent attention has been paid to older people due to ageing society in America (McEvoy and Cascio 1989) and the 'live longer and work longer' position in Europe (OECD 2006), limited research has turned the spotlight to younger workers in the past two decades. Reasons include older workers are more likely to suffer from ageism, and the consequences of such discrimination would appear to be more severe than for younger workers. Such imbalance in ageism literature can also be explained by the more negative attitudes towards old than young workers widely held by a society (Kite et al. 2005), since youth is a temporary status (Garstka et al. 2004; Iversen et al. 2009). However, there is evidence suggesting age discrimination experienced by younger workers is different from that experienced by older workers (Sargeant 2006). It may be the case that younger workers suffer more profoundly by particular aspects of employment, while older workers endure greater prejudice and unequal treatment on other aspects. Research reports that certain employment opportunities consider this specific age group too young and lacking required experience and skills (Butler 2005, 2009; North and Fiske 2012), whereas other job opportunities steer away from older workers, who are perceived as lacking motivation, resistant to change and inflexible (Arrowsmith and McGoldrick 1997). Hence, age discrimination can be negative for one age group (young workers) but positive for a competing age group (the aged group) and vice versa. Additionally, strategic human resource management (HRM) has noted that age discrimination is evident throughout various processes in HRM. Employee perceived age discrimination, for example, is documented in recruitment and selection, career advancement or promotion, opportunities for training, performance assessment and exit management (Acas 2014; Snape and Redman 2003). Researching age discrimination would appear to benefit from studying different age groups, which can provide insights for management within an organisational context to identify areas where workers are likely to suffer from unequal treatment and offer protection to workers at all ages. This has become especially important for socially responsible and high-performance organisations where a talent pool featuring diversity is pivotal for success.

Despite a steady increase in the number of ageism studies (especially those concerning older workers) in the past two decades, the definition of 'young' and 'old' workers is inconsistent among extant literature. Researchers often opt to follow the age norms held by the population within the researched countries or regions. Age norms represent commonly held beliefs regarding the standard or appropriate age that a person holds a particular job or occupation (Lawrence 1987, 1988). In practice, age norms depend on cultural, institutional and political factors. For instance, most industrialised countries define young people according to statutory minimum school-leaving age: for example, 18–24 years of age refers to 'young' in Britain, whereas many developing countries do not have a minimum school-leaving age (O'Higgins 2001). Despite such inconsistency in categorising young people between countries, United Nations defines 'youth' as those aged from 15 to 24 years inclusive (United Nations 1992), and an increasing number of researchers have started to adopt such a definition. In contrast to the generally convergent view of the high end of age band defining young people, the definition of old (or older) people varies significantly between countries as well as research. As discussed above, for example, the anti-age discrimination regulation that was brought into force in America in 1960s still maintains employees over forties as its older category and thereby outlaws any discrimination or unequal treatment towards this particular group of employees only. Contrastingly, to reflect the changing human life cycle where people are living longer and tend to work longer, for example, OECD (the Organisation for Economic Co-operation and Development) official reports recently categorise the population into three age groups: 15–24 as young age, 25–54 as prime age, and 55–64 as old age (OECD

2017). In Britain, some studies differentiate between four age groups: young (16–24), middle age (25–49), old (50–state pension age) and senior (over state pension age) (Sargeant 2006). As the state pension age is gradually changing for both men and women, there appears a trend to synchronise the categorisation of age bands with a gradually extended life cycle of people to ensure disadvantaged age groups will be protected from unequal treatment in workplaces.

Among extant literature, several theories emerge as a useful means to understand reasons behind unequal treatment experienced by workers on the grounds of their age. Human capital theory explains that age discrimination can be hidden in recruitment, training and exit scheme when perceived gains vary between age groups (Arrowsmith and McGoldrick 1997; Urwin 2006). For instance, older workers are perceived to possess a fast depreciating stock of human capital in front of fast-changing new technology and are frequently stereotyped as incapable of, or unwilling to, adapting to such new challenges. Related career development theory stresses work motivation and resultant performance against various age-related stages in the human life cycle (Super 1990): individuals moving on to establishment via skill building and stabilisation through work experience in their mid-twenties, maintaining in the mid-forties by continually adjusting and improving position, and eventually reaching decline with reduced output in the mid-sixties. Perceived as being either too young or too old, individuals are stereotyped and managed according to the age group they belong to through recruitment, training, performance assessment, promotion and exit. When such perception and stereotyping become internalised by the general mass belonging to that specific age groups, it starts to erode self-confidence and dampen the desire to pursue future employment opportunities (Gutek et al. 1996; Loretto and White 2006). Finally, labour market segmentation theory argues that there are two types of labour markets: the primary labour market targets developing and retaining firm-specific skills and establishing loyalty and focusing on younger people with a viewpoint for long-term employment relationship and succession; the secondary market comprises atypical forms of employment with marginal jobs requiring lower skills and a view of short-term employment contract (Arrowsmith and McGoldrick 1997). The flexibility presented by the latter has been argued to create mutual gains—older workers work shorter periods with flexible hours while employers benefit from numerical flexibility (McGregor and Gray 2003). When purposefully designed jobs start to target specific age groups in labour markets by emphasising person-job fit and at the same time stripping job security and fringe benefits, age discrimination becomes subtle and operates in silence.

Overall, research to date submits that age stereotypes are very common and likely lead to discriminatory HRM practice. While employers claim commitment to equal opportunities, they may stress that age-related disparities in recruitment and selection are due to younger candidates lacking extensive experience (Arrowsmith and McGoldrick 1997), or older workers being overqualified (Shen and Kleiner 2001). The practice of anti-age discrimination is likely to be bottlenecked especially in circumstances where multiple differentiators are intertwined and thus silence potential unfair treatment stemming from age discrimination. Given the hidden nature of age discrimination (Wood et al. 2009), legislation only presents a partial effect. This chapter therefore seeks to investigate the silenced nature of age discrimination from four perspectives: age-related employability, age-related pay differentials, age-related job quality and age-related gender inequalities.

4.2   Age-Related Employability

Both young and old workers experience age discrimination in recruitment and selection, although there are good reasons to believe employers are more likely to engage young workers than older workers. For instance, departing from human capital theory, older workers' higher pay makes them less attractive to employers, especially when younger workers are no less productive (Wood et al. 2009). On the one hand, older workers may well be overpriced; thus, hiring from the open labour market makes business sense if those workers are cheaper and flexible, rather than paying more for seniority. On the other, older workers are discouraged from following job leads in that they are 'over-qualified' or 'over-experienced' (Shen and Kleiner 2001), and they are likely to be placed in redundancy situations (Johnson and Neumark 1997; Walker 2005). However, the extent to which advantaging younger over older workers would occur begs further questioning. In fact, young people cannot realistically compete for jobs with skilled and experienced workers. Job descriptions for certain vacancies may require 'young' qualities such as adaptability, while other jobs may require more 'senior' qualities such as responsibility or reliability. While it is indeed the case that young workers are perceived to possess higher adaptability in relation to new technology than older workers, the apparent lack of experience or skills also renders ease of being dismissed and substituted (Abrams et al. 2011). Recent research also reports a number of undesirable or negative stereotypes associated with younger workers compared to older workers—for instance, stereotypes of younger workers as less conscientious, less reliable, less trustworthy and less motivated (Bertolino et al. 2011; North and Fiske 2012; Truxillo et al. 2012). A recent study drawing upon European Social Survey Round 4 Data 2008 reports that younger people (self) reported experiencing the highest levels of age discrimination (Bratt et al. 2018). However, the study also cautions the extent to which subjective experiences of age discrimination can reflect actual differences in age discrimination. A key issue in assessing the degree of inequality faced by youth in labour markets relates to their risk of experiencing unemployment compared to adults. Across countries, the risk varies enormously: the youth unemployment rate is largely twice the adult unemployment rate in developed economies, but higher in developing regions, for example, the youth unemployment rate is more than five times the adult's in South East Asia and Pacific region (Reinecke and Grimshaw 2015).

The unfavourable position of young workers could be because young people experience a period of 'emerging adulthood' in which they are not fully developed as adults and therefore lack the personal capacities needed for stable employment, which only develop in later life (Arnett 2000, 2004; Yates 2017). However, this type of essentialist explanation of the conditions of young people fails to adequately conceptualise young people as workers and situate them within the capital-labour relationship. Stemming from insecurity associated with precarious employment, young people may well be 'comfortable with uncertainty' (Roberts 2009, p. 262). These claims are challenged by studies suggesting that young people's engagement in non-standard, insecure work is more out of necessity than choice and that young people would work a greater number of regular hours if offered the opportunity to do so (Furlong and Kelly 2005; TUC 2014).

The contrasting approach to understanding age discrimination in employment towards specific age group compared to another suggests that some of the negative perceptions towards young workers (experience and/or skill gap) may well work positively for older workers (experienced and skilled), especially when the nature of the job requires a 'senior' element. A case study of targeted recruitment of mature staff for part-time work at NHS hospital in Britain reveals an employer's predilection of advantaging the aged (those in their forties, as stated in the research) over the younger. The case study reveals a list of positive stereotypes or perceptions of older workers held by the human resource (HR) department: reliable but less mobile; low absence rate due to fewer responsibilities for childcare; greater intrinsic value placed on dealing with customers and colleagues, and most importantly, older workers create less trouble at workplaces (Arrowsmith and McGoldrick 1997). These findings certainly explain why there are a growing number of social theorists advocating that organisational policies need to explore new ways of capitalising older workers' talent and experience rather than viewing them as a burden (Streb et al. 2008; Tikkanen 2011). It is also argued that higher costs associated with experience are likely to be offset by better performance (Cappelli and Novelli 2010). This is backed up by evidence that older workers mean qualities (e.g. higher loyalty, fewer accidents, lower absenteeism), which makes them relatively less costly compared to younger workers. Consequently, employers attach certain 'senior' elements (experience requirements) to the jobs, as well as a part-time nature associated with the new hires; the latter deliberately deters younger candidates from applying and/or likely disadvantages young people throughout the recruitment and selection process. The permeation of bias towards different age groups is subtly built into job design with a strong business case deliberation. This is widely accepted, and no one speaks about the inequalities which ensue since it is well 'engineered' into organisational management and thus successfully 'hidden' in workplaces.

Although numerous studies report that negative attitudes towards older workers (for review see, e.g., Posthuma and Campion 2009) hinder the employment of older candidates, the negative impact of employing older workers can be moderated by the positive attitudes towards older workers from managers and employers. In circumstances that employers had more favourable attitudes towards older workers (i.e. high competence), an older applicant was more likely to be shortlisted for a job interview (Krings et al. 2011). It is also worth noting that such positive perceptions towards older workers are largely documented in research focusing on customer service–driven industries (Arrowsmith and McGoldrick 1997; Chiu et al. 2001). Despite favourable justification for recruiting experienced mature candidates, a number of concerns regarding older employees' physical ability, the pressure/speed of work, training and new technology were also noted (p. 270). Overall, a recent review study concludes that the long-held negative perceptions and stereotypes of older workers by employers appear to outweigh countable positive perceptions (Harris et al. 2018).

Beyond the culture-free literature of age discrimination in employment predominately conducted in industrialised countries, research investigating multinational corporations seems to suggest that age norms reflecting specific characteristics and values attached to specific age group vary from country to country. Conventional wisdom stereotyped in Western studies indicates that there is less prejudice or discrimination towards older people in Chinese societies owing to their Confucian belief systems (Chou and Chow 2005). Against this, a comparative study between Hong Kong and the US unfolds greater negative perceptions towards the aged than towards the younger workers (Chiu et al. 2001). Recent research in Thailand's multinational corporates also notes that the influence of age seniority in management roles appears relatively diminishing as a result of 'intracorporate pressures for convergence' (Andrews et al. 2018). Whilst further study is needed to establish the impact (if any) of national culture upon age norms, existing research evidence undoubtedly point to the importance of researching age discrimination in context in order to appreciate the manifestation of age discrimination within specific national culture and develop effective anti-age discrimination measures across countries.

4.3   Age-Related Pay Differentials

Age-related pay literature commonly draws upon human capital theory, suggesting that pay reflects individual performance, in particular productivity. The perception of lacking experience and necessary skills and knowledge appears to justify why younger workers tend to be paid less compared to their older peers (Anderson and Smith 2010). Among the limited research that investigates lower pay among younger workers compared to older ones, minimum wages for younger workers are frequently at the centre of debate on hidden inequality related to age. Minimum wages are adopted as a tool to prevent abusive and discriminatory pay practices and improve the purchasing power of young workers (Grimshaw 2014). However, the minimum wage gap between young and adult workers, also termed as youth wage discount (Blanchflower and Freeman 1999), has been steadily increasing despite increased average level of education of young people and a decline in their share of the working age population which should have been favourable for their pay prospects. The widening of this gap has resulted in a reduced purchasing power of young workers compared to adult workers.

The youth wage discount varies across countries and the variation is enormous. A recent research of data collected from OECD countries suggests that young workers (aged 15–24) earned on average around 62 per cent the wages of older workers. Young workers in the USA are reported to face the highest wage discount by earning just 55 per cent of the wage of older workers. In the UK, the wage gap between young and all-age workers is 60 per cent, whereas the ratio in Norway suggests the lowest discount: young workers earn 73 per cent of the wage of older workers (Grimshaw 2014). Evidence also points to downward trends of young workers' earnings among many countries. For example, the ratio of young workers' pay (aged 16–24) against the average of all workers' pay dropped from 61 per cent to 58 per cent during 2006–2011 in the US, and from 70 per cent to 66 per cent in Australia among workers aged 20–24. The size of the youth wage discount is also mirrored by the dominance of young people in areas of employment that are associated with low-wage jobs. Young workers are more than four times as likely to be in low-wage (referring to earnings less than two-thirds of the median for all workers) employment as the overall average for a country. Further evidence even suggests young workers earn less than their marginal product and old workers more (Kotlikoff and Gokhale 1992; Anderson and Smith 2010). This finding does not only contrast the perception that age is negatively associated with productivity (Mahlberg et al. 2009), but also contradicts the principle held by labour economists that wages reflect individuals' productivity as justified by human capital theorists.

A possible explanation posits that there may well be an industry effect that needs to account for when interpreting why young workers are likely to be disadvantaged in pay when compared with other age groups. For instance, compared to middle-aged and older workers, a study shows that young employees in construction sector were underpaid but not in the service industry. This could be due to certain industries where the emphasis is more on experience than others, whilst age arguably often approximately mirrors experience. Using theory of deferred compensation (Lazear 1979; Medoff and Abraham 1980), labour economists also argue that workers and firms want to be engaged in long-term relationships whereby rising earnings do not necessarily fully reflect increased productivity. Human capital theory starts to lose its battle in reinstalling the principle of equality in relation to pay for performance; instead, it appears to be overridden by the perception of age reflecting experience. Empirical evidence confirms such 'hidden' discrimination embedded in age-related pay: workers with a shorter period of experience (8–15 years) are lower paid relative to their productivity, whereas highly experienced workers (more than 15 years) receive a wage premium that exceeds their relative productivity (Hægeland and Klette 1999).

A frequent accusation against older workers suggests that profound deterioration in mental ability, flexibility and physical activity is likely to happen when compared with their younger peers (Riach and Rich 2010). Part-time and precarious jobs with inferior pay, often providing no arrangement on fringe benefits, are ideal solutions for older workers. A big challenge to age, pay and productivity literature comes from an increasing number of research findings suggesting that there is no significant difference between the job performance of older workers and that of younger workers (Warr 1994, p. 309). Recent studies drawing upon longitudinal data show that older workers do not necessarily affect firm productivity (Göbel and Zwick 2009; Mahlberg et al. 2009, 2013), and wages often increase with age/seniority independently of productivity (Börsch-Supan and Weiss 2016). Hence, the pay-for-performance principle that often used to justify age-related pay differentials in a workplace begs further questions.

Further evidence continuously challenges the positive relationship between age and wage, or perceived overpayment of older workers. The average contribution of particular age groups to the productivity of firms indeed increases with age until 40–45 years of age but remains constant thereafter (Aubert and Crépon 2006). Similarly, a longitudinal study over a 22-year period in Portugal (mainly manufacturing and the private service sector) indicates that productivity increases until the age range of 50–54, whereas wages peak around the age range of 40–44 (Cardoso et al. 2011). This instead suggests wages increase in line with productivity gains at a younger age but wage increases start to lag behind performance gains when approaching prime age. Empirical evidence also suggests that the ageing effect on wages decreases as workers age (Lazear 1976), while years of work experience matter more after a certain age (25 years old in the study). As a result, on average, older workers may well contribute more to firm performance than their contribution to the wage bill.

4.4   Age-Related Job Quality

Against the stereotype of being dynamic, highly adaptable and able to respond fast to new technologies, there is instead some evidence pointing to 'an enduring, pervasive and deep set cultural prejudice against perceived "youth" in managerial positions/roles and an ensuing series of (again, perceived) organizational performance implications' (Andrews et al. 2018, p. 343). National statistics also confirm such managerial perceptions. For example, low-paid employment accounts for 21 per cent of all-age workers in the UK, 40 per cent for workers aged 21–25 years and 77 per cent for workers aged 16–20 years (Clarke and D'Arcy 2016, p. 20). Young workers often find themselves oscillating between precarious work and periods of unemployment (Gregg and Gardiner 2015). Young workers also have to tolerate the poor employment conditions because such jobs are not deemed as proper jobs but are instead 'student' or 'youth' jobs which are not worthy of decent pay or conditions due to the very fact that young people are employed in them (Sukarieh and Tannock 2014).

Different from the 'deliberation' in job designs targeting flexible older workers as discussed above, the age discrimination prevailing in the job design for 'students' or 'youths' is more due to changes in economic structure rather than a managerial bias. On one hand, the shrinking of the labour market sectors in terms of total employment pushes young workers to the back of job queues due to perceived lack of experience (Ashton et al. 1990). On the other hand, the increasingly 'hour-glass'-shaped internal and occupational labour markets indicate that whilst the number of mid-level and higher-level positions drops significantly, an increase in low-skilled, low-wage jobs occurs at the bottom end of the labour market (Anderson 2009; Goos and Manning 2007), where younger workers appear to dominate (Grimshaw 2014; Yates 2017). Further evidence also suggests greater incidence of precarious employment among young workers (15–24 years old) than among the prime age (25–54) group in all OECD countries except Australia (OECD 2006; Reinecke and Grimshaw 2015). For example, the share of temporary jobs among young and prime age category in Italy is 61.9 per cent versus 14.5 per cent and in Germany is 52.6 per cent versus 9.6 per cent (OECD 2018).

This partly explains why union membership among young workers is significantly lower: their lower average tenure in the workplaces and unions fails to keep up with the fast mobilising young age category. It is therefore unsurprising to observe that vulnerable young workers, coupled with lower tenure and less firm-specific human capital, are likely to be the target during downsizing (OECD 2018). This may also explain why young workers have limited access to some of the better conditions and employment rights often associated with the formal sector of the economy where trade unions often influence on management policies and practices (Yates 2017).

Repercussions of age discrimination towards young workers in labour markets are captured by government reports and academic research concerning job quality that young workers are likely to get involved. Recent research has deepened concerns over the labour process for young people employed in service-based occupations at the bottom end of the labour market. Yates' (2017) research of young workers in Greater Manchester reveals that over 80 per cent of young workers are employed in service sectors such as retail, hospitality and business services, where employers tend to adopt business strategies in which productivity gains are achieved through job intensification and long working hours, mirroring an old-fashioned 'sweat shop' (Taylor and Bain 1999). Young workers also face further challenges from increased competitiveness for decent jobs in labour markets. Increasing emphasis on qualifications results in 'credentialism' when employers require candidates to possess a degree for vacancies that previously was not required (UKCES 2012). At the same time, the number of university enrolment in the UK has increased by more than 50 per cent from 1995 to 2016 (Yates 2017). As a result, the majority of UK graduates (60 per cent) are now employed in non-graduate occupations, a situation which has led to over a third of UK graduates being employed in jobs in which they are overqualified or under-utilised: for example, in telesales, data entry and retailing (Yates 2017).

However, young workers being squeezed into such low-wage employment does not mean labour markets favour old workers or older workers always occupy the 'good' jobs. Numerical flexibility is more likely to be encountered in the later phases of an individual's working life when her/his bargaining position is weaker (Urwin 2004), and such arrangements are often available in the low-end service sector (Sargeant 2001). Older workers in financial need are 'doubly disadvantaged' in not having access to decent pensions and in having to compete with younger labour market entrants for poorly paid jobs (Taylor and Walker 1994).

Contrasting to the shocks researchers have brought out regarding young workers' experience of poor employment conditions and precarious work, research investigating older workers' job quality largely emphasises variations in work experiences among older workers. For example, older workers who have been in the same job for a long time likely report a different kind of work experience compared to poor job quality experienced by those older workers looking for new jobs. Studies of older workers searching for new jobs report that employers targeting older workers actually take advantage of the flexibility of this age group or the reality that older workers have no other choice compared to other competing age groups in the labour markets. This employment model appears to be easily justified by the human capital theory, and it makes business sense to reduce costs by employing expensive (experience) older workers on part-time basis.

Older workers were also found to be enduring more pressure within working environments and losing out financially relative to younger employees (Smeaton and White 2018), a context prone to older workers' disenchantment and deteriorating social and employment relations (White 2012). Moreover, there is evidence of declining organisational commitment and overall job attitudes of older workers, relative to younger ones (White 2012; White and Smeaton 2016). This is likely to weaken the older workers' position, and challenge their self-confidence and psychological empowerment, ultimately leading them to consider retirement (Schermuly et al. 2017) or risk being relegated to lower-quality jobs.

Older workers' inferior job experiences may also be explained by the negative perceptions from younger peers and/or being stereotyped by line managers. Numerous research studies suggest that performance measures inevitably rely on the managers' own subjective assessments and perceptions of the characteristics of older workers, making them permeable to their own stereotypes of older workers, despite the extensive provision of performance indicators (Principi et al. 2015). Such discriminatory treatment results in negative affective and calculative responses (Gutek et al. 1996) and potentially damages performance. It is also arguably true that workers tend to specialise more in a concentrated part of their jobs when they age and are less likely to be flexible or diverse in their work (Van Den Berg 2011; Thijssen 1992). The decline in skill variety affects intrinsic motivation. Given the growing number of part-time jobs are relatively low skilled, and older workers in new jobs tend to be influenced most by intrinsically rewarding work, there appears to be a growing mismatch between job design and those who are willing and also sought to fill it.

It is worth noting that young and older workers are not substitutable. When it comes to precarious jobs, those jobs with poor quality many young people often occupy do not mean older workers take most of the good jobs instead. What makes the understanding of unequal treatment at work challenging resides in the variation of individuals defining 'good' versus 'bad' jobs (Arrowsmith and McGoldrick 1997). While job quality is also a subjective measure that varies between individuals, an identification of inequality engineered in specific job design due to age discrimination becomes even more challenging. A good example is a part-time job that lacks all-round benefits which, often attached to full-time roles, would be viewed as inferior especially to individuals prioritising job security and continuity of income flow, but reported with high job satis-faction from those who value the flexibility such job design offers. A recent survey in Britain suggests that workers on zero-hour contract report relatively higher job satisfaction compared to those employed on a permanent contract (CIPD 2015). Hence, the perceived job quality var-ies not only between individuals from different age groups but also between those from the same age category who view flexibility differently. Hence, detection of any prejudice and/or discrimination on the grounds of age in relation to the design of job or job quality requires a closer look at how age discrimination is processed at workplaces, which is easily gone unnoticed by ignoring the fact that engagement in precarious work may well be due to individuals' limited choices.

4.5   Age-Related Gender Inequalities

Age discrimination in workplaces becomes even more subtle and hidden when it is examined intersectionally with gender. Intersectionality researchers poignantly argue that additive one-dimensional approach of investigating age discrimination alone fails to capture the complex and variable effects as a result of interactions between multiple differentiators such as gender, race, social status (Cho et al. 2013; Kelan 2014). Prior research indeed evidenced a fundamentally gendered view of age identity (Ainsworth 2002). Research shows that how 'young' and 'old' are defined varies widely and largely depends on perceptions associated with gender. For instance, female workers in their thirties can be perceived as 'too old' and 'too young' at the same time (Duncan and Loretto 2004). They are viewed as 'too old' due to their being assumed to soon opt out of work to bring up a family, yet they are simultaneously perceived to be 'too young' to be in senior leadership positions due to a presumed lack of experience (Kelan 2014).

However, the extent to which interactions between age and gender would shape managers' views and thereafter their way of managing a diverse workforce is nevertheless less understood; neither do we under-stand possible impact on individuals' experience at workplaces. This alerts that age and gender relations function as integrated social systems, and their interaction has different but related effects for men and women of various age. The enforcement of equality laws across most countries, particularly in the West, tends to present a rhetorical view that age inequality, alike gender, has become history (Coppock et al. 1995; McRobbie 2008). Nonetheless, juxtaposing age and gender may unfold potential hidden inequalities individuals likely experience in workplaces.

Further research findings not only reinforce the traditional perceptions towards gendered-age discrimination, but also reveal a silenced pattern of inequalities in relation to age between the genders. First of all, there is a denial of gender inequality among young (professional) women who view it as an issue that belongs to older generations; they presume organisations are based on ability and talent and that any excesses of gender inequality are due to choice (Broadbridge and Simpson 2011; Kelan 2014; Kelan and Jones 2010). Hence, age differences silence gender inequality among young female workers (professionals): the inequality they experience at workplaces is reduced to their choice to be mothers (Scharff 2011). They also reject the concept of feminism but instead individualise the responsibility for shaping their own life chances as opposed to vying for wider systemic change (Gill and Scharff 2013; Scharff 2011). Similar to gender inequality in modern workplaces, age discrimination is often buried under a strong rhetoric of diversity management (Eisenhart and Finkel 1998) or an issue dealt with by a previous generation, and thus age is used to make gender unspeakable (Gill 2002; Kelan 2014). The unspeakability of age-related gender inequality suggests that a denial of gender inequality is necessary to allow the young individuals rather than external structures to be in control. Consequently, by neutralising gender inequality, young workers may also silence certain aspects that would allow different views to emerge.

Contrasting to the disadvantaged position young female workers are likely to face compared to their male peers, older male workers tend to be significantly disadvantaged in comparison with older female workers. This is because older women appear to be relatively successful in gaining employment, compared to older male workers, and thus not in need of government assistance (Ainsworth 2002). Against the feminine versions of older worker identity being constructed as relatively advantaged com-pared to older men, more research reveals alarming concerns over the silenced nature of inequalities when age and gender juxtaposed in prac-tice. Older women perceive age as an impediment for entering or re-entering the labour market (Moore 2009). Womanhood is often considered in relation to appearance and sexuality, and women's bodies are viewed as less attractive as they age (Duncan and Loretto 2004). The reality, nevertheless, is that females' willingness to accept low-status, low-paid jobs is wrongly interpreted as they did not need help in the form of policy initiatives, while men deserve greater support because of their inflexibility (Ainsworth and Hardy 2007). Older female workers also face unfair treatment in relation to employment status in labour markets due to gender stereotypes. This results in older female workers being con-structed as 'nonworkers'. Traditional gender stereotypes of older women mean that they were not registered as unemployed because, for example, they were on other forms of government support such as sole parent ben-efits. Hence, the hidden unemployed remained hidden: female workers are "celebrated for their flexibility but rendered unproblematic and invis-ible, while older men were negatively labelled 'inflexible', and became targeted for 're-education' in the 'changing nature of the new labour mar-ket'" (Ainsworth 2002, p. 596).

A powerful revelation from intersectionality studies illustrates tremen-dous concerns of inequalities on various fronts in workplaces. Research indicates that young women's wages are more equal to young men's wages, and younger generations have historically driven much of the gender wage gap convergence (Blau and Kahn 2007; Roche 2017). However, a gender wage gap that does not exist in labour market entry (Fortin 2008) increases by nearly 25 per cent after ten years of experience, only half of which can be explained by differences in human capital (Manning and Swaffield 2005). An explanation for changes in the stock of human capital, especially experience-related, notes that women earn less than their male counterparts due to career interruptions and time spent child-rearing (Bertrand et al. 2010; Wu 2018). Hence, gender inequality has never gone; it is hidden behind the articulation of age by different age groups.

4.6   Methodology Issues

Four main methodological issues are identified from the literature review: (a) attention has been disproportionately paid to older workers than younger workers; there is (b) selection bias in sampling and (c) lack of research of inter-age-group discrimination; and (d) more research needs to adopt an intersectional approach to deepen our understanding of how age interacts with other differentiators and thus the impact on unfair treatment in workplaces. These will be discussed in turn as follows.

First, extant literature is overwhelmingly dominated by researching age discrimination towards older workers and discussing management initiatives to tackle such unspeakable bias. Age discrimination derived from research studying age stereotyping by one age group towards another competing age group is problematic in building up the knowledge base of the practice of age discrimination and then informing measures to tackle the reality of age discrimination (Gwenith et al. 2017). Such a research design unavoidably masks the hidden nature of age discrimination towards younger workers who are the future manpower. Without understanding potential bias towards them, a society and/or an employer may well deprive younger workers' opportunities for training, promotion, redeployment, which are essential to develop and prepare a talent pool and enable them to take on challenging roles that entail both 'young' and 'senior' elements. The omission of young workers in many current academic works may also mislead organisations to take on an imbalanced approach to hiring and firing. Leaving young people out of the debate of ageism, one would not appreciate the landscape of age-related bias, unequal treatment experienced by individuals at various ages.

Second, among the extant literature, there is great variation in the selection of research sample concerning their representativeness and potential constraints on extending their findings to more general applications. For example, considering the participants to the survey are part-time students of management courses in Hong Kong and Britain with a mean age of 31 and 33, respectively, one would anticipate the negative attitudes towards aged in their study could be due to inter-group discrimination. Similar concerns also apply to other studies that adopt similar research design. For example, drawing on data from 184 university students residing in the UK and 249 in Taiwan, with a mean age of 21.76 and 20.72, respectively, Vauclair et al. (2017) report greater negative views towards the aged in Taiwan than in the UK, particularly on a few societal factors. For instance, a pension system with its large expenses favouring the older may well explain feelings of contempt, especially when a younger generation is unlikely to benefit from these government expenses when they are old themselves. This also corresponds with findings from a meta-analysis suggesting that, contrasting to conventional wisdom held in Western literature, rises in population ageing predict negative elder attitudes in Eastern cultures, but positive in the West (North and Fiske 2015). Consensus in the research findings among these studies aside, using one specific age group (mostly are 'younger'—below forties) and gathering their views on older people (with a broad age band ranging from 40 to 70 or older) creates two issues for intellectual comprehension. First, again, it is younger workers' age discrimination towards older workers, which is only part of what ageism entails. Second, it is hard to anticipate a HR manager or recruiting officers in their twenties, thirties, forties, fifties or sixties would view older in the same way. This is because, according to social identity theory (Tajfel and Turner 1986), there is a desire to maintain a positive identity of their own age group: either younger or older workers may be motivated to hold negative evaluations of their colleagues from the competing age group (North and Fiske 2012).

Third, future research of ageism would benefit from examining inter-age-group discrimination by viewing young, middle-aged and old (the actually aged) as distinctive age groups. Negative workplace stereotypes about workers either too young or too old may not only prevent them from getting fully engaged at work and identified with the organisation but also foster intergenerational tensions (North and Fiske 2015; Oliveira and Cardoso 2018). Those tensions are likely to be intensified in ageist work settings marked by negative beliefs about what other age groups think of one's own group, a belief best described as negative age-based meta-stereotyping (Vauclair et al. 2016; Finkelstein et al. 2015). Those age threats in the organisational environment are more likely to be perceived by individual workers as a work stressor rather than a challenge (Dijkstra and Homan

2016), which potentially can damage these workers' well-being and performance. However, rather than predominantly examining age discrimination from the viewpoint of the prime age group, researching inter-age-group discrimination between any two age groups would provide nuanced understanding of various patterns of age discrimination so that management can develop targeted measures to tackle age discrimination in workplaces.

Fourth, future research would also benefit from adopting an intersectional approach by examining interactions between age and other differentiators such as gender, race, social status and job types. Previous research has revealed double jeopardy against applicants having a multiple stigmatised background (Derous et al. 2012). For instance, age-related hiring bias may differ in relation to whether the job role is of low or high status (Abrams et al. 2016). It has been argued that the intersectional approach sparks deepened inquiry into the dynamics of intersectionality both as an academic frame and as a managerial intervention in a world characterised by extreme inequalities (Cho et al. 2013). Emerging research has started applying such an approach to investigating the hidden nature of inequality associated with age in combination with other differentiators. Qualitative research appears to dominate this emerging research area, and thereby more quantitative analysis would certainly provide further insights into the generalisability of previous findings generated from qualitative studies.

4.7   Discussion and Conclusion

This chapter set out to review the literature of ageism and identify how age discrimination manifests through individuals' engagement in employment opportunities, pay, job quality and gender. The review is conducted by focusing on the experience from both young and old workers. The discourse on 'ageing' apparently suggests that the boundaries between 'younger' and 'older' are not as clear-cut as a first reading would suggest (Angouri 2012). The findings show that age discrimination can happen at various stages of human resource management in workplaces due to being either too young or too old. The challenges faced by individual employees as well as HR practitioners within an organisational context are the hidden nature of ageism influenced by perception, stereotyping, as well as human-designed procedures that reflect deeply rooted bias towards specific age groups. Such perceptions and stereotypes further channel into other forms of management which deepen unequal treatment for specific age groups through (a) their chances of securing an employment contract, (b) whether their wages or pay will have been penalised due to certain age stigma, (c) the type of jobs they are likely to get, and (d) most alarmingly, an even more subtle way of disguising age discrimination and potential negative impact on individuals' experience of unfair treatment at work when gender enters the equation of tackling age discrimination. It is therefore clear that age identity, like many others, is not something people 'have' or 'are' but something people 'do' (Holmes 2006; Coupland 2009).

The literature review on both young and older workers in this chapter also suggests that different age groups face different age stigmatisation. Although younger and older workers are not substitutes in employment, there is evidence suggesting employers encourage older workers to leave the labour force to free up job opportunities for young workers. This is a mistake: not only would this be ineffective in alleviating the problem of high and persistent unemployment, but also very expensive for the public purse (OECD 2006). A recent call for more research on additional work examining both disparate treatment towards and disparate impact on younger workers in order to understand the nature of age discrimination towards this age group and develop measures to improve their employment experience (Fisher et al. 2016).

Beyond the fact of increasing political concern with ageism, the literature review also reveals that there is a need for theoretical development to facilitate a better understanding of how an organisation would benefit from preparing a HR deployment that comprises a wide range of age groups, in addition to the principle of democracy. Current literature largely points to a business case argument by drawing upon human capital theory—pay for productivity or productivity-related experience. Given increasing evidence that there is no significant difference in productivity between young and old workers, human capital theory only finds its roots in the pay-for-experience scenario (Börsch-Supan and

Weiss 2016). Human capital theory may also backfire when HR practitioners design workplace training schemes: training is more productivity effective among younger or less experienced workers, whereas older workers are assumed experienced enough and hence no need for further training. It is therefore not surprising that older workers are unlikely to receive training compared to their younger peers, which is broadly viewed as a form of age discrimination towards older workers in workplaces.

Contrasting to human capital theory, both career development theory and labour market segmentation theory appear to more closely mirror how age discrimination can be tackled in workplaces through HR planning. Stressing work motivation and resultant performance at various age-related stages in the human life cycle (Super 1990), career development theory suggests an organisation could develop specific HR practices targeting different age groups within the workforce. For example, employers provide skill-building training and stabilisation through work experience for younger workers, career advancement planning to support mid-aged workers to naturalise the stock of skills and experience, and design jobs to elicit intrinsic motivation from older workers and allow their experience to benefit their organisations. According to labour market segmentation theory, employers develop their primary labour market through developing and retaining firm-specific skills, establishing loyalty by focusing not only on experienced (likely older) workers but also on younger people with a lookout for long-term employment relationship and succession, while at the same time, employers can develop secondary market by creating atypical forms of employment which are not necessarily marginal jobs requiring lower skills. In fact, often highly skilled work relies heavily upon experience so that candidates from various age groups would be considered mainly on the grounds of the skills and/or experience they have.

Findings in this chapter indeed suggest that robust regulations and legal frameworks are brought into force across the world to protect individuals from being discriminated against because of their characteristics. However, evidence also indicates that these principles are often violated in practice due to the hidden nature of age discrimination detected from various stages in organisational operation. Hence the limit that legislation can do in order to improve equality in workplaces points to the importance of identifying possible patterns of age discrimination and understanding how human 'designed' inequalities are hidden in management policies and practices, and areas where the implementation of certain policies and practices could have gone astray.

The literature review also points to the importance of researching cultural effects and/or institutional effects on age perceptions and stereotypes. North and Fiske's (2015) study reveals that cultural individualism significantly predicts respect for elders within rapidly ageing societies, whereas collectivist traditions may backfire. Their findings submit the importance of demographic challenges in shaping modern attitudes towards older workers. Similar to other research on ageism, there is a dearth of literature on cultural effects on age discrimination towards young workers.

Finally, an important note to take forward both in academic study and in practice is the intersectional approach in investigating hidden inequalities as a result of interactions between age and other differentiators. The review of age-related gender inequality, in particular, reveals that the concept of postfeminism, for example, may well mask the reality that gender equality has yet been achieved (Coppock et al. 1995; McRobbie 2008), given age discrimination experienced varies between men and women (Kelan 2014). It is therefore important to bring the shaping power of gender back into the spotlight (Lewis 2006) in order to unfold the disguised and systemic nature of discrimination at play (Meyerson and Fletcher 2000; Nash 2008).

Turning to managerial implications, employers should pursue a strategy that will lead to adopt a more active stance in managing an age-diverse workforce. The strategy includes (a) growth-enhancing structural reforms (e.g. organisational structure supported by job designs that blend in a diverse range of individual characteristics, career paths and experience) that have the potential to benefit both internal and external labour market outcomes of both young and old workers; (b) targeted active career development policies to help young and older workers with specific problems of finding or staying in employment; and (c) installing HR policies and practices that embrace age diversity to shape a positive age climate and an age-friendly organisational culture. Previous research has shown that intergenerational contact may be able to facilitate positive views towards older people at work (Henry et al. 2015; Iweins et al. 2013). In workplaces, regular and high-quality exchanges among decision-makers from different age groups and job design emphasising teamwork may therefore be effective in transforming negative attitudes into positive views towards individuals either too young or too old.

References

Abrams, D., P.S. Russell, M. Vauclair, and H.J. Swift. 2011. *Ageism in Europe: Findings from the European social survey*. London: Age UK.

Abrams, D., H.J. Swift, and L. Drury. 2016. Old and unemployable? How age-based stereotypes affect willingness to hire job candidates. *Journal of Social Issues* 72: 105–121.

Acas. 2014. *Age and the workplace: A guide for employers and employees*. London: Acas.

———. 2017. *Equality and discrimination: Understand the basics*. London: Acas.

Ainsworth, S. 2002. The "feminine advantage": A discursive analysis of the invisibility of older women workers. *Gender, Work and Organization* 9: 579–601.

Ainsworth, S., and C. Hardy. 2007. The construction of the older worker: Privilege, paradox and policy. *Discourse & Communication* 1: 267–285.

Anderson, P. 2009. Intermediate occupations and the conceptual and empirical limitations of the hourglass economy thesis. *Work, Employment and Society* 23: 169–180.

Anderson, A., and L. Smith. 2010. Dynamic matching and evolving reputations. *The Review of Economic Studies* 77: 3–29.

Andrews, T., C. Rowley, K. Nimanandh, and R. Banomyong. 2018. Age negotiation at the Asian corporate subsidiary: Challenges of managerial 'youth' in Thai-based subsidiaries of Western multinationals. *Asia Pacific Business Review* 24: 330–350.

Angouri, J. 2012. "The older I get the less I trust people" constructing age identities in the workplace. *Pragmatics*. Quarterly Publication of the International Pragmatics Association 22: 255–277.

Arnett, J.J. 2000. Emerging adulthood: A theory of development from the late teens through the twenties. *American Psychologist* 55: 469–480.

———. 2004. *Emerging adulthood: The winding road through the late teens and twenties*. Oxford: Oxford University Press.

Arrowsmith, J., and A.E. McGoldrick. 1997. A flexible future for older workers? *Personnel Review* 26: 258–273.

Ashton, D., M. Maguire, and M. Spilsbury. 1990. *Restructuring the labour market: The implications for youth*. London: Palgrave Macmillan.

Aubert, P., and B. Crépon. 2006. Age, wage and productivity: Firm-level evidence. http://www.crest.fr/ckfinder/userfiles/files/Pageperso/crepon/Age%20Wage%20and%20Productivity.pdf. Accessed 16 May 2018.

Bertolino, M., D.M. Truxillo, and F. Fraccaroli. 2011. Age as moderator of the relationship of proactive personality with training motivation, perceived career development from training, and training behavioral intentions. *Journal of Organizational Behavior* 32: 248–263.

Bertrand, M., C. Goldin, and L.F. Katz. 2010. Dynamics of the gender gap for young professionals in the financial and corporate sectors. *American Economic Journal: Applied Economics* 2: 228–255.

Blanchflower, D.G., and R.B. Freeman. 1999. The declining economic status of young workers in OECD countries. http://www.dartmouth.edu/~blnchflr/papers/DecliningYouth.pdf. Accessed 30 May 2018.

Blau, F.D., and L.M. Kahn. 2007. The gender pay gap: Have women gone as far as they can? *Academy of Management Perspectives* 21: 7–23.

Börsch-Supan, A., and M. Weiss. 2016. Productivity and age: Evidence from work teams at the assembly line. *The Journal of the Economics of Ageing* 7: 30–42.

Bratt, C., D. Abrams, and H.J. Swift. 2018. Perceived age discrimination across. Age in Europe: From an ageing society to a society for all ages. *Developmental Psychology* 54: 167–180.

Broadbridge, A., and R. Simpson. 2011. 25 years on: Reflecting on the past and looking to the future in gender and management research. *British Journal of Management* 22: 470–483.

Butler, R.N. 1995. Ageism. In *Encyclopedia of aging*, ed. G. Maddox, 38–39. New York: Springer.

———. 2005. Ageism: Looking back over my shoulder. *Generations* 3: 84–86.

———. 2009. Combating ageism. *International Psychogeriatrics* 21: 221.

Cappelli, P., and B. Novelli. 2010. *Managing the older worker: How to prepare for the new organizational order*. Boston: Harvard Business Press.

Cardoso, A.R., P. Guimarães, and J. Varejão. 2011. Are older workers worthy of their pay? An empirical investigation of age-productivity and age-wage nexuses. *De Economist* 159: 95.

Chiu, C.K.W., A.W. Chan, E. Snape, and T. Redman. 2001. Age stereotypes and discriminatory attitudes towards older workers: An east-west comparison. *Human Relations* 54: 629–661.

Cho, S., K.W. Crenshaw, and L. McCall. 2013. Toward a field of intersectionality studies: Theory, applications, and praxis. *Signs: Journal of Women in Culture and Society* 38: 785–810.

Chou, K.L., and N.W. Chow. 2005. To retire or not to retire: Is there an option for older workers in Hong Kong? *Social Policy and Administration* 39: 233–246.

CIPD. 2015. *Zero-hours and short-hours contracts in the UK: Employer and employee perspectives.* London: Chartered Institute of Personnel and Development.

Clarke, S., and C. D'Arcy. 2016. *Low pay Britain 2016.* London: Resolution Foundation.

Coppock, V., D. Haydon, and I. Richter. 1995. *The illusions of 'post-feminism'– new women, old myths.* London: Routledge.

Council Directive 2000/78/EC on Employment Equality Framework Directive.

Coupland, J. 2009. Discourse, identity and change in mid-to-late life: Interdisciplinary perspectives on language and ageing. *Ageing and Society* 29: 849–861.

Derous, E., A.M. Ryan, and H. Nguyen. 2012. Multiple categorization in resume screening: Examining effects on hiring discrimination against Arab applicants in field and lab settings. *Journal of Organizational Behavior* 33: 544–570.

Dijkstra, M., and A.C. Homan. 2016. Engaging in rather than disengaging from stress: Effective coping and perceived control. *Frontiers in Psychology* 7: 1415.

Duncan, C., and W. Loretto. 2004. Never the right age? Gender and age-based discrimination in employment. *Gender, Work and Organization* 11: 95–115.

Eisenhart, M.A., and E. Finkel. 1998. *Women's science: Learning and succeeding from the margins.* Chicago: The University of Chicago Press.

Finkelstein, L.M., E.B. King, and E.C. Voyles. 2015. Age metastereotyping and cross-age workplace interactions: A meta view of age stereotypes at work. *Work, Aging and Retirement* 1: 26–40.

Fisher, G.G., D.S. Chaffee, and A. Sonnega. 2016. Retirement timing: A review and recommendations for future research. *Work, Aging and Retirement* 2: 230–261.

Fortin, N.M. 2008. The gender wage gap among young adults in the United States the importance of money versus people. *Journal of Human Resources* 43: 884–918.

Furlong, A., and P. Kelly. 2005. The Brazilianisation of youth transitions in Australia and the UK? *Australian Journal of Social Issues* 40: 207–225.

Garstka, T.A., M.T. Schmitt, N.R. Branscombe, and M.L. Hummert. 2004. How young and older adults differ in their responses to perceived age discrimination. *Psychology and Aging* 19: 326–335.

Gill, R. 2002. Cool, creative and egalitarian? Exploring gender in project-based new media work in Euro. *Information, Communication and Society* 5: 70–89.

Gill, R., and C. Scharff. 2013. *New femininities: Postfeminism, neoliberalism and subjectivity*. New York: Springer.

Göbel, C., and Zwick, T. 2009. *Age and productivity—Evidence from linked employer employee data*. Discussion Paper 09-020. Centre for European Economic Research.

Goos, M., and A. Manning. 2007. Lousy and lovely jobs: The rising polarization of work in Britain. *The Review of Economics and Statistics* 89: 118–133.

Gregg, P., and L. Gardiner. 2015. *A steady job? The UK's record on labour market security and stability since the millennium*. London: Resolution Foundation.

Grimshaw, D. 2014. *At work but earning less: Trends in decent pay and minimum wages for young people*. Employment Policy Department EMPLOYMENT Working Paper No. 162. International Labour Office, Employment and Labour Market Policies Branch. Geneva: ILO.

Gutek, B.A., A.G. Cohen, and A. Tsui. 1996. Reactions to perceived sex discrimination. *Human Relations* 49: 791–813.

Gwenith, G.F., D.M. Truxillo, L. Finkelstein, and L.E. Wallace. 2017. Age discrimination: Potential for adverse impact and differential prediction related to age. *Human Resource Management Review* 27: 316–327.

Hægeland, T., and T.J. Klette. 1999. Do higher wages reflect higher productivity? Education, gender and experience premiums in a matched plant-worker data set. In *The creation and analysis of employer–employee matched data*, ed. J.C. Haltiwanger, J. Lane, J. Theeuwes, and K. Troske, 231–259. Amsterdam: Elsevier.

Harris, K., S. Krygsman, J. Waschenko, and D.L. Rudman. 2018. Ageism and the older worker: A scoping review. *The Gerontologist* 5: e1–e14.

Henry, H., H. Zacher, and D. Desmette. 2015. Reducing age bias and turnover intentions by enhancing intergenerational contact quality in the workplace: The role of opportunities for generativity and development. *Work, Aging and Retirement* 1: 243–253.

Holmes, J. 2006. Workplace narratives, professional identity and relational practice. *Studies in Interactional Sociolinguistics* 23: 166.

Iversen, T.N., L. Larsen, and P.E. Solem. 2009. A conceptual analysis of ageism. *Nordic Psychology* 61: 4–22.

Iweins, C., D. Desmette, V. Yzerbyt, and F. Stinglhamber. 2013. Ageism at work: The impact of intergenerational contact and organizational multi-age perspective. *European Journal of Work and Organizational Psychology* 22: 331–346.

Johnson, R., and D. Neumark. 1997. Age discrimination, job separations and employment status of older workers. *Journal of Human Resources* 32: 779–811.

Kelan, E.K. 2014. From biological clocks to unspeakable inequalities: The intersectional positioning of young professionals. *British Journal of Management* 25: 790–804.

Kelan, E.K., and R.D. Jones. 2010. Gender and the MBA. *The Academy of Management Learning and Education* 9: 26–43.

Kite, M.E., G.D. Stockdale, B.E. Whitley, and B.T. Johnson. 2005. Attitudes toward younger and older adults: An updated meta-analytic review. *Journal of Social Issues* 61: 241–266.

Kotlikoff, L.J., and J. Gokhale. 1992. Estimating a firm's age-productivity profile using the present value of workers' earnings. *The Quarterly Journal of Economics* 107: 1215–1242.

Krings, F., S. Sczesny, and A. Kluge. 2011. Stereotypical inferences as mediators of age discrimination: The role of competence and warmth. *British Journal of Management* 22: 187–201.

Lawrence, B.S. 1987. An organizational theory of age. In *Research in the sociology of organizations*, ed. S. Bacharach and N. DiTomaso, 37–71. Greenwich: JAI Press.

———. 1988. New wrinkles in the theory of age: Demography, norms, and performance ratings. *Academy of Management Journal* 31: 309–337.

Lazear, E. 1976. Age, experience and wage growth. *The American Economic Review* 66 (4): 548–558.

———. 1979. Why is there mandatory retirement? *Journal of Political Economy* 87: 1261–1284.

Lewis, J. 2006. Work/family reconciliation, equal opportunities and social policies: The interpretation of policy trajectories at the EU level and the meaning of gender equality. *Journal of European Public Policy* 13: 420–437.

Loretto, W., and P. White. 2006. Employers' attitudes, practices and policies towards older workers. *Human Resource Management Journal* 16: 313–330.

Mahlberg, B., I. Freund, and A. Prskawetz. 2009. Firm productivity, workforce age and vocational training in Austria. In *Labour markets and demographic change*, ed. M. Kuhn and C. Ochsen, 58–84. Wiesbaden: VS Verlag.

Mahlberg, B., I. Freund, J.C. Cuaresma, and A. Prskawetz. 2013. Ageing, productivity and wages in Austria. *Labour Economics* 22: 5–15.

Manning, A., and J. Swaffield. 2005. *The gender pay gap in early career wage growth*. CEP Discussion Paper No. 700.

McEvoy, G., and W. Cascio. 1989. Cumulative evidence of the relationship between employee age and job performance. *Journal of Applied Psychology* 74: 11–17.

McGregor, J., and L. Gray. 2003. *Older worker employment transition*. Palmerstone North: Massey University.

McRobbie, A. 2008. *Gender culture and social change: In the aftermath of feminism*. London: Sage Publication Ltd.

Medoff, J.L., and K.G. Abraham. 1980. Experience, performance and earnings. *Quarterly Journal of Economics* 95: 703–736.

Meyerson, D.E., and J.K. Fletcher. 2000. A modest manifesto for shattering the glass ceiling. *Harvard Business Review* 78: 126–136.

Moore, S. 2009. No matter what I did I would still end up in the same position' age as a factor defining older women's experience of labour market participation. *Work, Employment and Society* 23: 655–671.

Nash, J.C. 2008. Re-thinking intersectionality. *Feminist Review* 89: 1–15.

North, M.S., and S.T. Fiske. 2012. An inconvenienced youth? Ageism and its potential intergenerational roots. *Psychological Bulletin* 138: 982–997.

———. 2015. Modern attitudes toward older adults in the aging world: A cross-cultural meta-analysis. *Psychological Bulletin* 141: 993–1021.

O'Higgins, N. 2001. *Youth unemployment and employment policy: A global perspective*. Geneva: International Labour Office.

OECD. 2006. *Live longer, work longer—Ageing and employment policies*. Paris: OECD Publishing.

———. 2017. OECD Employment Outlook 2017. https://doi.org/10.1787/empl_outlook-2017-en. Accessed 18 May 2018.

———. 2018. *Temporary employment (indicator)*. Paris: OECD.

Oliveira, E., and Carlos Cabral Cardoso. 2018. Stereotype threat and older worker's attitudes: A mediation model. *Personnel Review* 47: 187–205.

Palmore, E.B. 1990. *Ageism: Negative or positive?* New York: Springer.

———. 1999. *Ageism: Negative and positive?* 2nd ed. New York: Springer Publishing Company.

Posthuma, R.A., and M.A. Campion. 2009. Age stereotypes in the workplace: Common stereotypes, moderators, and future research directions. *Journal of Management* 35: 158–188.

Principi, A., P. Fabbietti, and G. Lamura. 2015. Perceived qualities of older workers and age management in companies: Does the age of HR managers matter? *Personnel Review* 44: 801–820.

Reinecke, G., and D. Grimshaw. 2015. Labour market inequality between youth and adults: A special case? In *Labour markets, institutions and inequality: Building just societies in the 21st century*, ed. J. Berg, 361–398. New York: International Labour Office.

Riach, P.A., and J. Rich. 2010. An experimental investigation of age discrimination in the English labor market. *Annals of Economics and Statistics/Annales d'Économie et de Statistique* 99/100: 169–185.

Roberts, K. 2009. Opportunity structures then and now. *Journal of Education and Work* 22: 355–368.

Roche, K. 2017. Millennials and the gender wage gap in the US: A cross-cohort comparison of young workers born in the 1960s and the 1980s. *Atlantic Economic Journal* 45: 333–350.

Sargeant, M. 2001. Lifelong learning and age discrimination in employment. *Education and the Law* 13: 141–154.

———. 2006. The employment equality (age) regulations 2006: A legitimization of age discrimination in employment. *Industrial Law Journal* 35: 209–244.

Scharff, C. 2011. Disarticulating feminism: Individualization, neoliberalism and the othering of 'Muslim women'. *European Journal of Women's Studies* 18: 119–134.

Schermuly, C.C., V. Büsch, and C. Graßmann. 2017. Psychological empowerment, psychological and physical strain and the desired retirement age. *Personnel Review* 46: 950–969.

Shen, G., and B. Kleiner. 2001. Age discrimination in hiring. *Equal Opportunities International* 20: 25–32.

Smeaton, D., and M. White. 2018. Britain's older employees in decline, 1990–2006: A panel analysis of pay. *Work, Employment and Society* 32: 93–113.

Snape, E., and T. Redman. 2003. Too old or too young? The impact of perceived age discrimination. *Human Resource Management Journal* 13: 78–89.

Streb, C.K., S.C. Voelpel, and M. Leibold. 2008. Managing the ageing workforce: Status quo and implications of the advancement of theory and practice. *European Management Journal* 26: 1–10.

Sukarieh, M., and S. Tannock. 2014. *Youth rising? The politics of youth in the global economy*. London: Routledge.

Super, D.E. 1990. A life-span, life-space approach to career development. In *The Jossey-Bass management series and the Jossey-Bass social and behavioral science series. Career choice and development: Applying contemporary theories to practice*, ed. D. Brown and L. Brooks, 197–261. San Francisco: Jossey-Bass.

Tajfel, H., and J.C. Turner. 1986. The social identity of intergroup behaviour. In *Psychology of intergroup relations*, ed. S. Worchel and W.G. Austin, 7–24. Chicago: Nelson Hall.

Taylor, P., and P. Bain. 1999. An assembly line in the head': Work and employee relations in the call Centre. *Industrial Relations Journal* 30: 101–117.

Taylor, P.E., and A. Walker. 1994. The ageing workforce: Employers' attitudes towards older people. *Work, Employment and Society* 8: 569–591.

Thijssen, J. 1992. A model for adult training in flexible organizations: Towards an experience concentration theory. *Journal of European Industrial Training* 16: 5–15.

Tikkanen, T. 2011. From managing a problem to capitalizing on talent and experience of older workers. *International Journal of Human Resource Management* 22: 1217–1220.

Trades Union Congress (TUC). 2014. More than two-thirds of agency workers aged under 30 are looking for permanent jobs. https://www.tuc.org.uk/economic-issues/labour-market-and-economic-reports/labour-market/economic-analysis/more-two-thirds. Accessed 1 June 2018.

Truxillo, D.M., E.A. McCune, M. Bertolino, and F. Fraccaroli. 2012. Perceptions of older versus younger workers in terms of big five facets, proactive personality, cognitive ability, and job performance. *Journal of Applied Social Psychology* 42: 2607–2639.

UK Commission for Employment and Skills. 2012. *The youth employment challenge*. London: UKCES.

United Nations. 1992. *Statistical charts and indicators on the situation of youth, 1970–1990*. New York: United Nations.

Urwin, P. 2004. *Age matters: A review of existing survey evidence. Employment relations*, Research series 24. London: Department of Trade and Industry.

———. 2006. Age discrimination: Legislation and human capital accumulation. *Employee Relations* 28: 87–97.

van Den Berg, P.T. 2011. Characteristics of the work environment related to older employees' willingness to continue working: Intrinsic motivation as a mediator. *Psychological Reports* 109: 174–186.

Vauclair, C.M., M.L. Lima, D. Abrams, H.J. Swift, and C. Bratt. 2016. What do older people think that others think of them, and does it matter? The role of meta-perceptions and social norms in the prediction of perceived age discrimination. *Psychology and Aging* 31: 699.

Vauclair, C.M., K. Hanke, L.L. Huang, and D. Abrams. 2017. Are Asian cultures really less ageist than Western ones? It depends on the questions asked. *International Journal of Psychology* 52: 136–144.

Walker, A. 2005. The emergence of age management in Europe. *International Journal of Organisational Behaviour* 10: 685–697.

Warr, P. 1994. Age and employment. In *Handbook of industrial and organizational psychology*, ed. H.C. Triandis, M.D. Dunnette, and L.M. Hough, 485–550. Palo Alto: Consulting Psychologists Press.

White, M. 2012. Older employees under pressure? Theorizing reasons for declining commitment. *Work, Employment and Society* 26: 447–463.

White, M., and D. Smeaton. 2016. Older British employees' declining attitudes over 20 years and across classes. *Human Relations* 69: 1619–1641.

Wood, G., G. Wilkinson, and M. Harcourt. 2009. Age discrimination and working life: Perspectives and contestations—A review of the contemporary literature. *International Journal of Management Reviews* 10: 425–442.

Wu, N. 2018. Flexible working: Are we ready for this? In *Hidden inequalities in the workplace*, ed. V. Caven and S. Nachmias, 127–154. Cham: Palgrave Macmillan.

Yates, E. 2017. Reproducing low-wage labour: Capital accumulation, labour markets and young workers. *Industrial Relations Journal* 48: 463–481.

5

Hidden Care(e)rs: Supporting Informal Carers in the Workplace

Louise Oldridge

5.1 Introduction

The UK has an ageing population; people are not only living longer but doing so with health problems and increasing rates of disability (Grierson 2017; White 2013; Pickard 2008; Heitmueller 2007). At the same time, the government has been investing less in adult social care services, and we await an updated national carers strategy following consultation which closed in 2016 (Carers UK 2018; Petrie and Kirkup 2018; Green 2017). As a result, we have seen an ever-increasing, and unrecognised, reliance on care provided on an informal basis by friends and family with decreasing formal support, leading to a widely reported 'social care crisis' often detailed in the media (White 2013; BBC 2017; Grierson 2017; Slawson 2017). Successive governments adopting neoliberal ideologies have emphasised the importance of family as a mechanism of care and

L. Oldridge (✉)
Department of Human Resource Management, Nottingham Business School,
Nottingham Trent University, Nottingham, UK
e-mail: louise.oldridge@ntu.ac.uk

© The Author(s) 2019
S. Nachmias, V. Caven (eds.), *Inequality and Organizational Practice*, Palgrave
Explorations in Workplace Stigma, https://doi.org/10.1007/978-3-030-11647-7_5

have continued to rely on them as a policy initiative, only stepping in when there is a failure in care provision (Gilbert and Powell 2005). This is alongside policies to increase the employment rates of older workers to meet the needs of the ageing population (Kirton and Greene 2016) and government objectives to encourage carers to remain in employment (Care Act 2014). The terms 'unpaid', 'family' and 'informal' carer or caregiver are used interchangeably in literature and caring resources. Carers UK states,

> A carer is someone of any age who provides unpaid support to family or friends who could not manage without this help due to illness, disability, mental ill-health or a substance misuse problem. (Grayson 2017, p. 5)

This is the definition used for this chapter to describe notions of 'informal care' and 'informal carers' of adults in particular. Currently 6.5 million people in the UK are reported to provide informal care, saving the state an estimated £132 billion per year (Carers UK 2017a, 2018). Census records show that the highest provision of care is provided by mid-life women (aged 50–64), with one in four women of this age self-identifying as a carer (ONS 2011). Yet, not all those providing care are comfortable with the term 'carer', and would not identify as such, seeing the help/care provided as part of their normal familial role or responsibility (O'Connor 2007). As a result, the actual number could be even greater. At the same time, in the UK in 2016, 65.6 per cent of women aged 50–64 registered as employed (ONS 2017). One in seven people in the workforce are reported to be carers (Carers UK 2019), with 13.3 per cent of employed women overall combining work and care (ONS 2011). Employers for Carers (2015) offer a definition of working carers as,

> [e]mployees with significant caring responsibilities that have a substantial impact on their working lives. These employees are responsible for the care and support of disabled, elderly or sick partners, relatives or friends who are unable to care for themselves. (Grayson 2017, p. 5)

Previous research on working carers has tended to focus on their labour market status and includes findings which demonstrate that carers may reduce the number of hours they work and levels of responsibility or even leave their jobs entirely (Carers UK 2017a, 2018, 2019; Yeandle et al. 2007). Few studies have examined mid-life women (aged 45–65) in detail or, more specifically, the effect of caring on their careers in paid employment and the levels of support received at work. With not all employers being aware of the caring lives of their employees (Employers for Carers 2013), due to the burdens on carers to disclose, this could lead to the existence of carers being hidden amongst our workforces. Furthermore, where women have had to make sacrifices to their paid employment in light of this unrecognised caring work, we see their formal careers becoming a hidden inequality as care responsibilities take priority where inflexible and unsupportive employment practices prevail. With insufficient attention given to the plight of mid-life women working and caring, the career and support inequalities they face in the workplace have been little documented.

This chapter goes on to examine existing literature and legislation surrounding working carers. It reviews findings from interviews conducted in 2016 with 30 women aged 45–65 across Leicestershire combining paid employment and informal care, with reference to their careers, and organisational and line manager support. This is particularly significant given the large number of mid-life women caring, alongside careers commentary referring to women of this age being at their professional peak. Whilst empirical research was conducted with mid-life women, the findings and resulting conclusions and recommendations are relevant to all working carers, employers, local and national government offices seeking to address the work inequalities faced due to caring responsibilities. As a result, the chapter closes with recommendations for employers and policymakers.

5.2   Informal Care and Employment

Carers UK (2014) reported that 45 per cent of carers have had to give up work due to their caring responsibilities (Carers UK ibid). This is despite the 2008 carers strategy which noted, '[I]t is crucial that we place a much higher priority on supporting people of working age with caring responsibilities to remain in work, if they wish to do so' (HM Government 2010). Indeed, a duty is placed upon local authorities to meet the needs of carers when their 'involvement in employment' is at risk (The Law Commission 2011). However, it is not always clear to local authorities when a carer's employment is at risk or their obligations in this respect (The Law Commission 2011).

Carers' strategies (HM Government 1999, 2008) and the Care Act 2014 recognise that the possible adverse effects of caring include the capacity to remain in employment (Carers UK 2016a). The government's position is that carers who remain active in the labour market are protected through employment and pension rights (Gilbert and Powell 2005), which are arguably limited. Furthermore, if carers have no option but to leave employment due to caring, the state fails to offer adequate financial recompense (Carers UK 2016b). This is seen through the earnings limit set on carer's allowance and the fact that a carer earning over £120 per week would lose their allowance (HM Government 2018).

Providing informal adult care, which is often unpredictable in nature, could affect an individual's employment in a number of ways: leaving work or taking early retirement; reducing working hours and not taking up developmental opportunities (Carmichael and Charles 2003; Van Houtven et al. 2013). Indeed, 36 per cent of women surveyed in the recent State of Caring Survey (2018) by Carers UK noted that their work had been negatively impacted by caring. Hutton and Hirst (2000) reported that carers suffer worse working conditions than their colleagues. Additionally, carers have perceptions of the types of roles they believe they would be able to carry out and possible working practices of organisations, particularly in terms of flexibility, which means they may not apply for roles (Arksey and Glendinning 2008; Carmichael et al. 2008). Working carers also demonstrate longer length of service records with the same employer than non-carers, indicating a potential lack of mobility, inhibiting career development (Carers UK 2016b). Ensuring working hours are met, despite caring commitments, could lead to long working hours inclusive of caring and employment, and thus have an impact on formal career opportunities (Arber and Ginn 1995). Hence, it is important to understand the levels of support offered to working carers by employers.

5.3   Informal Care and Organisations

Limited studies have focused on organisations and informal care, with a scarcity of recent work. Nevertheless, it is significant to examine the levels of organisational support and policies in place discovered by existing research as this will undoubtedly affect the careers of those employed by them. A study by Arksey in 2002 demonstrated that both large and small employers offered forms of flexible working practices to their working carers. This could be formally at large organisations, with policies in place to support employees. Only 2 large employers out of 13 organisations studied had specific provisions in place for carers. It is notable that they were in the retail sector and employed a high proportion of women over the age of 45. Yet, a small employer in the study also recounted how they could quickly respond to employee needs, avoiding the formal bureaucracy often associated with large organisations. Whilst part-time working hours were on offer in all of the organisations studied, it was highlighted it would be difficult for more senior staff to work part-time hours in some occupations, such as engineering. Other provisions in place among those organisations studied included flexitime, working from home and compressed working hours (Arksey 2002).

It is also worth examining the sector that carers are employed in, to see if this makes a difference to support levels provided by organisations. Yeandle et al. (2007) found that two-thirds of working carers reported their employers as being supportive. However, only half of those employed in the private sector said their employer was 'carer friendly', compared with 68 per cent of public sector employees and 78 per cent in the voluntary sector. Furthermore, 527 out of 810 working carers worked in the public sector and felt working practices were more flexible than in the private sector. Additionally, in the public and private sectors, those in more senior positions had been able to adopt informal flexible working practices because their roles were mainly focused on output as opposed to monitoring working hours (Yeandle et al. 2007). A survey by Employers for Carers (2013) found that 88 per cent of 223 employers who responded had awareness of employees with caring responsibilities, mainly by large organisations, the public and voluntary sector. Employers responded that they supported carers through both individual needs and organisational policies. This included flexible working, leave arrangements, remote working and provision of information (Employers for Carers 2013).

The Chartered Institute of Personnel and Development (CIPD) surveyed 554 senior HR professionals in 2016. Only 26 per cent of respondents' employers had formal policies in place to support carers, and 20 per cent measured how many of their employees had caring responsibilities (CIPD 2016). The support provisions reported included flexible leave (49 per cent) and work arrangements (48 per cent), use of telephones and private time for calls (32 per cent), counselling and employee assistance programmes (22 per cent). Only 13 per cent of organisations offered training to line managers to assist them managing working carers (CIPD 2016).

Most recently, Sethi et al.'s (2017) study in Canada referred to the significance of line managers and their approach, in addition to formal organisation policies. Participants noted an overall lack of awareness of carer-friendly policies, and that work accommodation was dealt with on a case-by-case basis. As a result, one of the suggested recommendations from the study was for managers to be offered support in dealing with issues associated with working carers. Indeed, the role of line managers has been a focus of wider human resource management literature (e.g., Winkelmann-Gleed 2012; Hutchinson 2013). Guidance for organisations employing working carers, such as that by Employers for Carers (2018), also highlights the importance of line managers supporting employees. In a recent report on juggling work and unpaid care, of all interventions, carers reported that having a supportive line manager would be most helpful (Carers UK 2019). The case for supporting working carers is outlined in the next section.

5.3.1   Supporting Working Carers

To support working carers, the UK government has introduced a number of initiatives and legislation. These include the Carers (Recognition and Services) Act 1995, the National Strategies for Carers in 1999 and 2008 (HM Government 1999, 2008), the Carers and Disabled Children Act in 2000, the Health and Social Care Act 2001, the Carers (Equal Opportunities) Act 2004, provisions contained in the Employment

Relations Act 1999, the extended Flexible Working provisions from April 2007 (Arksey and Glendinning 2008) and the Care Act 2014. Workplaces are also expected to review possible adjustments which can be made to support those employees with caring responsibilities, enabling them to stay in employment (Acas 2014). Furthermore, protection against direct discrimination and/or harassment due to caring responsibilities is also prohibited under the Equality Act 2010, due to a carer's 'association' with an individual covered by a protected characteristic, such as age or disability. Yet, to gain access to provisions designed to support carers involves an individual firstly identifying as a carer.

With reduced adult social care funds and the government aims for employment levels, employers are encouraged to support their working carers (Grayson 2017). Research conducted by Employers for Carers (2013) examined what employers felt the benefits of supporting their working carers were. The results demonstrated staff morale and loyalty, improved rates of retention, and reduced leave and sickness absence. This was alongside staff engagement, improved people management, effective teamwork, improved service delivery, higher productivity, reduced training and recruitment costs, and improved employer branding and cost savings (Employers for Carers 2013).

More recently, Grayson (2017, p. 5) has noted that caring is a 'universal human experience', with one in nine employees having care responsibilities. He outlines that it is in the interest of employers to address the social, political and economic challenges of caring. His justifications for doing so include issues with lost productivity; retention and recruitment concerns; addressing skills gaps and responding to an ageing workforce. Overall, though, supporting working carers can lead to greater employee engagement (Grayson 2017). Resources on assisting employers to support carers can be found on websites such as Employers for Carers (2018).

Despite government protestations, policy provisions and employment legislation, support of working carers is limited, notwithstanding the recognition that caring is predicted to have a negative impact on careers. It is clear that whilst some employers studied have the requisite policies in place, actual practices employed vary, depending on sector, role/level and line manager approach. This is in spite of those working to publicise the benefits of supporting working carers. Having provided the context of this research and examined existing literature, the chapter now moves on to focus on this particular study.

5.4   Methodological Considerations

The study undertaken adopted an interpretive approach to understand the experiences of participants in their own words (Berger and Luckmann 1967; Burrell and Morgan 1979). Taking an interpretive approach is said to demand 'insider knowledge' on the part of the researcher to understand data produced (Lacity and Janson 1994). I have always been interested in women's work and career experiences, particularly those factors which influence their development. In 2009, my mother made changes to her patterns of work to accommodate caring for my maternal grandmother. What struck me was that her empathetic employer allowed her to formally work flexibly as well as offering informal support when she had to leave work suddenly, leading to increased loyalty from my mother. Despite this, she recognised that her career would not progress with her employer and that similarly she was unable to take on the challenges of a new job.

Adopting a life course approach (Giele and Elder 1998), calendar interviews were held with 30 women to review key events, behaviours and emotions over a period of time (Belli and Callegaro 2009). Adding open-ended interview questions provided further explanation of particular events, creating an autobiographical narrative framework (Harris and Parisi 2007; Nelson 2010). Ahead of the interviews, a focus group was formed to consult on the proposed calendar and interview schedule to ensure authenticity of the research and that the experiences of the participants remained a focus (Aldridge 2015).

In total, 30 women from Leicester and Leicestershire were interviewed. Purposive, snowball and self-selection sampling methods (Noy 2008) were used to identify the research population to ensure they had experience of combining caring and working, and were between the ages of 45 and 65. The majority of participants were between the ages of 50 and 59. Twenty-two were employed, 3 were self-employed, 2 were retired and 3 participants were unemployed at the time of their research interview. Participants worked across the private, public and third sectors in a range of different positions, with most holding professional occupations.

Thematic synthesis was used to analyse and organise the data into themes-based participant experiences. In exploring the themes in the next sections, quotations from participants are used to provide insight into, and illustrate, their experiences. Whilst a multitude of themes were covered at interview, this chapter focuses on participants' career experiences and support in their workplace taking account of their caring. Participant pseudonyms are used throughout the discussions to preserve the anonymity of those involved.

5.5   Findings and Discussion

5.5.1   Careers Hidden by Caring

Almost all participants of this study spoke about their caring responsibilities having an impact on their employment, and thus the progression of their careers. Twenty-six out of 30 participants demonstrated upwards linear career progression prior to caring, with movement between employers in order to advance their careers. After the point at which they reported they began to identify as carers, they made career decisions in the short term, regarding concerns linked to working hours and needing to be at home, alongside confidence in the levels of work responsibilities they felt they might be able to manage. Such career decisions are reflected in literature advocating the notion that women's careers are relational, and that they make decisions on the basis of those around them, and other responsibilities, not just considering formal career opportunities (Mainiero and Sullivan 2005).

As a result, the careers of participants appear to plateau. An example was Mary, who said, "I haven't really had any" career development, since caring started. She wished to take a qualification to progress but needed to stay employed as she was the main 'breadwinner'. Also evident were reductions in working hours and responsibilities, career breaks and terminations of employment in relation to overall caring responsibilities. These findings are in line with existing research, which has focused on the negative impact of caring on careers (Carers UK 2017a; Yeandle et al. 2007). The findings also support quantitative data which has suggested that caring would negatively impact career progression (Heitmueller and Inglis 2007) and that women cannot be assumed to be able to seek work free from constraints (Arthur 1994).

In making decisions regarding their careers, participants reported considerations of their workplace reputation and worries that the level of empathy and understanding from colleagues and managers may not be replicated in a different role or organisation. In some cases, such worries led to participants staying longer with employers than they would have liked and withdrawing job applications, or not putting themselves forward for opportunities. For example, at the focus group, Whitney said,

> I was offered a job a couple of months ago managing the [name] team … but I decided not to take it and it's gutt[ing] really because I was really excited about it but I thought where I am I've got credibility. They know me, they know I work hard, they know I do my best and I thought I can't risk going somewhere where you're the newbie because you've got... so if I need to go off at the drop of a hat you know then things might be seen very differently from somewhere where you've worked for quite a few years.

Nonetheless, participants spoke of their employment offering a break from caring and, in many cases, were keen to continue combining work and care. Employment was seen as being interesting and fulfilling, offering an opportunity for generativity (sharing knowledge with younger workers) and for participants to add value to employing organisations and society. Such reasons support Grayson's (2017) recent publication on employing carers, which argues that employers should consider the mechanisms they can utilise to support their employees. Failure to do so, and where carers have no other option but to leave employment, workplaces face a loss of talent and tacit knowledge (Grayson 2017). Hence, the extent of workplace support was also examined.

5.5.2   Extent of Workplace Support

Key to enabling working carers to continue to care and work in paid employment are mechanisms of support. Participants spoke of varying degrees of adjustments offered, management and colleague support which led to the enabling, or constraining, of caring. In a single and unique case, Pema's small employer had made a number of significant arrangements designed to help her. They allowed her to go to work as and when it suited her and the care of her husband. They had also bought practical items to help them in their home.

In most participant cases, employers had formal policies in place designed to support carers, irrespective of sector or size. This is despite the CIPD's (2016) research indicating otherwise. Policies included flexible working, care of dependants and emergency leave, long-term carers leave and, in some cases, 'carers' passports' (a document identifying a carer and setting out their support requirements). As an example, Hannah's employer allowed her to work from home as she was not always required to be present in the office. Whilst Kate's voluntary sector employer was a small organisation, they had in place all of the necessary policies according to legislation. Similarly, employed in the public sector, Sara felt that her organisation wanted to set a good example, and as a result, they were very flexible. Such findings link with existing literature on the significance of support for working carers (Zuba and Schneider 2013; Appannah and Biggs 2015).

Participants noted that it was important to them to know about the existence of supportive workplace policies. When she was looking for a new job, Tracey said that she had examined the relevant human resource management policies. At the time of the interview, she had been recently appointed but had since noted that her employer was bringing in a new absence management policy with trigger warnings, which was worrying her.

> I understand the need to do that, erm, but actually doing it in such a kind of formalised way, means that you end up, erm, discriminating against people who have genuine reasons and it means that, erm, as an employee you can feel pressurised that, you know, "oh my God, how many days have

I had off?" Erm, so I don't, I don't, think it's particularly helpful for anybody, you know, who's got a disability, or cares for somebody, or has problems in their lives.

Participants employed in the public sector often had access to carers' passports. These were designed such that if a participant moved department or manager, this document would move with them and the support be replicated. At Christine's last place of work, she had been the one pushing for carers' passports to be implemented. They were also in place at Wendy's organisation, but she actually found them frustrating. At the focus group she had said,

> I know they designed this wonderful form … talking about registering as a carer and I'm bored to death after page 1, trust me, I'm not filling it in. And they were saying HR had designed it all about caring at work and being at work and I can't be bothered, no. Don't ask me all of that.

Whilst Wendy found the nature of carers' passports intrusive, Vanessa had concerns that the documents were in fact a "tick box exercise" and that they were "not worth the paper they were written on". She reported a "complete lack of empathy" and support in the workplace, which had affected her ability to make internal career moves. Though her employer advertised being "carer friendly", she had found that departments operated in silos and that whilst flexible working was available in some departments and roles, it was not universally available.

More significantly, a key finding from most research interviews was that employers had a number of policies in place, but their application, use and value depended heavily on line managers' understanding and interpretation. Participants were concerned that policies were not clear in the way they were written, and having different managers led to different experiences and interpretations. This finding has ramifications for the ongoing support of working carers, illustrated by Dawn at the focus group, who said,

> You can have all the policies in the world but it depends on the way your manager interprets it and how personally sympathetic they are.

In spite of her employer having organisational policies around flexible and mobile working, when Vanessa was exploring internal job vacancies, she had found that the approach in operation was not that of the organisation's formal policy, saying,

> Every single interview you have to go, "Well, are you carer friendly? Do you do flexible working?" And I just find the whole thing appalling. Appalling. Short of having a tattoo across my forehead, I have got to ask the question. And I don't… it's degrading. I don't feel that I should have to do that. I do not. If there's a policy, it should apply to everybody, and everything.

Several of the study's participants reported that their employers had technology in place which would support working from home, but that it was only allowed in some parts of the organisation. Whilst it was recognised that there are of course roles which cannot be carried out from home, Christine reported that some of her team were allowed to work from home because of their caring responsibilities, but said,

> I was never, ever, even with my husband having mental health difficulties, never ever allowed to work from home. At all. And that's because my boss was a control freak.

Even where flexible working arrangements were in place, two participants reported feeling under pressure to work above their hours or change their previously agreed working patterns. Patricia reported that her manager would repeatedly ask why she could not attend a meeting on a non-working day, when she was caring for her mother. Stephanie's manager had said that she could work compressed hours but then later told her that she could not take a day off every week. She reported that now the first thing she is asked in every performance development review (PDR) is if she still wants to continue with her compressed hours.

Participants also reported varying approaches of support from line managers. Several of them described being in the same role for some time but having had a number of different managers in this time, each with differing style. Wendy had grown tired of her previous manager who would repeatedly ask her, "How's the caring going?" during their one-to-one meetings. Whilst she knew he was trying to be supportive, she felt he was not entirely comfortable with it and did not know how to approach it and wished he would stop asking her. Whereas, at the time of interview, Winnie had just had a new manager,

> and she actually nursed her Mum through cancer about a year or 18 months or so ago, erm, so she, she's got an understanding of what it's like to juggle work and family and, erm, caring.

Additionally, there was also a difference by organisation level, with those working in more senior positions with employers reporting that it was easier to adopt informal flexible working practices, in line with existing research (Yeandle et al. 2007). This included local agreement with line managers whereby their exact location or work undertaken did not need to be known at all times. Having examined workplace and line manager support in general, this chapter now turns to the support of participants' formal career development.

5.5.3   Extent of Support in Career Development

Study participants recalled the different approaches managers had regarding the development of their careers within the workplace alongside their caring. What was promising to note was that many did report career discussions taking place, in accordance with existing literature (Hutchinson 2013). This was often by way of appraisal, or annual PDR. Participants had a variety of responses to such discussions. Sometimes they were valued, such as by Judith, who had enjoyed having the opportunity to talk about training, development and other aspects of her role and what was going on in her life. Alternatively, Wendy said,

> We have the, we have annual ones as part of our process anyway, our PDR process. I, mine, usually the answer is the same – I'm not looking for career development, I'm looking at my exit plan rather than anything.

Similarly, Patricia reported that she had access to career development discussions but that she had "made it very clear that they weren't appropriate". She said she did not wish to progress with her employer. Rather, saying, "My aspirations were about doing the best that I could in the time that I have left to do it". She felt she was coming towards the end of her career and thus was less ambitious, but that also she could not work full-time or look for other opportunities because of her caring. Likewise, when asked about career development, Bridget had told her employer, "Actually my personal circumstances don't allow it at the moment". At the time of the interview, Winnie had just had an appraisal, but she said that as she was at the top of her salary band she did not perceive any financial benefit in trying to do any more than she was doing. Stephanie reported the impact that caring could have on performance at work, with her continued employment having been at risk at one stage, saying,

> I think when you're actually in it, when you['re] doing 'stuff', it can be, it can become all consuming … and you don't sleep and you're rushing around like a headless chicken and I think…. You start to lose your concentration and your confidence. I certainly lost a lot of my confidence, and I've just started to get it back. Erm… I think you lose your confidence, your ability to concentrate for everything. You know, you can't be everything to all people, but you're trying to. You're trying to juggle all these responsibilities. Erm, you know, I can remember, what, just before my mum died, this particular manager I talked about wanted to put me on an Action Plan – performance improvement.

She felt her development had been stymied because she perceived that she was seen as inflexible, working four days a week. As a result, she said, "I'm still in the same position now, on the same salary grade that I've been since 1999".

A number of participants spoke about the impact their managers' actions had had in respect of career development. Recent literature has explored the notion of benign paternalism (Rawat and Lyndon 2016) by line managers. This is where a manager may interfere with an individual's opportunity to choose, perceived to be for a valuable reason, but doing so without the individual's consent. Dawn reported that before her ex-husband was ill she had taken on a number of areas of responsibility at work, but when he fell ill her department head said she "wasn't firing on all cylinders", and took a project off her. Whilst she was relieved at the time, at interview Dawn reflected on the negative impact it may have had on her career. Having cared for six individuals over the last 25 years, Christine also spoke of the "perception of other people that they won't give you additional responsibility because they don't want to add to your burden".

Alternatively, Vanessa described how she had been made to attend courses, without discussion. She was frustrated that there was "absolutely no consideration" to her circumstances. She had previously had to attend a course with ten hours of study associated with it. She had asked her manager when she would be able to fit in the study, in addition to working and caring, saying, "And basically he told me to read it on me sunbed and I weren't very happy at all". The day after the interview she was due to attend a further course, which she reported her employers were "enforcing" on her.

A number of participants reported that they did not have discussions with their line managers about career development. Further, Rachel did not even have a line manager to have a discussion with. Whilst in most cases, career development discussions existed, several participants voiced concern that they were a 'tick box' exercise only, without proper time or attention given to them. Indeed, Tracey said, "I must confess, when I had my appraisal with my previous line manager, erm, it was very much a kind of tick boxy exercise". Meanwhile, Mary had received "a snippet of 5 minutes here and there", without a proper meeting time devoted to such discussions. Evidently, working carers' experiences vary, but workplace and career development support greatly influence the possibilities of combining work and care. With these findings in mind, there are a possible number of implications for future organisational practice, to which this chapter now turns.

5.6   Conclusion and Implications

As previous literature has suggested, this study has shown that adult care responsibilities do inhibit women's career progression. Despite many of the participants of this study wishing to continue to work, or return to employment, caring impacted working hours, roles and responsibilities. For many participants, their formal careers were shrouded by caring, with limited opportunities for development.

It is clear that whilst organisations of all sizes and sectors can have formal policies and procedures in place with a view to assisting those with caring responsibilities, the most important support element for participants in this study was the role of line managers, their interpretation and application of such policies, and overall approach. Those participants with supportive line managers, who offered both formal and informal flexible arrangements, found it easier to combine work and care, with some still developing their career. Nonetheless, some experiences of participants of this study support existing work that indicates the negative impact caring can have on workplace experiences and careers, including interactions with line managers who fail to support their employees. Furthermore, most participants were offered support only in line with existing employment legislation, which, it is argued, does not address the reality, or moral obligations, of supporting working carers, and concerns remain over the integrity of development and performance discussions.

The findings point to the importance of engaging with carers as individuals rather than making assumptions about the forms of support they may or may not need, relating to hours, responsibilities and career development opportunities. It is apparent that lack of engagement with carers and misinterpretation, or minimal awareness of supportive policies and practices, contributes to caring responsibilities eclipsing women's careers. This is particularly apparent when faced with paternalistic management styles, and decisions being made without consultation.

As this study was carried out within the context of a growing 'social care crisis' (BBC 2017; Grierson 2017; Slawson 2017), the reliance on informal carers is only set to increase, with greater pressure and less support (Grierson 2017; White 2013; Pickard 2008; Heitmueller 2007). With caring considered to be a 'universal human experience' (Grayson 2017, p. 5), the reality is that at some point in our lives each of us will have been both cared for and be carers. As one of my participants, Vanessa, said,

I hope it doesn't happen to you, but it is going to happen to you.

At the same time, the government is keen for carers to remain in employment (HM Government 2014), which many of the study's participants desired to do. It is apparent that care and employment policies are in opposition with each other. If working carers are not better supported, we face a reduction in the number of women in professional occupations, who have no option but to leave the labour market (Petrie and Kirkup 2018).

The UK government has a key role in ensuring that employment legislation addresses the realities of combining work and care, and in publicising the value in supporting carers in the workplace and the moral obligation and significance of doing so (Grayson 2017). The newly created Department of Health and Social Care has set out its plan for the future, and the green paper on social care is expected alongside a Carers Action Plan (Carers UK 2017b). In the meantime, Carers UK (2018) has called for rights to paid time off work to care for up to ten days and tailored support for carers. National and local governments need to provide reliable, quality and affordable care services to enable carers to maintain careers (Carers UK 2018). Furthermore, they need to publicise the value and necessity of supporting working carers, providing the business case illustrated by Grayson (2017) to employers.

In addition to influencing policy, there are implications for human resource management and organisational practice. Currently nearly five million people combine work and care in the UK (Carers UK 2019), and with neoliberal policy continuing to rely on informal carers (Gilbert and Powell 2005), this number is set to increase. In response, employers should be examining the ways in which they can support and manage working carers effectively, to maintain their commitment and motivation to their organisational roles, and assist them in continuing to work. The potential consequences of not doing so are those carers being forced to leave work, with a loss of talent, tacit knowledge and productivity (Grayson 2017). The argument has been put forward that employers must understand the business and moral case of supporting carers to maintain employment. This includes recognition of how many carers they employ (Petrie and Kirkup 2018), gender equality, diversity and inclusion, creating an engaged workforce and a great place to work

(Grayson 2017) where carers feel supported and empowered to respond to their caring needs (CIPD 2016).

In respect of developing equality and diversity practices in the UK (Kirton and Greene 2016), this research calls for a personalised approach to managing working carers. Each caring situation is unique. Whilst people may be perceived to be in similar situations, what support is required may differ. The key is for engagement and discussion to be held with working carers, rather than assumptions being made on their behalf, to ensure that the sacrifice of formal careers does not continue to generate hidden career and workplace inequalities at the expense of caring.

Organisations face a balancing act here in creating policies, structured enough to offer consistency of support, but flexible enough to be adapted to individual circumstances. At the very least, policies should reflect UK legislation, taking account of leave provisions and flexible working practices, for example. Organisations should ensure an inclusive culture, which recognises employee responsibilities outside of the workplace, and one in which employees feel supported. They should also offer coaching and guidance to managers to ensure they are equipped to respond to their employees' needs in line with their obligations, policies and culture. As this research has demonstrated, experiences vary depending on the line manager, regardless of organisational policy and established practice. Furthermore, organisations should ensure that time and attention are provided for genuine development conversations to take place, not just as part of an annual appraisal process, seeking to understand the needs and aims of individual employees and their own situations.

References

Acas. 2014. The right to request flexible working: An Acas guide. http://www.acas.org.uk/media/pdf/1/7/The-right-to-request-flexible-working-the-Acas-guide.pdf. Accessed 6 May 2018.

Aldridge, J. 2015. *Participatory research: Working with vulnerable groups in research and practice*. Bristol: Policy Press.

Appannah, A., and S. Biggs. 2015. Age-friendly organisations: The role of organisational culture and the participation of older workers. *Journal of Social Work Practice* 29: 37–51.

Arber, S., and J. Ginn. 1995. Gender differences in the relationship between paid employment and informal care. *Work, Employment and Society* 9: 445–471.

Arksey, H. 2002. Combining informal care and work: Supporting carers in the workplace. *Health and Social Care in the Community* 10: 151–161.

Arksey, H., and C. Glendinning. 2008. Combining work and care: Carers? decision-making in the context of competing policy pressures. *Social Policy and Administration* 42: 1–18.

Arthur, M. 1994. The boundaryless career: A new perspective for organizational inquiry. *Journal of Organizational Behavior* 15: 295–306.

BBC. 2017. Labour leader Jeremy Corbyn vows pay rise for 'unsung hero' carers. http://www.bbc.co.uk/news/uk-politics-39627689. Accessed 14 May 2018.

Belli, R., and M. Callegaro. 2009. The emergence of calendar interviewing: A theoretical and empirical rationale. In *Calendar and time diary methods in life course research*, ed. R. Belli, F. Stafford, and D. Alwin, 31–52. Los Angeles/London: Sage.

Berger, P., and T. Luckmann. 1967. *The social construction of reality*. London: The Penguin Press.

Burrell, G., and G. Morgan. 1979. *Sociological paradigms and Organisational analysis*. Hants: Ashgate Publishing Ltd.

Care Act. 2014. (c.23) London: The Stationery Office.

Carers UK. 2014. Carers UK. http://www.carersuk.org/. Accessed 22 Apr 2018.

———. 2016a. *State of caring 2016*. London: Carers UK.

———. 2016b. *Walking the tightrope: The challenges of combining work and care in later life*. London: Carers UK.

———. 2017a. State of Caring 2017 Report. https://www.carersuk.org/for-professionals/policy/policy-library/state-of-caring-report-2017. Accessed 11 May 2018.

———. 2017b. Carer charities welcome Minister's commitment to action plan of support for carers. https://www.carersuk.org/news-and-campaigns/news/joint-response-to-ministerial-announcement-of-an-action-plan-on-support-for-carers. Accessed 2 May 2018.

———. 2018. State of Caring 2018 Report. https://www.carersuk.org/news-and-campaigns/state-of-caring-survey-2018. Accessed 13 May 2018.

———. 2019. Juggling work and unpaid care: A growing issue. http://www.carersuk.org/images/News_and_campaigns/Juggling_work_and_unpaid_care_report_final_0119_WEB.pdf. Accessed 05 Mar 2019.

Carmichael, F., and S. Charles. 2003. The opportunity costs of informal care: Does gender matter? *Journal of Health Economics* 22: 781–803.

Carmichael, F., C. Hulme, S. Sheppard, and G. Connell. 2008. Work-life imbalance: Informal care and paid employment in the UK. *Feminist Economics* 14: 3–35.

Chartered Institute of Personnel and Development (CIPD). 2016. Creating an enabling future for carers in the workplace. https://www.cipd.co.uk/knowledge/culture/well-being/enabling-carers. Accessed 19 June 2018.

Employers for carers. 2013. Employers for carers task and finish group: Employers business benefits. http://www.employersforcarers.org/resources/research/item/809-employers-business-benefits-survey. Accessed 22 Jan 2018.

———. 2018. Resources – Supporting carers at work: Essential Guides. https://www.employersforcarers.org/resources/supporting-carers-at-work-essential-guides. Accessed 6 May 2018.

Equality Act. 2010. (Chapter 15). London: The Stationery Office.

Giele, J., and G. Elder. 1998. Life course research: Development of a field. In *Methods of life-course research, qualitative and quantitative approaches*, ed. G. Giele and G. Elder, 5–27. London: Sage.

Gilbert, T., and J. Powell. 2005. Family, caring and ageing in the United Kingdom. *Scandinavian Journal of Caring Sciences* 19: 53–57.

Grayson, D. 2017. *Take care: How to be a great employer for working carers*. Bingley: Emerald Publishing Limited.

Green, D. 2017. Government to set out proposals to reform care and support. https://www.gov.uk/government/news/government-to-set-out-proposals-to-reform-care-and-support. Accessed 11 Jan 2018.

Grierson, J. 2017. 928 carers in England quit a day as social care system 'starts to collapse'. https://www.theguardian.com/society/2017/apr/11/900-carers-in-england-quit-a-day-as-social-care-system-starts-to-collapse. Accessed 6 May 2018.

Harris, D., and D. Parisi. 2007. Adapting life history calendars for qualitative research on welfare transitions. *Field Methods* 19: 40–58.

Heitmueller, A. 2007. The chicken or the egg? Endogeneity in labour market participation of informal carers in England. *Journal of Health Economics* 26: 536–559.

Heitmueller, A., and K. Inglis. 2007. The earnings of informal carers: Wage differentials and opportunity costs. *Journal of Health Economics* 26: 821–841.

Her majesty's government. 1999. *Caring about carers: A national strategy for carers*. London: Her Majesty's Government.

———. 2008. Carers at the heart of 21st-century families and communities. https://assets.publishing.service.gov.uk/government/uploads/system/uploads/attachment_data/file/136492/carers_at_the_heart_of_21_century_families.pdf. Accessed 30 Apr 2018.

———. 2010. Recognised, valued and supported: Next steps for the carers strategy. https://assets.publishing.service.gov.uk/government/uploads/system/uploads/attachment_data/file/213804/dh_122393.pdf. Accessed 30 May 2018.

———. 2014. Carers strategy: Second national action plan 2014–2016. https://assets.publishing.service.gov.uk/government/uploads/system/uploads/attachment_data/file/368478/Carers_Strategy_-_Second_National_Action_Plan_2014_-_2016.pdf. Accessed 5 Feb 2019.

———. 2018. Carer's allowance. https://www.gov.uk/carers-allowance/eligibility. Accessed 20 June 2018.

Hutchinson, S. 2013. The role of line managers in managing performance. In *Performance management: Theory and practice*, ed. S. Hutchinson, 73–94. London: Chartered Institute of Personnel and Development.

Hutton, S., and M. Hirst. 2000. *Informal care over time.* Research Works, Research Findings from the Social Policy Research Unit.

Kirton, G., and A. Greene. 2016. *The dynamics of managing diversity: A critical approach.* 4th ed. Oxon: Routledge.

Lacity, M., and M. Janson. 1994. Understanding qualitative data: A framework of text analysis methods. *Journal of Management Information Systems* 11: 137–155.

Mainiero, L., and S. Sullivan. 2005. Kaleidoscope careers: An alternative explanation for the 'opt-out' revolution. *Academy of Management Executive* 19: 106–123.

Nelson, I. 2010. From quantitative to qualitative: Adapting the life history calendar method. *Field Methods* 22: 413–428.

Noy, C. 2008. Sampling knowledge: The hermeneutics of snowball sampling in qualitative research. *International Journal of Social Research Methodology* 11: 327–344.

O'Connor, D. 2007. Self-identifying as a caregiver: Exploring the positioning process. *Journal of Aging Studies* 21: 165–174.

Office for national statistics. 2011. Census. https://www.ons.gov.uk/census/2011census. Accessed 6 May 2018.

———. 2017. UK Labour Market: September 2017. https://www.ons.gov.uk/employmentandlabourmarket/peopleinwork/employmentandemployeetypes/bulletins/uklabourmarket/september2017. Accessed 6 May 2018.

Petrie, K., and J. Kirkup. 2018. Caring for carers: The lives of family carers in the UK. http://www.smf.co.uk/wp-content/uploads/2018/07/Caring-for-Carers.pdf. Accessed 6 May 2018.

Pickard, L. 2008. *Informal care for older people provided by their adult children: Projections of supply and demand to 2041*. Personal Social Services Research Unit (PRSSU), London. Discussion paper 2515.

Rawat, P., and S. Lyndon. 2016. Effect of paternalistic leadership style on subordinate's trust: An Indian study. *Journal of Indian Business Research* 8: 264–277.

Sethi, B., A. Williams, and R. Ireson. 2017. Supporting caregiver employees: Managers' perspective in Canada. *International Journal of Workplace Health Management* 10: 25–41.

Slawson, N. 2017. UK Social care sector in crisis due to staff shortages. https://www.theguardian.com/society/2017/mar/08/uk-social-care-crisis-staff-shortages. Accessed 6 May 2018.

The law commission. 2011. *Adult social care*. London: The Stationery Office.

Van Houtven, C., N. Coe, and M. Skira. 2013. The effect of informal care on work and wages. *Journal of Health Economics* 32: 240–252.

White, C. 2013. 2011 Census analysis: Unpaid care in England and Wales, 2011 and comparison with 2001. https://www.ons.gov.uk/peoplepopulationandcommunity/healthandsocialcare/healthcaresystem/articles/2011censusanalysisunpaidcareinenglandandwales2011andcomparisonwith2001/2013-02-15. Accessed 6 May 2018.

Winkelmann-Gleedd, A. 2012. Retirement or committed to work? Conceptualising prolonged labour market participation through organisational commitment. *Employee Relations* 34: 80–90.

Yeandle, S., C. Bennett, L. Buckner, G. Fry, and C. Price. 2007. *Managing caring and employment*. University of Leeds: Carers UK, 2.

Zuba, M., and U. Schneider. 2013. What helps working informal caregivers? The role of workplace characteristics in balancing work and adult-care responsibilities. *Journal of Family and Economic Issues* 34: 460–469.

6

The Take-Up and Quality of Part-Time Work Among Men

Amanda Thompson and Daniel Wheatley

6.1 Introduction

Within most advanced societies, patterns of employment are changing as a consequence of a flexibilisation of the labour market (Raess and Burgoon 2015), a trend which has, in turn, led to growing heterogeneity in the employment experiences of both men and women (Wilson et al. 2016). However, irrespective of a shifting context for work and employment legislation providing men and women with the right to request to work flexibly, the evidence to date shows that women are still much more inclined to utilise flexible working practices than men (CIPD 2013;

A. Thompson (✉)
Nottingham Business School, Nottingham Trent University, Nottingham, UK
e-mail: amanda.thompson@ntu.ac.uk

D. Wheatley
Department of Management, Birmingham Business School, University of Birmingham, Birmingham, UK
e-mail: d.wheatley@bham.ac.uk

© The Author(s) 2019
S. Nachmias, V. Caven (eds.), *Inequality and Organizational Practice*, Palgrave Explorations in Workplace Stigma, https://doi.org/10.1007/978-3-030-11647-7_6

EHRC 2013). Patterns of part-time employment remain deeply gendered, while the quality of part-time work among women is often poor (Fagan et al. 2012; Wheatley 2017). Part-time work refers to working reduced hours, usually under 30 hours per week, although definitions vary in the upper limits which are considered to reflect working part-time. Of the 32.3 million recorded people in employment in the UK in 2018 (January to March), only 13.1% of employed men reported working part-time, compared with 41.5% of employed women (ONS 2018). In part, these patterns are a product of most flexible working arrangements, and part-time employment in particular, being commonly considered as a work pattern ideally suited to those combining paid work with domestic and/or caring responsibilities (Atkinson and Hall 2009, p. 659). Although a substantially smaller proportion (and numerical total) of men work part-time, compared to the proportion and volume of women working part-time, this form of employment, nevertheless, accounts for approximately 1.7 million male employees in the UK (ONS 2018) and is a growing phenomenon.

Past evidence has tended to centre on part-time work as something men actively choose at particular points in their lives, notably as students and young men setting out in careers, and as a preferred way of 'winding down' to retirement or continuing to work, post-retirement, in older age groups (Delson 1998; Gregory and Connolly 2008). However, a significant rise in the last 20 years, from around 1-in-20 to 1-in-5, of men in low-paid employment working part-time questions the extent to which men are entering part-time work voluntarily and willingly. As Belfield et al. (2017) highlight, the combination of low pay and low hours of work is particularly undesirable, and so it would be reasonable to assume that, for some at least, this permutation is borne from compromise rather than active choice. Green and Livanos (2015, p. 1226) concur, suggesting that low pay and low hours inevitably result in the under-employment of some workers.

Developments in paid work, including the shift from employment in production to services and associated move from occupations requiring manual to cognitive and interpersonal skills (Glover and Kirton 2006), are considered, at least at the level of job creation, to have resulted in a more favourable climate for women to increase their participation in paid work.

For men, these changes potentially represent both a rise in involuntary part-time employment (reflecting under-employment) and, simultaneously, greater opportunities for them to choose different work patterns, and for couples and families to reshape traditional gendered notions of working, living, caring, and leisure. At a macro-level, the wider distribution of part-time work across male groups and thus a greater proportion of men working shorter hours can be positioned as a positive development, which has the potential to rebalance gender inequalities, both at work and in the home. Set against this context, and amidst predictions that men's take-up of part-time work is expected to increase by around 20% in the period to 2024 (Wilson et al. 2016), it is timely to explore the relative quality of part-time work among men, their reasons for working part-time, and their experiences of this particular mode of working.

The chapter begins with a brief discussion of the gendered nature of flexible working, and part-time work more specifically, acknowledging the widespread use of part-time work by women as a key way of combining paid work with domestic and/or caring labour (see, e.g. Fagan and Walthery 2011; Lewis and Humbert 2010; Plantenga and Remery 2010; Wheatley 2017). We move on to recognise changes in the context of employment in recent decades and consider the impact on men and masculinity. Next, we consider the extant literature surrounding the quality of part-time work, referred to as job quality, and explore the extent to which part-time jobs offer autonomy, variety, skills acquisition, and training and development. The relative pay and job security associated with part-time work also forms part of this discussion. The chapter subsequently briefly describes the methodology underpinning our research into men's uptake of part-time work and the quality of part-time work among men, before presenting our key empirical findings, conclusions, and associated implications for policy and practice.

6.2   The Gendering of Part-Time Employment

Flexible working is a familiar and much researched topic (see Atkinson and Hall 2009; Davies and Freedland 2007; Fagan et al. 2012; Wheatley 2017); there is, however, less recognition of tacit assumptions regarding the gendering of flexibility (Lewis and Humbert 2010, p. 242). Since 1997, successive UK governments have promoted flexible working, initially using the term 'family-friendly working practices' and latterly with reference to 'work-life balance'. The *Flexible Working Regulations*, introduced in 2003, for parents of young and disabled children, have been incrementally extended and broadened, most recently in 2014, such that they now apply to all workers with 26 weeks' service.[1] In addition, Shared Parental Leave (SPL) regulations were introduced in December 2014, presenting greater options for parents of babies born after 5 April 2015 to determine how to structure work and caring responsibilities, including the possibility for men to take up to 50 weeks of parental leave (Gov.uk 2016). While legislation has forged ahead, research carried out by the Department of Business Innovation and Skills (DBIS) prior to the introduction of SPL revealed considerable scepticism on the part of employers that male employees would take advantage of their soon-to-be, new, entitlement, given it was 'not the culture for men to take large amounts of leave' (DBIS 2014, p. 40). This cynicism has turned out to be well founded. The law firm, EMW, suggested only 8700 couples used the scheme between April 2016 and March 2017, amounting to just 1% of eligible couples; the Department for Business was slightly more optimistic in its calculations putting the figure at closer to 3% of those eligible (BBC 2018).

The practical, ground-level response to the introduction of SPL is an illustration that despite use of gender-neutral language and persistent effort to rally inclusiveness and universalism of access to leave arrangements and patterns of working that are more conducive to work-life balance, there is still a stubborn underlying presumption that the business of accommodating paid work and caring/domestic labour rests predominantly with women (Lewis and Humbert 2010). Not surprisingly, therefore, evidence to date demonstrates that, as a group, women are much more inclined to utilise flexible working practices than men (CIPD 2013; EHRC 2013; Wheatley 2017). Part-time work, as perhaps the most

---

[1] The Flexible Working (Procedural Requirements) Regulations, SI 2002/3207, and Flexible Working (Eligibility, Complaints and Remedies) SI 2002/3236 are amendments to the Employment Act 2002, s47, consolidated in the Employment Rights Act 1996, ss80F–80I.

traditional and well-recognised form of flexible working, remains dominated by women.

Viewed in contrast to its well-documented use among women, part-time work is still less common among men as already outlined but is particularly unusual within senior roles and the professions. In the UK, only 3.8% of male directors, managers, and senior officials are employed part-time, for example, and just 5.9% of men in professional occupations use this mode of working (ONS 2017). The equivalent figures for women are 15% and 26.3%, respectively. Work is infused with cultural meanings. Work, but specifically full-time, permanent employment is considered to hold central importance for men and be a defining feature of male identity. The domain of paid work has long been inextricably linked, not just to men but to the performance of masculinity (Cockburn 1983; Guerrier and Adib 2004). As a rule, men have been expected to adopt the breadwinner role, supported by women whose primary allegiance is to the home (Connell 2009). For men, being in a position to do this is regarded as a signifier of manliness and masculinity, and the loss or erosion of this role diminishes masculine identity and power (Besen 2007). Work, therefore, has been considered an important space in which men trial and demonstrate their masculinity (Gaylin 1992), and achieve credibility and legitimacy as men. Biologically, men are predisposed to this pattern of employment, not hampered or hindered by childbirth. Indeed, men's careers are often taken more seriously, propelled and strengthened by the onset of fatherhood, whilst motherhood has a 'scarring effect' on women's careers. Full-time, permanent work has developed as the normative, and assumed gender neutral, career model, yet as Sheridan (2004) notes, it is, in reality, saturated with male values. Hegemonic masculinity is not just associated with work, but it is more acutely associated with work that entails long hours and behaviours to demonstrate prioritisation of the needs of the employer over and above personal and family time (Lewis and Humbert 2010)—necessarily full-time work. The resultant employment pattern is that, *women predominate in a raft of low-paid jobs, especially part-time, whilst men are better represented in full-time and higher paid jobs* (Kirton and Greene 2016, p. 20).

Men who work part-time fail to conform to the dominant masculinised career model and usual experience of male paid work. Past evidence has described men's usage of part-time employment as 'U-shaped', as a way of highlighting the pronounced spikes in the incidence of part-time employment among young men and young male students, on the one hand, and older men approaching retirement, on the other (Delson 1998; Gregory and Connolly 2008). However, the recent, and expected continued, growth in part-time work among men is more diverse in nature. It is not only a product of increases among young and older workers, but it is also found among middle-aged men, single men, married men, and those with and without children (Belfield et al. 2017). These changes appear to be signalling an end to the relatively static patterns that have even until recently characterised men's participation in part-time work. In the period 2002–2011, for example, men's participation in part-time work increased by just three percentage points (EHRC 2013). A new male cohort of part-time workers is fast developing in employment, arising not it seems as a result of progressive, 'father-friendly' parental leave and flexible working arrangements, but largely because of the rising flexibilisation of paid work, and continued job growth in sectors traditionally dominated by women, such as retail and hospitality where part-time jobs are commonly found (Raess and Burgoon 2015; UKCES 2016). The extent to which these new patterns of work among men are driven by choice and agency is debatable.

6.3   Contextual Change

The UK has witnessed changes in the nature of employment and in the occupational structure of the labour market in recent decades, attributable to a host of factors including, but not limited to, globalisation, competition, changes in consumer demand and rapid technological developments. A notable example is the declining relative importance of manufacturing, which has meant that, over time, the volume of occupations associated with manufacturing has similarly declined, while the share of occupations associated with the delivery of business services, and retail, for example, has increased. Sissons (2011) claims that over the longer term, the economy will shift away from routine production towards a knowledge base, causing new jobs to be created in large numbers in high-skill, high-wage managerial and professional occupations. However, the last decade or so has also seen substantial growth in lower-wage service occupations, combined with a reduction in middle-wage occupations as advances in technology and the forces of globalisation 'hollow out' demand for routine workers, semi-skilled work in administrative and secretarial, and process, plant, and machine operatives (Wilson et al. 2016). The term 'hourglass economy' has been coined to reflect this changing occupational structure. In essence, the routine tasks that can be replaced by technology are neither the managerial roles at the top nor the low-skilled ones at the bottom, such as cleaning, bar work, or shelf-stacking. The roles that are most vulnerable are in fact those in the middle of the occupational structure, including blue collar/manual work, and it is these jobs that are being scaled back. Concern is expressed that an hourglass-shaped economy will result in stark polarisation between high-wage 'lovely' occupations and low-wage 'lousy' occupations (Holmes and Mayhew 2012); this is a concept that we return to later in this chapter, in relation to the quality of part-time jobs.

In parallel to changes to the occupational structure, the Trades Union Congress (TUC) (2015) highlights labour market shifts in favour of more low-paid, short hours, casualised, and exploitative forms of employment, designed to provide employers with optimal flexibility, a lean cost base, and consequently greater potential to leverage competitive advantage. Men's employment has not been insulated in the midst of these changes. On the contrary, Philpott (2011), reflecting on the deep economic recession triggered in 2008, uses the term 'mancession' to describe the way in which men were more acutely affected than women, as a result of blue-collar job losses in the private sector, notably in construction and manufacturing. The effects of the recession and its aftermath still reverberate in the economy, as employers pursue employment strategies designed to minimise costs, maximise adaptability, and thus strengthen their resilience to economic decline.

The nature and pace of change described within this section has arguably created a more difficult environment for men to maintain the breadwinner role and for men themselves, couples and families, to rely on the notion that men will engage in full-time paid work throughout their careers. Traditional working-class-based masculinities constructed around manual labour, grit, and muscle are threatened when the structural base of manufacturing and production industries within which they have developed and flourished is eroded (Glover and Kirton 2006). Men's assured status as the breadwinner is no longer intact (Besen 2007); however, it could be argued that women's greater presence in paid work provides new freedoms and wider choices for men and means they need not necessarily adopt the breadwinner role (Kelan 2009). Alongside change in the public sphere, within the private sphere of the home too, male patriarchal authority is no longer automatic as divorce and separation force a reconsideration of masculine identity. Such changes impact on men and construct men in a multitude of ways. As Kelan (2009, p. 6) has argued, *gender as a practice can take different shapes when the economy itself is transforming*. It is against this changing economic and social backdrop that we seek to develop a more advanced understanding of men's patterns of participation in part-time employment, their motives for working part-time, and the quality of the part-time jobs they occupy.

6.4   The Quality of Part-Time Work

The quality of work, often referred to as job quality, reflects the characteristics of paid work which have positive (good characteristics) and negative (bad characteristics) impacts on a worker, including to physical and psychological well-being (Green 2006). Characteristics of high-quality job are usually considered to include autonomy, variety, skill, training and development, better pay and security, and work-life balance policies including flexible working arrangements (Holman 2013, pp. 477–78). In contrast, bad or low-quality jobs exhibit low levels of autonomy, skill, pay, and training and are often associated with highly flexibilised, precarious, employment including zero-hour contracts and agency work (Gregory and Milner 2009). A number of taxonomies of job quality has been developed (see Bartling et al. 2012; Karasek and Theorell 1990; Connell and Burgess 2016; Holman 2013; Vidal 2013). Consistent in these different taxonomies is that good jobs exhibit higher levels of task discretion and autonomy, higher pay and job security, and opportunities for training and development (Bartling et al. 2012). Salient to a discussion of part-time employment, Choi et al. (2008, p. 436) suggest that the ability to choose where and when to work is more common where there is a highly skilled and 'high discretion' workforce, who can be trusted to use autonomy yet remain dedicated to the work role (Bartling et al. 2012). It should, though, be noted that jobs rarely fit neatly into one or other category, as recognised in Vidal's taxonomy, which has 18 subgroups (Vidal 2013, p. 600). High-quality jobs may, for example, exhibit negative characteristics including intense working routines (high demand) and work-family conflict (Kalleberg 2012).

The increased flexibility that part-time employment offers is perceived as a positive development since it can be an effective way of organising work from both an employer and employee perspective (Fagan et al. 2012; Plantenga and Remery 2010). Part-time employment enables employers to use workers more effectively to navigate peaks and troughs in demand and reduce costs accordingly, while it simultaneously offers opportunities for those who wish to work non-standard hours. Rubery et al. (2016, p. 236), however, argue that flexibility is not the panacea it is often depicted to be, rather it *has a way of biting back*, giving rise to issues that cannot be predicted and are difficult to ameliorate, given the tide of contemporary labour market conditions. Rubery et al. (2016) plot the major forms of flexible working arrangements using the standard employment relationship (SER) as a benchmark, where the SER is described as predictable, regular, and usually full-time hours with the ability to voluntarily work additional hours for additional reward (overtime), and where terms and conditions of employment, at least, meet statutory minima and reflect sector and occupational norms. The model positions a range of flexible working arrangements using a horizontal axis, representing at one extreme employer-oriented temporal flexibility and at the opposite end worker-oriented flexibility, and a vertical axis, where the highest point denotes high labour costs and the lowest point, low labour costs. The SER is set centrally at the intersection between the two axes. The majority of flexible working arrangements are plotted in the lower half of the model, demonstrating the low costs to employers of adopting flexibility as a resourcing strategy. Most part-time employment is located in the bottom right-hand quadrant with employees accepting poorer pay and terms and conditions in exchange for a degree of employee-oriented flexibility, while a smaller proportion of part-time employment is set inside the bottom left-hand quadrant, recognising that for some part-time workers, hours and patterns of employment are less employee friendly and primarily organised to suit the employer's needs. In such cases, part-time work is seen as analogous with other low-quality forms of employment, such as zero hours and agency working (Gregory and Milner 2009, p. 123). The quality of part-time work is much debated and diverse as can be seen by the taxonomy summarised in Table 6.1.

Working reduced hours offers some benefits to employees, for example, through enabling improved work-life balance while allowing employees to maintain an organisational presence (Lewis and Humbert 2010). Benham et al. (2018) finds, for instance, that part-time workers have higher satisfaction with work-life balance than full-time workers, and their level of satisfaction increases the fewer hours they spend at work. Working part-time has also been shown to potentially increase job satisfaction (Gregory and Connolly 2008), although evidence of this is conflicting (Wheatley 2017). Meanwhile, part-time work can have positive effects through reducing the pressure associated with combining work and nonwork (Russell et al. 2009). In a Swedish study, for example, fathers who had chosen parental part-time work reveal that part-time work represents for them a way to reconcile their separate identities as professionals and as involved fathers (Larsson and Bjork 2017). On the other hand, there is also a growing body of evidence that part-time workers and those engaging in other forms of flexible working experience work intensification. Walsh (2007) found that whilst employees in her study generally liked part-time work, there was evidence that fragmented work schedules, mandated overtime, and difficulties in taking time off work at times to suit the employee created tensions in both the work and family sphere. Kelliher and Anderson (2010) also present findings to show that employees who worked from home for part of the week and employees working reduced hours experienced work intensification.

Part-time work evidently can represent an 'accommodation' option that employees voluntarily choose to improve work-life integration. However, it can also reflect an involuntary form of employment, driven by constraint arising due to household responsibilities and/or employer demands (Fagan et al. 2012; Fagan and Walthery 2011), in particular,

Table 6.1 Taxonomy of part-time employment

Type of part-time employment	Employee characteristics	Job quality dimensions
Good part-time employment	High proportion with a partner and with parenting responsibilities More likely to have a higher household income contribution More likely than those in other groups to report higher educational and experience requirements associated with their job	More work hours Supervisory responsibilities Permanent status More flexibility than part-time workers in other groups Higher pay
Bad part-time employment	High proportion with a partner and with parenting responsibilities Income contribution also relatively high Lower educational and experience requirements	Fewer work hours and supervisory responsibilities Lower incidences of permanent status Less flexibility Lower pay
Student part-time employment	Lower percentages of respondents with a partner or children High percentages enrolled in a programme of study Contribution to household income mostly in the lowest category Very low percentages reporting having a job elsewhere	Few hours worked Least likely to report supervisory responsibilities Lower percentages of individuals in this group report high levels of flexibility or permanent status.
Transitional part-time employment (likely to represent early career stage employment)	Low educational and experience requirements Not likely to have a partner or children Over 40% reported being enrolled in a programme of study Contribution to household income low relative to good and bad part-time employment, but more than in the student group Educational and experience requirements are low relative to good part-time employment, but higher than in the student group	The percentage of individuals in this group reporting more work hours is much higher than in the student group and higher than in bad part-time employment About twice as likely to report supervising or managing other employees than are individuals in bad or student groups Higher pay levels than in the student group There is less flexibility in the transition group than in the good part-time employment group, but more than in the student group. A higher percentage reported a permanent status in the transition group than in the student group

Source: Haines et al. (2018)

where employers apply these arrangements as an 'optimal staffing' mechanism for generating numerical flexibility. Data from the UK *Labour Force Survey* offers insight into the involuntary nature of part-time employment for some workers, as over 15% of those working part-time in 2015 reported doing as a result of a lack of a full-time alternative, an increase from just over 8% in 2006 (Green and Livanos 2015; ONS 2015). As a result of the often highly flexibilised and involuntary nature of part-time work, it is often perceived as a poor quality and temporary form of employment (Fagan et al. 2012). Part-time work imposes costs on the employee through work intensification and lower pay (Lewis and Humbert 2010). Other low-quality characteristics range from lack of responsibilities and reduced opportunities for development and promotion, high work intensity associated with part-time workers completing full-time workloads and/or not taking breaks, and poor workplace support (McDonald et al. 2009). Overwhelmingly, it is involuntary part-time workers who experience poorer job quality with reference to key job quality dimensions such as training opportunities, career development, job insecurity, and autonomy at work (Kauhanen and Natti 2015).

6.5   Method

Data from wave 4 (2012–2013) of *Understanding Society* are used to explore patterns of part-time employment among men and the relative quality of work these men encounter, including reported well-being derived from paid work.[2] *Understanding Society* is a multi-topic longitudinal sample survey of 40,000 households, aiming to improve understanding of social and economic change in Britain at household and individual levels (University of Essex 2014) The analysis focuses on men employed part-time, and, as such, does not include self-employed men reporting part-time hours. Exploratory analysis is conducted, using two-step cluster analysis, which focuses on the quality of work encountered

---

[2] Wave 4 (2012–13) of Understanding Society is used as the most recently available dataset at the time the research was conducted, wave 5 (2013–14), did not include the module containing questions on the quality of work including levels of autonomy.

by men working part-time. Cluster analysis is particularly suited to exploratory analysis. It groups cases into homogenous groups or clusters, differing from many other research techniques as it does not require any prior assumptions about the distribution of the data (Witte et al. 2009). Two-step cluster analysis is applied as it is suitable for large data sets, and unlike hierarchical cluster analysis, it allows the analysis of both continuous and categorical variables, and it automatically fits the data to the most appropriate number of clusters rather than requiring the number of clusters to be specified (Norušis 2012). The analysis of part-time men generates three clusters determined by the largest increase in *Bayesian Information Criterion* (BIC) and the maximum *Ratio of Distance Measures* (1.966), that is, the solution where clusters are most distinct (Amato and Hohman-Marriott 2007; Witte et al. 2009). The exploratory cluster analysis is extended using multinomial logistic regression, comparing the three clusters using a cluster membership variable derived from the cluster analysis, and offering additional comparison with men reporting full-time employment. The regression analysis focuses on the relative quality of paid work reported by men which is reflected in the independent variables included in the model.

6.6   Empirical Analysis and Findings

Approximately 13% of men in the *Understanding Society* sample report part-time employment, a marginal over-representation in comparison with UK national averages. Data from *Understanding Society*, summarised in Fig. 6.1, is consistent with Delson (1998) and Gregory and Connolly (2008) in showing that men are particularly likely to work part-time when they are young or when they are older, whilst men aged 30–39 and 40–49 are least likely to work part-time. It should be noted, though, that while these patterns are evident in the proportions of men working part-time, the number of men working part-time, represented by the line on the secondary axis in Fig. 6.1, reveals a more nuanced pattern. The numbers reporting part-time employment are more distributed, and while a U-shape is evident with fewer men aged 22–29 and 30–39 reporting part-time work, a notable number of middle-aged men work part-time,

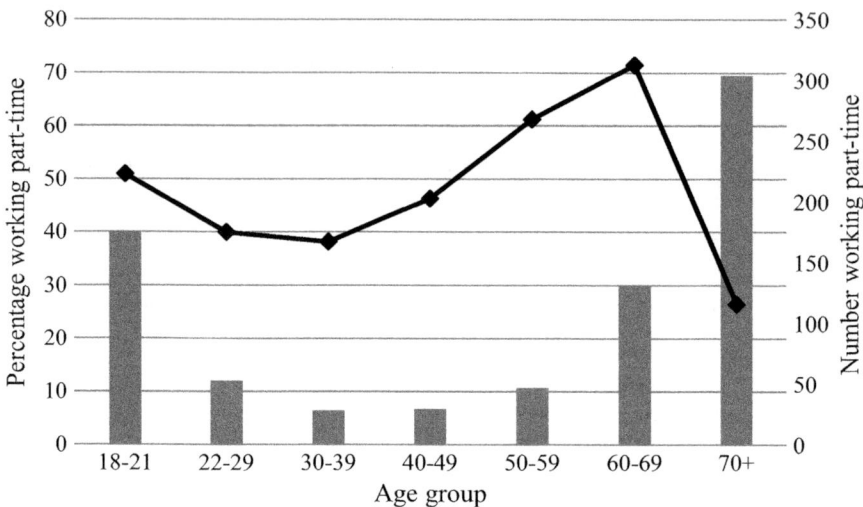

Fig. 6.1 Patterns of part-time work among men. (Source: Wave 4, 2012–13, Understanding Society)

and the numbers working part-time grow as men enter their 50s and 60s. Part-time work may not be that common proportionally among middle-aged men, but notable numbers are, nevertheless, engaged in this form of employment. Male part-time workers are present in varying proportions across a range of occupation groups; however part-time work is least prevalent in highly skilled occupations, consistent with the Office for National Statistics (ONS) data from the *Labour Force Survey* (ONS 2017). Men who do work part-time in highly skilled occupations are, on average, older at around 56 years of age, compared to the youngest occupation group, sales and customer service, where the average age is 31 years.

Extending these broad patterns by exploring other demographics, married men are found to be less likely to work part-time (11.6%), as are those who report being divorced/separated (10.1%). These results are perhaps not surprising, given the familial and other financial commitments encountered by men in these groups. However, number of children is positively associated with working part-time among men, suggesting some effect may be present in some cases related to childcare. Men in part-time work report contributing more to the household as they report lengthier hours of housework (6.2 hours per week) than their full-time counterparts (5.5 hours), but this still represents only around half of the household contribution of working women. Men working part-time also report greater caring commitments for ill/elderly relatives or friends and are more likely to possess a disability or long-term illness themselves: around 30% of men working part-time report a disability or long-term illness, compared with 22% of men in full-time employment. Overall, while broad patterns of part-time employment among men follow past research, a more nuanced and complex picture emerges when a range of demographic and occupational factors are considered, consistent with recent patterns observed by Belfield et al. (2017). In order to explore these patterns in more detail, and gain insight into the quality of work encountered by men working part-time, cluster analysis is performed using the data from *Understanding Society*.

6.6.1   Two-Step Cluster Analysis

Table 6.2 summarises the three clusters generated by the two-step cluster analysis. Cluster 1 comprises older men (averaging 54 years old), reflecting those who work part-time as part of phased or partial retirement, evident in the high proportions employed in highly skilled managerial, professional, and associate professional occupations, accounting for 43.7% of this cluster, and those in bridge employment who often trade down to less skilled elementary occupations (17.6% of this cluster). Members of this cluster more often report good jobs characterised by relatively higher levels of autonomy, the highest levels of flexibility including the ability to work at home, high pro-rata pay (averaging £26,000), and high levels of job satisfaction (mean value of 5.7). Financial security is also a feature of this cluster, as just over 40% report their financial status as 'living comfortably'. Continued engagement in paid work for this cluster is likely to represent a greater degree of choice, although around a quarter do report a preference to stop paid work. Members of this cluster are also the most likely to engage in unpaid voluntary work in addition to paid work, consistent with the greater engagement in volunteering among men nearing retirement reported in other research (Hardill and Wheatley 2017; Schlosser and Zinni 2010).

Table 6.2 Two-step cluster analysis

	Cluster		
	1 *n* = 471	2 *n* = 258	3 *n* = 356
Demographic variables			
Age (mean)	54.2	39.5	21.9
Marital status (%)	67.1 (married/ civil partnership)	58.9 (married/civil partnership)	95.8 (single/ never married)
Highest qualification (%)	41.2 (no qualifications)	36.8 (no qualifications)	43.8 (intermediate qualifications)
Disability/long-term illness (% 'yes')	38.9	30.6	9.6

Number of children in
  household aged 0–2
  (mean)
	0.0	0.2	0.0

Number of children in
  household aged 3–4
  (mean)
	0.0	0.2	0.0

Number of children in
  household aged 5–11
  (mean)
	0.1	0.4	0.0

Number of children in
  household aged 12–15
  (mean)
	0.1	0.2	0.0

Time-use variables (per week)			
Working hours (mean)	16.2	18.9	13.5
Overtime hours (mean)	0.8	0.9	1.2
Housework hours (mean)	7.0	6.6	3.8
Care (ill/elderly) hours (mean)	1.6	4.6	0.4
Volunteering hours (mean)	4.2	2.1	1.2
Occupation variables			
Private sector (%)	61.4	84.5	85.7
Major occupation group (SOC) (%)	17.6 (elementary occupations)	32.6 (elementary occupations)	45.8 (elementary occupations)
Annual personal income (mean £000s)	26.1	15.4	6.1
Work location (%)	71.5 (employer premises)	79.5 (employer premises)	89.3 (employer premises)
Quality of work variables			

(*continued*)

Table 6.2 (continued)

	Cluster		
	1 *n* = 471	2 *n* = 258	3 *n* = 356
Autonomy over job tasks (%)	49.9 (a lot)	40.7 (none)	37.6 (some)
Autonomy over work pace (%)	58.8 (a lot)	32.9 (none)	35.7 (some)
Autonomy over work manner (%)	66.0 (a lot)	33.7 (none)	37.9 (some)
Autonomy over task order (%)	59.7 (a lot)	33.7 (none)	32.3 (some)
Autonomy over working hours (%)	34.6 (none)	63.9 (none)	53.9 (none)
Informal flexibility (%)	55.2 (yes)	58.5 (no)	48.6 (yes)
Would like training (% 'yes')	24.8	47.3	42.7
Would like new job with different employer (% 'yes')	17.8	66.7	58.9
Would like to start own business (% 'yes')	15.9	34.9	30.6
Would like to stop paid work (% 'yes')	25.7	24.8	6.7
Tense about job (%)	49.0 (never)	37.6 (some of the time)	52.8 (never)
Uneasy about job (%)	69.2 (never)	32.9 (some of the time)	79.0 (never)
Worried about job (%)	75.4 (never)	41.9 (never)	87.1 (never)
Depressed about job (%)	90.4 (never)	47.3 (never)	93.0 (never)
Gloomy about job (%)	82.0 (never)	39.9 (never)	84.8 (never)
Miserable about job (%)	88.3 (never)	43.0 (never)	82.9 (never)
Subjective financial status (%)	40.6 (living comfortably)	39.5 (just about getting by)	48.3 (doing alright)

(*continued*)

Table 6.2 (continued)

	Cluster		
	1 n = 471	2 n = 258	3 n = 356
Satisfaction with job (mean)	5.7	4.3	5.5

Source: Understanding Society, wave 4 (2012–13)
Notes: Table shows means or most frequent responses
Work location has four options: 'at employer premises', 'driving or travelling around', 'at one or more places', and 'work at home'
Questions regarding autonomy levels have four possible responses: 'a lot', 'some', 'a little', and 'none'
Questions regarding preferences for changes in paid work, e.g. would like training, have two possible responses: 'yes' and 'no'
Questions regarding negative perceptions of paid work, e.g. tense about job, have five possible responses: 'all of the time', 'most of the time', 'some of the time', 'occasionally', and 'never'
Informal flexibility has three possible responses: 'yes', 'some' and 'none'
Subjective financial status has five possible responses: 'living comfortably', 'doing alright', 'just about getting by', 'finding it quite difficult', and 'finding it very difficult'
Satisfaction with job is measured on a 7-point Likert scale, where 1 = completely unsatisfied, 4 = neither satisfied or unsatisfied, and 7 = completely satisfied

Cluster 2 consists of men who are engaged in part-time work through constraint, due to either the impact of unpaid work or lack of full-time labour market opportunities. Men in this cluster are predominantly middle-aged (averaging 40 years old), but with a notable degree of deviation from the mean (standard deviation of 13.5). In line with their reported age, members of this cluster are the most likely to report dependent children, in particular, school-aged children, and be married or in a civil partnership. They work the longest part-time hours and report significantly greater unpaid work, both housework and care for ill/elderly relatives and friends, than members of other clusters. Men in this cluster work in low-skilled sales and customer service and elementary occupations, and report low-quality jobs which have little autonomy and lack flexibility, resulting in low job satisfaction and higher levels of negative feelings towards work. Two-thirds of men in this cluster report they would like a new job with a different employer, supporting the assertion of some members of this cluster being in involuntary part-time employment due to lack of an alternative (Green and Livanos 2015; ONS 2015). Despite working longer hours than other men working part-time and reporting higher earnings (averaging £15,000) than members of cluster 3, men in this cluster report financial insecurity. Approximately one-third of this cluster report they are either 'finding it quite difficult' or 'finding it very difficult' to get by financially. This is likely to be a product of the greater financial pressure felt by these men as parents and/or carers for others. Despite their jobs having a number of low-quality characteristics consistent with cluster 2, members of cluster 3 do report some autonomy in aspects of paid work, and relatively high satisfaction with their job, reflecting the blurred boundaries present in the quality of work (Kalleberg 2012; Vidal 2013). This cluster comprises younger, single men (averaging 22 years old), who are in their early career and/or are likely to engage in paid work alongside education, reflecting transitional and student part-time work, respectively (Haines et al. 2018). They work in low-skilled sales and customer service and elementary occupations, and report the shortest working hours (13.5 hours per week) and lowest pay (£6000). Part-time work for these individuals is likely to be, at least perceived as, a short-term mode of employment undertaken in order to gain experience and/or income, in some cases while studying.

6.6.2   Multinomial Logistic Regression

The multinomial logistic regression model is used to add additional robustness to the results of the cluster analysis, comparing cluster 2, which comprises those men working part-time through constraint, with the other two clusters using the cluster membership variable, and additionally includes comparison with men reporting full-time employment. Table 6.3 summarises the multinomial regression model. The results of the model confirm that relative to cluster 2, men in cluster 1 work shorter hours and are more likely to be employed in highly skilled professional occupations. Moreover, men in cluster 1 report better quality jobs, reflected in statistically significant higher autonomy levels (over job tasks, work pace, and task order), flexibility measured in terms of informal

Table 6.3 Multinomial logistic regression: quality of work among men working part-time

	Phased retirement (cluster 1) compared to constrained part-time (cluster 2)	Early career/ education (cluster 3) compared to constrained part-time (cluster 2)	Full-time compared to constrained part-time (cluster 2)
Constant	3.320**	7.265***	−50.368***
Work-time variables (per week)			
Working hours	−0.052**	−0.067**	1.828***
Overtime hours	−0.046	0.043	1.740***
Occupation variables			
Public sector	−1.446***	−0.273	−0.041
Major occupation group (SOC): Reference category is elementary occupations			
Managers, directors and senior officials	1.080	−0.929	0.295
Professionals	2.034**	−19.072	1.266
Associate professional and technical	0.698	−0.239	0.212
Administrative and secretarial	2.035***	0.797	−0.230
Skilled trades	0.110	−0.835	0.808
Caring, leisure and other service	0.068	−0.236	0.238
Sales and customer service	−0.973*	−0.094	1.081
Process, plant, machine operatives	−0.034	−2.226***	−0.311
Annual personal income (£,000 s)	−0.004	−0.278***	−0.016
Work location: Reference category is employers premises			
At home	19.646***	18.858***	23.074***
Driving or travelling around	−0.103	−1.065*	−0.334
At one or more other places	0.328	0.564	2.215*
Quality of work variables			
Autonomy over job tasks: Reference category is none			
A lot	1.169**	−0.442	1.490
Some	0.629	0.611	0.601
A little	0.625	0.868*	1.252

(*continued*)

Table 6.3 (continued)

	Phased retirement (cluster 1) compared to constrained part-time (cluster 2)	Early career/ education (cluster 3) compared to constrained part-time (cluster 2)	Full-time compared to constrained part-time (cluster 2)
Autonomy over work pace: reference category is none			
A lot	1.749***	0.053	0.724
Some	1.546***	0.250	1.722*
A little	0.647	0.157	1.060
Autonomy over work manner: reference category is none			
A lot	0.976	0.526	−1.290
Some	−0.096	0.713	−1.586
A little	−0.434	0.485	−0.486
Autonomy over task order: reference category is none			
A lot	1.047*	0.655	1.104
Some	0.730	0.878	0.322
A little	0.333	1.266**	−0.688
Autonomy over working hours: reference category is none			
A lot	0.311	−1.328**	0.091
Some	0.153	−0.166	0.643
A little	0.642	0.731	1.290
Informal flexibility: Reference category is none			
Yes	0.620*	1.002***	0.443
No	−0.427	0.225	0.884
Would like training	−0.691**	−0.062	0.099
Would like new job with different employer	−1.311***	−0.060	0.845
Would like to start own business	−0.742**	0.352	−0.548
Would like to stop paid work	0.964***	−0.992**	0.766
Negative feelings expressed toward paid work[a]	−3.343***	−4.551***	−1.545***
Subjective financial status: Reference category is 'finding is very difficult'			
Living comfortably	2.548***	3.382***	0.319
Doing alright	1.351**	2.906***	−0.605
Just about getting by	0.488	1.194	−1.173
Finding it quite difficult	−0.163	0.474	−1.324

(continued)

Table 6.3 (continued)

	Phased retirement (cluster 1) compared to constrained part-time (cluster 2)	Early career/ education (cluster 3) compared to constrained part-time (cluster 2)	Full-time compared to constrained part-time (cluster 2)
Satisfaction with job	0.194*	0.157	0.393*
Model diagnostics			
−2 log likelihood	854.160		
Chi-square	8092.623		
Sig.	0.000		
Cox and Snell	0.593		
Nagelkerke	0.941		
McFadden	0.905		
No. observations	9006		

Source: Understanding Society, wave 4 (2012–13)

Notes: Dependent variable is cluster membership variable. Significance levels of 1%, 5% and 10% are denoted by ***, ** and * respectively

[a]Questions regarding negative perceptions of paid work e.g. tense about job have been combined into one composite index (negative feelings expressed toward paid work) due to multicollinearity concerns when variables entered separately

flexibility, and propensity to work at home. It should be noted that cluster 2 is the least likely to report working at home. Members of cluster 1 are also less likely to report negative feelings towards paid work, captured in the regression analysis in a single composite variable, and report greater job satisfaction than those in cluster 2. Also consistent with the cluster analysis, members of cluster 1 are significantly more financially secure.

Men in cluster 3, similarly to cluster 1, are more likely to work shorter hours than those in cluster 2. They also report significantly lower pay. The results pertaining to autonomy actually suggest that younger workers may report relatively little autonomy, especially over hours, but that even 'a little' autonomy reported by younger workers may be more than the autonomy encountered by men in cluster 2. Members of cluster 3 are likely to report fewer negative feelings towards work, although the greater likelihood of reporting higher levels of job satisfaction found in the cluster analysis is statistically insignificant, casting some doubt over some aspects of the differences in the relative quality of work encountered by men in clusters 2 and 3. Finally, comparing cluster 2 to men in full-time employment, we find that men working full-time report higher levels of job satisfaction and fewer negative feelings towards work, reflecting the greater degree of choice, on average, present among men engaged in this form of employment. Overall, the analysis highlights the diversity of men working part-time. While some men working part-time conform to documented patterns reported by Delson (1998) and others, some men do not fit into these broad patterns. Meanwhile, the quality of work encountered by men in part-time employment suggests quite contrasting experiences, highlighting the presence of both voluntary and involuntary part-time employment.

6.7   Conclusions and Implications

This chapter facilitates a greater understanding of men's reasons for participating in part-time employment and the quality of part-time work they experience. Using data from *Understanding Society*, we have shown that patterns of part-time employment, while broadly following a U-shape (Delson 1998; Gregory and Connolly 2008), are more complex and diffuse consistent with the assertions of Belfield et al. (2017) and analogous with the typology developed by Haines et al. (2018) embracing good and bad student and transitional part-time work. Correspondingly, quite contrasting experiences are found pertaining to the quality of part-time work among men. The chapter illuminates the gender division in part-time work, yet in empirically focusing specifically on men's participation in part-time work demonstrates that there has been a loosening of the male breadwinner model and corollary part-time (female) worker, homemaker, and carer. It is apparent that not all men in part-time work consciously choose to work reduced hours; rather, they are propelled into part-time work due to the scarcity of more attractive, full-time, employment options.

The experiences of men fall into both categories of part-time work identified in Rubery et al.'s (2016) presentation of flexible employment types, as some men benefit from better quality employee-oriented flexibility, albeit at some cost in terms of pay and working conditions, while others are subject to employer-driven flexibilised part-time work which is low quality and can equate to under-employment (Green and Livanos 2015). However, our findings also suggest that part-time work can occupy a further quadrant (top right) of Rubery et al.'s (2016, p. 237) model, as we find evidence of high-paid part-time work among highly skilled older men. The factors contributing to men's participation in part-time employment are diverse, representing both freedom and contentment for some, including older men nearing the end of their working lives and young male workers typically working while studying, yet for others, life and/or labour market circumstances result in little choice but to work part-time. In particular, our research identifies a phenomenon which is less well recognised—men in middle-age groups in part-time employment— where working patterns are constrained and conflicted by an unsatisfactory array of personal, familial, and external labour market factors.

Given the predicted growth and heterogeneity among men working part-time, these findings have important implications for both organisations, including those seeking to recruit and retain part-time workers, and for public policy. Currently, we find that access to good quality part-time work and employee-oriented flexibility is a perk reserved for the privileged—in other words, for those with superior skills, qualifications, financial, and/or cultural capital to vie for the better positions and terms, and who are able to make active choices to work part-time. For many women, as already widely reported in existing research, part-time employment represents poor pay, poor prospects, and a career cul-de-sac within which it is easy to get stuck. For a portion of men, their experiences are analogous. For men and women, poor quality part-time work is the price paid in some cases for seeking to find a means of combining paid work and care, and in other cases, it is the involuntary compromise forced upon workers as a consequence of the quality and availability of jobs in the economy. Part-time jobs can be high quality though, as evident in our findings. It is important for the well-being of workers and their families that future growth in part-time employment is located among good quality jobs, as opposed to the further proliferation of low quality, low-paid positions, which exacerbate the problem of under-employment. As such, efforts should be made by both employers and policymakers to improve the quality of part-time work. In particular, increasing opportunities for training and development, and the level of autonomy and discretion available to workers, could improve the quality of part-time work without imposing significant additional costs to the employer. In addition, perceptions regarding 'what it is to work part-time' and 'what constitutes a part-time job' need to be revisited. Organisations should place greater value on part-time work outside of the most common, stereotypical scenarios and so begin to respond positively, imaginatively, and responsibly to workers' diverse lifestyles, circumstances, preferences, and associated working needs, irrespective of gender, age, and other personal and social characteristics. Such moves, if realised, would see an end to the hidden patterns of inequality many men (and women) experience when engaging in part-time work. Significant benefits could be attained from restructuring employment opportunities for both men and women through (re) designing jobs so that they can be encapsulated in part-time working routines.

References

Amato, P.R., and B. Hohman-Marriott. 2007. A comparison of high and low distress marriages that end in divorce. *Journal of Marriage and Family* 69: 621–638.

Atkinson, C., and L. Hall. 2009. The role of gender in varying forms of flexible working. *Gender, Work and Organisation* 16: 650–666.

Bartling, B., E. Fehr, and K. Schmidt. 2012. Screening, competition and job design: Economic origins of good jobs. *American Economic Review* 102 (2): 834–864.

BBC. 2018. Shared parental leave take up may be as low as 2%. http://www.bbc.com/news/business-43026312. Accessed 10 June 2018.

Belfield, C., R. Blundell, J. Cribb, A. Hood, R. Joyce, and A. Norris Keiller. 2017. *Two decades of income inequality in Britain: The role of wages, household earnings and redistribution.* London: The Institute for Fiscal Studies.

Benham, B., S. Drobnic, P. Prag, A. Baieri, and J. Eckner. 2018. Part-time work and gender inequality in Europe: A comparative analysis of satisfaction with work-life balance. *European Societies* 1461 (6696): 1–25.

Besen, Y. 2007. Masculinities at work. *Equal Opportunities International* 26: 256–260.

Choi, S., J. Leiter, and D. Tomaskovic-Devey. 2008. Contingent autonomy technology, bureaucracy, and relative power in the labor process. *Work and Occupations* 35: 422–455.

CIPD. 2013. *Flexible working provision and uptake*. London: CIPD.

Cockburn, C. 1983. *Brothers, male dominance and technological change*. Michigan: Pluto Press.

Connell, R. 2009. *Gender: In world perspective*. 2nd ed. Cambridge: Polity Press.

Connell, J., and J. Burgess. 2016. Strategic HRM and its influence on quality of work: Evidence from nine Australian organisations in HRM and organisational effectiveness. In *Asia Pacific human resource management and organisational effectiveness*, ed. A. Nankervis, Ch. Rowley, and N.M. Salleh, 171–192. London: Elsevier.

Davies, P., and M. Freedland. 2007. *Towards a flexible labour market: Labour legislation and regulation since the 1990s*. Oxford: Oxford University Press.

Delson, L. 1998. Why do men work part time? In *Part-time prospects; An international comparison of part-time work in Europe, North America and the Pacific Rim*, ed. J. O'Reilly and C. Fagan, 57–76. London: Routledge.

Department for Business, Innovation and Skills (DBIS). 2014. Improvement plan. https://assets.publishing.service.gov.uk/government/uploads/system/uploads/attachment_data/file/298523/bis-14-682-department-for-business-improvement-plan-march-2014.pdf

Equality and Human Rights Commission. 2013. Women, men and part-time work. www.equalityhumanrights.com. Accessed 12 Jan 2015.

Fagan, C., and P. Walthery. 2011. Individual working-time adjustments between full-time and part-time working in European firms. *Social Politics* 18: 269–299.

Fagan, C., C. Lyonette, M. Smith, and A. Saldaña-Tejeda. 2012. *The influence of working time arrangements on work-life integration or 'balance': A review of the international evidence*. Conditions of Work and Employment No. 32. New York: ILO.

Gaylin, W. 1992. *The male ego*. New York: Viking.

Glover, J., and G. Kirton. 2006. *Women, employment and organisations*. Abingdon: Routledge.

Gov.uk. 2016. Shared parental leave. https://www.gov.uk/shared-parental-leave-and-pay-employer-guide/overview. Accessed 12 May 2018.

Green, F. 2006. *Demanding work. The paradox of job quality in the affluent society*. Princeton: Princeton University Press.

Green, A., and I. Livanos. 2015. Involuntary non-standard employment and the economic crisis: Regional insights from the UK. *Regional Studies* 49: 1223–1235.

Gregory, M., and S. Connolly. 2008. Feature: The price of reconciliation: Part-time work, families and women's satisfaction. *The Economic Journal* 118: F1–F7.

Gregory, A., and S. Milner. 2009. Trade unions and work-life balance: Changing times in France and the UK? *British Journal of Industrial Relations* 47: 122–146.

Guerrier, Y., and A. Adib. 2004. Gendered identities in the work of overseas tour reps. *Gender, Work and Organisation* 11: 334–350.

Haines, I., P. Dorey-Demers, and V. Martin. 2018. Good, bad and not so sad part-time employment. *Journal of Vocational Behaviour* 104: 128–140.

Hardill, I., and D. Wheatley. 2017. Care and volunteering: The feel good Samaritan? In *Time well spent: Subjective well-being and the work-life balance*, ed. D. Wheatley, 52–86. London: Rowman and Littlefield International.

Holman, D. 2013. Job types and job quality in Europe. *Human Relations* 66: 475–502.

Holmes, C., and K. Mayhew. 2012. *The changing shape of the UK job market and its implications for the bottom half of earners*. London: Resolution Foundation.

Kalleberg, A.L. 2012. Job quality and precarious work: Clarifications, controversies, and challenges. *Work and Occupations* 39: 427–448.

Karasek, R.A., and T. Theorell. 1990. *Healthy work: Stress, productivity, and the reconstruction of working life*. New York: Basic Books.

Kauhanen, M., and J. Natti. 2015. Involuntary temporary and part-time work, job quality and well-being at work. *Social Indicators Research* 120: 783–799.

Kelan, E. 2009. *Performing gender at work*. Basingstoke: Palgrave.

Kelliher, C., and D. Anderson. 2010. Doing more with less? Flexible working practices and the intensification of work. *Human Relations* 63: 83–196.

Kirton, G., and A. Greene. 2016. *The dynamics of managing diversity: A critical approach*. 4th ed. Abingdon: Routledge.

Larsson, J., and S. Bjork. 2017. Swedish fathers choosing part-time work. *Community, Work and Family* 20: 142–161.

Lewis, S., and L. Humbert. 2010. Discourse or reality? Work life balance, flexible working policies and the gendered organisation. *Equality, Diversity and Inclusion: An International Journal* 29: 239–254.

McDonald, P., L. Bradley, and K. Brown. 2009. 'Full-time is a given here': Part-time versus full-time job quality. *British Journal of Management* 20: 143–157.

Norušis, M. 2012. *IBM SPSS statistics 19 statistical procedures companion.* Upper Saddle River: Prentice Hall.

Office for National Statistics (ONS). 2015. Time Series: LFS: Part-time workers: % could not find full-time job: UK: All: SA. http://www.ons.gov.uk/employmentandlabourmarket/peopleinwork/employmentandemployeetypes/timeseries/ycda. Accessed 12 May 2018.

———. 2017. *Labour force survey.* Quarter 2, April–June 2017.

———. 2018. *UK labour market: May 2018, estimates of employment, unemployment, economic inactivity and other employment related statistics for the UK.* Statistical Bulletin.

Philpott, J. 2011. *How men and women have fared in the post-recession UK jobs market.* London: CIPD.

Plantenga, J., and C. Remery. 2010. *Flexible working time arrangements and gender equality: A comparative review of 30 European countries.* Luxembourg: European Commission (Publications Office of the EU).

Raess, D., and B. Burgoon. 2015. Flexible work and immigration in Europe. *British Journal of Industrial Relations* 53: 94–111.

Rubery, J., A. Keizer, and D. Grimshaw. 2016. Flexibility bites back: The multiple and hidden costs of flexible employment policies. *Human Resource Management Journal* 26: 235–251.

Russell, H., P. O'Connell, and F. McGinnity. 2009. The impact of flexible working arrangements on work–life conflict and work pressure in Ireland. *Gender, Work and Organisation* 16: 73–97.

Schlosser, F., and D. Zinni. 2010. Transitioning ageing workers from paid work to unpaid work in non-profits. *Human Resource Management Journal* 21: 156–170.

Sheridan, A. 2004. Chronic presenteeism: The multiple dimensions to men's absence from part-time work. *Gender, Work and Organisation* 11: 207–225.

Sissons, P. 2011. *The hour glass and the escalator: Labour market change and mobility.* London: The Work Foundation.

TUC. 2015. *Living on the margins: Black workers and casualization.* London: Equality and Employment Rights Department.

University of Essex. Institute for Social and Economic Research and NatCen Social Research. 2014. *Understanding society: Waves 1–5, 2009–2014* [computer file]. 7th ed. Colchester: UK Data Archive [distributor], November 2015. SN: 6614, Retrieved from https://doi.org/10.5255/UKDA-SN-6614-7.

Vidal, M. 2013. Low-autonomy work and bad jobs in postfordist capitalism. *Human Relations* 66: 587–612.

Walsh, J. 2007. Experiencing part time work; Temporal tensions, social relations and the work family interface. *British Journal of Industrial Relations* 45: 155–177.

Wheatley, D. 2017. Employee satisfaction and patterns in availability and use of flexible working arrangements. *Work, Employment and Society* 31: 567–585.

Wilson, R., N. Sofroniou, R. Beaven, M. May-Gillings, S. Perkins, M. Lee, P. Glover, H. Limmer, and A. Leach. 2016. *Working futures 2014–2020, evidence report 100*. London: UKCES.

Witte, T.K., K.A. Timmons, E. Fink, A.R. Smith, and T.E. Joiner. 2009. Do major depressive disorder and dysthymic disorder confer differential risk for suicide? *Journal of Affective Disorders* 115: 69–78.

7

Identifying and Addressing Hidden Structural and Cultural Inequalities in the Workplace

Evanthia Kalpazidou Schmidt

7.1 Introduction

Recent studies in science and technology organisations reveal how a multilayered set of hidden factors of different nature and depth interact in the workplace and produce negative effects on gender equality. In the same vein, existing research underlines the complexity of addressing hidden structural and cultural gender inequality in the workplace of scientific organisations (Kalpazidou Schmidt and Cacace 2017). Such hidden features demonstrate a robust capacity to take on new forms and strength, adjusting to organisational and other environmental transformations. These features are embedded in cultures, procedures and practices, language, behavioural patterns and beliefs that are widespread in the workplace but are mostly unknown to the stakeholders (Cacace 2009).

E. Kalpazidou Schmidt (✉)
Department of Political Science, Danish Centre for Studies in Research and Research Policy, Aarhus University, Aarhus, Denmark
e-mail: eks@ps.au.dk

© The Author(s) 2019   **159**
S. Nachmias, V. Caven (eds.), *Inequality and Organizational Practice*, Palgrave Explorations in Workplace Stigma, https://doi.org/10.1007/978-3-030-11647-7_7

Scholars and practitioners therefore emphasise the importance of research on structural and cultural features producing inequalities to enable organisations to address them (Timmers et al. 2010). Yet hidden, deeply rooted structural and cultural gender biases in scientific organisations remain an understudied area. In particular, insights into concrete actions and good practices to effectively address hidden structural barriers are highly necessary to avoid marginalising inequality issues due to the fact that they are complex and difficult to deal with (Nielsen 2015).

Based on two studies—one on gender equality interventions at more than 100 science and technology organisations worldwide and another on action research carried out at five research institutions in different countries in Europe—this chapter outlines these typically subtle and difficult to grasp structural and cultural inequalities. While the general focus lies on the hidden inequalities in the workplace, the specific aim of the chapter is twofold: first, it draws attention to the areas where structural and cultural inequalities in scientific organisations have been identified, and second, it explores organisational practices to mitigate exclusion of women by addressing these areas through systematic actions that have been successfully implemented in scientific organisations. The chapter thus contributes to the literature on cultural and structural gender inequalities by mapping strategic areas for intervention and suggesting how to address them in complex, for instance scientific, organisations. More specifically, it demonstrates concrete strategies and actions that have proven effective in achieving sustainable structural and cultural changes. A number of recommendations are presented in broad strategic areas, namely in the fields of (1) organisational management and communication, (2) culture and environment, and (3) visibility, networking and women empowerment.

The chapter is organised as follows: first, the theoretical and conceptual framework is presented, followed by some methodological reflections. Second, the findings and their implications for policymaking and management are discussed, and concluding remarks are offered in the last section.

7.2 Theoretical and Methodological Reflections

Recent studies reveal that diverse research teams demonstrate higher degree of productivity and creativity (Elsevier 2017). Similarly, dynamic and innovative research organisations have been found to have a greater proportion of female researchers among their staff (Graversen et al. 2002). In a review of literature on teams, Müller et al. (2016) conclude that one of the key effects of gender diversity—or lack thereof—on team performance is related to gender biases. They demonstrate that the lack of gender diversity can have a negative impact on performance because available expertise in teams is not used due to a range of factors related to gender biases. Such biases (e.g. homophily, power relations, status differentials, etc.) can counterwork the sharing of knowledge and information among the members of a team, which can have a negative impact on research productivity (Müller et al. 2016).

Despite this knowledge, and the fact that the share of female PhD students in Europe is almost 50% and the share of women graduates is 60%, gender inequality in science is a persistent problem in Europe and worldwide. The total share of female researchers is still low across all scientific areas. The share of women among researchers is 30%, while it is only 20% among high-level academic positions (European Commission 2013). The underrepresentation of women in high-level academic positions is particularly striking in the field of science and technology, where only 13% of engineering, technology and natural sciences professors are women (European Commission 2016). Thus, the extent of gender equality varies based on the discipline's culture, which produces noteworthy differences across different faculties even within the same organisation. Moreover, gender competency expectations vary across scientific disciplines, depending on the status of women in them and on whether or not women constitute a minority within a team in the workplace. This implies that competency expectations for women in male-dominated teams (such as within engineering or information and communication technologies) are resilient (Callerstig and Müller 2016). Such expectations might lead to limitations in information sharing in the workplace, resulting in the 'silencing [of] often non-redundant and most valuable information from low status-low power members' such as female researchers (Callerstig and Müller 2016, p. 87).

Gender inequality in organisations is linked to structural power differences embedded in the values of the organisations (Bleijenbergh et al. 2013; van den Brink and Benschop 2012; Benschop and Verloo 2006). As underlined by Bleijenbergh et al. (2008), gender dynamics are strongly interconnected with other organisational issues. Thus, the structure of scientific organisations reproduces inequalities and gender stereotypes (Benschop and Brouns 2003; Priola 2007; van den Brink and Stobbe 2009). Moreover, as gender inequalities are persistent due to their strong embeddedness in cultural and structural factors, they are often taken for granted, are unknown to stakeholders and thus typically remain unchallenged (Parsons and Priola 2013; Bagilhole and Goode 2001; Gherardi and Poggio 2007; Meyerson and Tompkins 2007). University leadership and faculty members for a long time have largely disregarded how structural and cultural barriers operate in the workplace and produce inequalities (Bird 2010). Similarly, other studies on workplace practices, for example, regarding the promotion of scientific staff, have revealed various biases in favour of male faculty members (Bornmann et al. 2007; Van den Brink et al. 2006; Cole et al. 2004; Foschi 2000). Explaining these biases, researchers point to the hidden and unconscious stereotypes that are embedded in the structures and cultures of scientific organisations (Greenwald and Banaji 1995; Greenwald et al. 2002).

While there is a strand of research focusing on the sources of inequality, the lack of studies on the implemented measures and their efficacy as to addressing hidden structural and cultural inequalities is striking (Kalpazidou Schmidt and Cacace 2017; Kalev et al. 2006; Timmers et al. 2010). In particular, there is a deficiency of evidence-based recommendations for actions to effectively address structural and cultural barriers (Czarniawska 2006; Nielsen 2015). This chapter sets to provide insights into the most persistent areas of inequality and to offer evidence-based recommendations for addressing them.

7.3   Conceptual Framework

The underlying assumption of this chapter's conceptual framework is that complex organisations, such as scientific organisations, are characterised by unique features and dynamics. Institutional contexts play a decisive role in shaping the gender balance profile in science (Castaño et al. 2010). This implies that the same strategies and solutions may have different impacts depending on the contextual features of the organisation and the dynamics at play, since key variables and links between them are seldom identical (Kalpazidou Schmidt and Cacace 2017). Similarly, Glass and Minnotte (2010) and Kalpazidou Schmidt and Cacace (2017) point to the complexity of the gender equality issue, demonstrating that even when focus lies on only one particular aspect of gender inequality (e.g. promotion or funding), one kind of intervention may not be enough to establish gender-balanced conditions because there is a range of interrelated factors of different nature that produce those imbalances. Complexity also arises from the fact that the features producing and reproducing gender inequality in science constitute an integral part of the structures and cultures of the organisations.

The institutional, organisational and scientific context is hence at the centre of the complex phenomenon of hidden inequalities in the workplace. Cullen et al. (2008) state that there is clear evidence pointing to the complexity of a mix of different structural, cultural and institutional factors that generate gender imbalances, which calls for integrated and strategic answers. Since unequal outcomes between genders are determined by multiple factors, the issue has to be addressed from different viewpoints in an integrated approach that targets structural, cultural and organisational dimensions, accounting for the complexity of the issue (Kalpazidou Schmidt and Cacace 2018). As Morley (2013) notes, single approaches are 'fundamentally flawed', including those only targeting the institutional level. Timmers et al. (2010) claim that the structural approach, rather than focusing on individuals or roles, targets the nature of existing structures and the organisation of work. Likewise, Schiebinger and Klinge (2013) highlight that women-centred approaches (seeking answers to the problem in the choices and actions of individual researchers) alone are not sufficient to understand the complexity of female underrepresentation; there is a need to combine them with organisation-centred approaches (seeking explanations in the organisation of science). However, literature on the adoption of an integrated approach addressing hidden gender inequalities in scientific organisations is lacking (Kalpazidou Schmidt and Cacace 2017).

Overall, this chapter relies on two tenets: first, it adopts the *complexity approach*[1] in identifying and addressing hidden structural and cultural inequalities in scientific organisations, and second, it accounts for the importance of the *contextual factors* and the dynamics surrounding structural, organisational and cultural features (which can provide support in addressing inequalities but may also serve as hindering factors in the process of implementing equality strategies). Adopting a holistic viewpoint, this chapter hence seeks to study and analyse gender inequalities in the workplace through an integrated perspective, unveiling the many interconnected layers of the complex problem in focus.

7.4   Methods and Data

As mentioned earlier, this chapter is based on the results of two studies aimed at identifying and addressing gender inequalities in scientific organisations. The first study was carried out within the framework of the PRAGES[2] project that aimed at taking stock of gender imbalances by identifying areas where action was needed due to slow inclusion of female researchers in science. The project identified strategies and measures that had proven effective in promoting gender equality in scientific and technological organisations. A combination of different methodological steps was employed to achieve project objectives: first, a comparative approach was adopted to analyse the identified gender equality initiatives in different European countries, as well as in Australia, Canada and the United States. The second step was based on an analytical approach aimed at

---

[1] For a detailed description of the complexity and complex concepts, see (Rogers 2008).

[2] The PRAGES (Practicing Gender Equality in Science) project, funded by the EU, was carried out between 2007 and 2009.

highlighting the complexity of the relationship between science and gender to identify appropriate strategies and tools to tackle it. Finally, a benchmarking approach was used to detect the most successful interventions, enabling suggestions about adaptation and transferability to similar contexts. Thus, concrete initiatives, implemented in specific institutional contexts, were studied, comprising both one-issue interventions (such as mentoring or networking) and larger programmes (such as mainstreaming) to attain more inclusive organisations. Interventions from public, private and not-for-profit scientific organisations were included in the study, with public organisations accounting for most of the cases (Cacace 2009; Kalpazidou Schmidt and Cacace 2017).

The second study was conducted in the framework of the STAGES[3] project and was based on a structural[4] change strategy to identify structural and cultural gender inequalities in scientific institutions and systematically address them through tailor-made action plans, introducing long-term sustainable solutions. Concrete strategies were launched targeting structures and cultures in the workplace from an integrated perspective to make scientific organisations an enabling environment for female researchers, promoting women in scientific leadership positions as well as promoting the sex and gender dimension in the image of science, and in the process and content of research. A line of actions based on negotiation with all institutional stakeholders relevant for the implementation of the tailor-made action plans was adopted (cf. Benschop and Verloo 2011). The study also focused on the dynamics of change and on the actual and potential transformational actors, engaging a growing number of stakeholders and attaining their support in the implementation of the action plans (Kalpazidou Schmidt and Cacace 2018).

In both projects, context sensitivity, consideration of the strong contextual character of the interventions and attention to the complexity of the issue and the implementation processes were central to the research. Organisational settings, structures, cultures, practices and procedures,

---

[3] The STAGES (Structural Transformation to Achieve Gender Equality in Science) project, funded by the EU, was carried out between 2012 and 2015.
[4] For a definition of gender equality structural change in research organisations, see European Commission (2012).

leadership and attitudes of the relevant stakeholders to equality and gender biases were taken into account during the planning and implementation process. In the following sections, some of the key findings of the abovementioned projects are presented—and their implications for policy and management discussed—along with recommendations on how to launch and promote structural and cultural changes in scientific organisations.

7.5 Findings and Implications for Policy and Management

7.5.1 Strategic Intervention Areas

The analysis of gender equality promoting interventions at more than 100 scientific organisations[5] identified three risk areas in the structures and cultures of scientific organisations: (1) the *working environment* (science as an unfriendly environment for women), (2) *science contents and methods* (science as gender-insensitive) and (3) *female leadership* (scientific leadership lacking women) (Cacace 2009; Kalpazidou Schmidt and Cacace 2017).

Based on this analysis, three corresponding *strategic areas for intervention* have been identified. The *first* area of creating a women-inclusive environment comprises actions aimed at making scientific institutions an inclusive environment for women's working life and career advancement, targeting cultural and other features (both formal and informal), promoting work-life balance and providing early-stage career support. Interventions encompass modifying the cultural and behavioural patterns by promoting awareness-raising initiatives, stimulating early-stage

---

[5] In total, 125 gender equality programmes were included in the study, implemented in Europe (66 programmes), North America (33 programmes) and Australia (26 programmes). As for the quality of the programmes, the study revealed that North American programmes demonstrated a slightly higher level of quality than the European and Australian. A weak point of the programmes was efficiency, while relevance and sustainability represented strong points. Nine programmes out of 109 evaluated as to impact, demonstrated an excellent impact level, while 40 were assessed as having a good impact.

career development through training, mentoring and funding, and facilitating work-life balance through flexible organisational arrangements. In the analysis, the following lines of action[6] have been identified as to the promotion of women-inclusive environments. The *first* is related to the lack of knowledge and data on the factors creating discriminatory conditions and the need to document and counteract the tendency—among staff and leadership—to deny the existence of the problem or underestimate its impact on the organisation. Systematic and participatory collection of data as to gender offers the opportunity to demonstrate the systemic character of the problem and raise awareness involving key stakeholders. The *second* line of action addresses the gender pay gap and its monitoring. Gender pay gaps are not immediately visible due to their non-public character and because the mechanisms that produce them are complex and subtle. Making pay gaps visible and discussing their reasons contribute to our understanding of discrimination dynamics at the workplace. The *third* line of action focuses on keeping of women's issues in the foreground by developing specific communication strategies and information tools, targeting in particular the leaders in the organisation and providing space for discussion of common problems (networks, workshops, seminars, newsletters, webzines, interactive portals, etc.). The *fourth* addresses the promotion of research and teaching on gender issues. Relevant activities include supporting gender-related research or establishing a research unit specialising in gender or providing funds for gender studies or training and introductory courses on gender issues and effects on the organisation. The *fifth* line of action aims at promoting the integration of women in the research environment by fighting women's isolation and providing direct support to women in difficulty (e.g. through welcome events, specific services for newcomers or by providing facilitators, mentoring opportunities and tools to deal with discrimination and harassment). The *sixth* line of action refers to the involvement of senior leaders and managers in the change process by promoting a direct and visible commitment of the leadership in the organisation. Proactive involvement of the senior leadership is evidently of pivotal importance for mobilising the necessary resources and developing the required

---

[6] For a detailed description of the different lines of action, see www.pragesdatabase.eu

initiatives to trigger cultural and structural change. The *seventh* line of action addresses the work-life balance by promoting the creation of a network of services and information on available resources and services (new in-house services, offices of childcare and family resources, modification of parental leave policies, part-time and dual-career arrangements, modification of assignments of duties). Finally, the *last* line of action refers to supporting early-stage career development through regulation and policy, assistance and training and providing women funds for professional development (through career advice, mentoring programmes, critical junctures initiatives, networking, training of hiring committee and staff search committee members).

The *second* strategic area comprises actions geared towards integrating the gender dimension in the process of science and innovation design to influence the identification of research priorities, subjects, methods and innovation drivers to combat the male-centred stereotypes of science. Interventions involve challenging gender stereotypes linked to the image of science as the domain of men, on the one hand, and gendering science and methods by questioning scientific priorities, theoretical and methodological approaches and in general the design of scientific research and education, on the other. The following lines of action have been identified as to the promotion of gender-aware science. The *first* involves the challenging of gender stereotypes by collecting and disseminating information contrasting stereotypes and by adopting gender-sensitive language and educational material (e.g. by producing guides to non-sexist language). The *second* line of action addresses the horizontal segregation issue through a systematic analysis of female distribution as regards scientific careers in different sectors and disciplines, pointing out stereotypes in career choices and in the allocation of tasks, thus making segregating mechanisms more visible. The *third* encompasses the gendering of scientific contents and methods (by inserting the gender dimension in the research design and content and funding research on gender dynamics) and the incorporation of gender awareness in education and teaching (in particular in the STEM fields). Finally, the *last* line of action refers to acknowledging women's visions and expectations. This involves the identification and addressing of women's critical issues in relation to science (such as barriers to women's participation in STEM fields), pointing out the role women scientists can play in enhancing research and innovation. The *third* strategic area refers to the promotion of women in scientific leadership positions within management, science communication, scientific practice, innovation and societal engagement. Three different areas are thus the target of interventions in scientific organisations, that is, (1) advancement in the academic career to leadership positions (such as professorships and other decision-making positions in the organisation) through specific funding, training, mentoring, mobility and support for creation of positions targeting women, (2) support to develop research management skills and to access committees and boards, and (3) support to increase the visibility of women (both internally and externally) and their involvement in the management of the science and society relationship. The following lines of action have been identified in this strategic area. *First*, more women in leadership positions requires support to attain key positions in the practice of research through systematically disseminating information and data on high-profile female scientists and supporting women scientists to pursue high-level positions. This involves dissemination of information about available positions, organisation of leadership training programmes and presentation of successful scientists as role models. The *second* line of action refers to introducing new organisational bodies and regulations to redress gender imbalances and modification of rules and procedures for appointing boards and committee members, as well as for monitoring of the impact of new policies and regulations as a specific organisational task with a particular person/team in charge. The *third* line addresses the provision of women with reserved funds, resources and opportunities for professional development (such as reserved positions for female scientists, mobility grants, transparency in appointments). The *forth* line of action refers to supporting women to attain gender balance in key positions in the management of science. This requires monitoring of women's presence on boards and committees through the systematic and enduring collection of data (creating a database of candidates), making women candidates available and visible for boards and committees, and providing training in writing applications to serve in boards and committees. The *fifth* action line involves the strengthening of women's visibility in scientific communication (also by communicating and rewarding female scientific excellence) and supporting their role in communication management through training in communication skills. Finally, the *last* action line addresses the influence of women in innovation and the science and society relationship. This involves the development of specific innovation-oriented funding schemes and of research environments, linking innovation to diversity, the promotion of training initiatives on innovation and the facilitation of contacts with other innovative environments (for instance by providing mobility grants).

Within the above-discussed three strategic areas, based on the outcome of the PRAGES project, concrete instruments have been created, tailored to the needs of the scientific organisations, aimed at achieving structural change. The results of the project were used by the European Commission to formulate (and fund) a new gender equality strategy (adopted by many EU countries) moving away from an emphasis on 'fixing the women' to 'fixing the system' and 'fixing the knowledge' approach.

7.5.2   Triggering Structural Change to Address Hidden Inequalities

The abovementioned strategic areas prepared the ground for the implementation of action plans in different scientific organisations in Europe. Thus, based on the strategic areas, concrete tailor-made fields of action have been recognised to launch structural change processes. As mentioned earlier, considering the strong contextual character of the actions and the complexity of the issue was the central focus at this stage of the studies. The point of attention was fixing the women (individual), fixing the culture (beliefs and language, everyday processes) and fixing the structures (organisational hierarchies, rules and procedures) approaches, which were used in an integrated, all-encompassing strategical intervention that accounted for emerging issues in dynamic environments, such as the scientific organisations in focus. The strategic intervention aimed to attain sustainable change (Schiebinger 2008; Kalpazidou Schmidt and Cacace 2018).

In addressing the inequalities, building on existing resources has been central to the implementation process. The subsequent important step was to mobilise different actors to identify the areas of intervention and to tailor-make the actions to be implemented. Such actors included internal women's groups, internal gender equality units or bodies, leadership and management of the involved organisations, female and male researchers and decision-makers in the organisations, local, regional or national authorities or associations. A continuous and evolving planning process has been crucial to the success of the implementation of actions. As Kalpazidou Schmidt and Cacace (2018) emphasise, to be able to face the challenges of the complexity of structural change, three steps in the process are of imperative significance, that is, deciding which actions to implement, estimating the required effort and designing the concrete steps in the implementation process. The importance of these steps is also evident from other studies: for instance, Kalev et al. (2006) highlight the responsibility structures referring to bodies that can promote change in the organisation. In the same vein, Cacace et al. (2015) discuss the role of transformational agents within an organisation, who are able to trigger the transformation process, activating the dynamics of change and mobilising other agents, internal and external to the organisation.

Central to the intervention and its impact are the breadth and depth of the implemented action plan. Structural and cultural changes require the involvement of many components of different nature in the organisation to attain sustainable outcomes. Changes can be considered structural only when they are institutionalised and become sustainable in the medium and long run or when interventions can demonstrate a potential to trigger further change processes in the future, allowing for new agents or bodies in the organisation to carry on additional gender equality activities (Kalpazidou Schmidt and Cacace 2017).

7.6   Outcomes and Recommendations

The tailor-made to each organisational context interventions produced tangible outcomes in terms of more women in senior and decision-making positions. In the same way, they created the *conditions for further change* through efforts to embed the actions into the equality policies of the organisations and by institutionalising study and training courses;

making the gathering of gender equality data permanent; establishing transformation bodies and networks and modifying rules, procedures and practices. Thus, the interventions ensured the safeguarding of continuity of at least some actions after the finalisation of the concrete action plans (Cacace et al. 2016).

The outcome of the implementation of the action plans point to the most effective interventions, which have generated the following key areas to be targeted in future interventions: (1) collecting data on and monitoring gender equality, (2) engaging leadership, (3) influencing policymaking and attaining institutionalisation, (4) intensifying networking and empowering women to take action, (5) integrating gender in education and research and (6) strengthening communication and visibility (Cacace et al. 2015). These areas are obviously interrelated and thus actions in one category may reinforce actions in another, producing the conditions for medium- or long-term changes.

The first category—collecting data and monitoring gender equality—involves mapping of available information and data, and identifying and assessing existing policies and practices, but also initiating efforts to produce new information that will enable analysis and monitoring of gender equality as well as provide evidence for future policy. Moreover, this evidence and knowledge are essential to awareness-raising initiatives and may support further data collection, monitoring and policy assessment endeavours in the organisation. From a sustainability perspective, data collection and monitoring of gender equality developments is imperative for the visibility of the issue and is a prerequisite for the commitment of central organisational actors to continue the actions. Carrying on efforts to combat subtle inequalities requires that the issue is kept on the organisational agenda.

The second category implies linking gender equality to institutional strategies to gain internal legitimacy by framing the actions as addressing current and forthcoming key challenges in the organisation. Gaining internal legitimacy may entail mapping the leadership and their attitudes towards gender equality, raising their awareness and involving organisational leaders in action design and implementation, as well as supporting already existing gender equality bodies and initiatives. To gain legitimacy internally may also require the involvement of support from external stakeholders and bodies, such as scientific and other organisations, ministries, research councils, which constitute the wider environment of the organisation and which may sometimes, due to legislation or other regulations and conditions, be pivotal for the internal organisation and structure of scientific institutions and their functioning.

The third category—influencing policymaking and increasing institutionalisation of actions—entails creating internal bodies to be institutionalised by inserting actions in the regular functioning of the organisation and by continuously adapting them to address emerging issues. The aim is to enable these bodies to carry on also after the finalisation of the initial action plan implementation, with at least some parts of the original actions. In regard to targeting policymaking to institutionalise and thus sustain actions and programmes, key elements include promoting change in internal strategical documents and regulations, provisions and procedures. Institutionalisation implies that gender equality actions are taken over by the organisation that carries on and sustains concrete activities through existing or newly established institutional bodies.

The fourth category implies empowering women to take action, for example, in design and implementation of gender equality initiatives, by integrating top-down (leadership-initiated) and bottom-up (staff-initiated) approaches, through planning as well as through establishing new or supporting existing gender equality networks and other activities empowering women scientists. Supporting existing and promoting new networks in the organisation may facilitate sustainability of actions in the long run as the bodies engaged in the actions very often continue with the activities after the finalisation of the initial action plan.

The fifth category targets the integration of the gender dimension in the content of scientific endeavours in order to improve the scientific quality and societal relevance of the produced knowledge, technology or innovation. This can be achieved by promoting courses at different levels or integrating gender and sex analysis in research design and methodology. Moreover, organising events and disseminating information on gendering science content and methods are other intervention areas that may help increase awareness of science as a female-inclusive area, where science priorities and contents are gendered.

Finally, the last category has a twofold target. First, it aims to enhance the visibility of women, their voices and contributions (such as presentations of profiles of women, women's days and awards, 'name and fame' actions), as well as the visibility of gender research tools used to change the masculine image of science, through sophisticated communication strategies. Second, communicating concrete actions and achievements, through a diversified communication plan incorporating attractive messages adapted to the organisation and tailored to the specific context and stakeholders, has proven effective. Contextual factors are crucial in communication processes and in making gender issues visible: communication can be hindered if messages miss the target groups using context-insensitive form, language and content.

The recommendations discussed above constitute an inspiration catalogue for policymakers and managers to be adapted and tailored to other specific contexts in order for the transformed interventions to provide successful outcomes and effects. Evidently, as organisational profiles and dynamics may differ greatly, transferability has to be based on a systematic analysis of the contextual factors and future interventions need to be tailored to the requirements of the specific environment.

7.7   Concluding Remarks

In this chapter, we have identified the most compelling strategic areas to intervene in addressing hidden structural and cultural inequalities in the workplace of scientific organisations. We have also identified and described effective intervention approaches and concrete actions, pointed to the actors and mechanisms to mobilise and types of instrumentation to employ while working towards mitigation of deeply rooted organisational inequalities. In addition, we highlighted the importance of accounting for the contextual factors and the complexity of the issue in order to attain sustainable outcome and effects and—equally important—to enable the transferring of intervention outcomes to similar contexts.

Research on the forces at work triggered by effective gender equality interventions is rare. The strategies and instrumentation presented in this chapter have been applied in specific, varied as to gender balance contexts in Europe and produced outcome with acknowledged impact. These strategies and interventions have delivered on the task to unveil some hidden gender inequalities and foster an inclusive workplace and can constitute an important input to efforts concerning transformation of other scientific organisations. The effects of implemented measures have received less attention in the literature, in particular in relation to the contextual frame and its structural and cultural characteristics. Thus, looking across more contexts might provide additional evidence-based knowledge to policymakers, practitioners and researchers, and contribute to deepening the reservoir of knowledge on how to identify and successfully address hidden structural and cultural gender inequality. To conclude, it is evident that structural and cultural gender equality changes require a strategic approach, detailed planning and long-term implementation; but above all, they require continuous efforts that can enable policymakers, practitioners and transformational agents to address emerging challenges, as hidden inequalities and biases have proved to be persistent and vigorous, adjusting to changing conditions, taking on numerous forms and manifestations.

References

Bagilhole, B., and J. Goode. 2001. The contradiction of the myth of individual merit, and the reality of a patriarchal support system in academic careers: A feminist investigation. *European Journal of Women's Studies* 8: 161–180.

Benschop, Y., and M. Brouns. 2003. Crumbling ivory towers: Academic organizing and its gender effects. *Gender, Work and Organization* 10: 194–212.

Benschop, Y., and M. Verloo. 2006. Sisyphus' sisters: Can gender mainstreaming escape the genderedness of organizations? *Journal of Gender Studies* 15: 19–33.

———. 2011. Gender change, organizational change, and gender equality strategies. In *Handbook of gender, work and organization*, ed. L. Emma, D. Knights, and P. Martin, 277–290. Chichester: Wiley.

Bird, S.R. 2010. Unsettling universities' incongruous, gendered bureaucratic structures: A case-study approach. *Gender, Work and Organization* 18: 202–230.

Bleijenbergh, I.L., Y. Benschop, and J. Vennix. 2008. *Making gender equality a shared problem in organizations: Group model building as a gender mainstreaming method. Paper presentation.* Los Angeles: Critical Management Studies Research Workshop, USC.

————. 2013. Group model building to support gender equality change. In *Op zoek naar het andere, een liber amicorum voor Hans Doorewaard,* ed. J. Achterbergh, Y. Benschop, P. Hendriks, and A. van de Ven, 81–96. Den Haag: Boom Lemma.

Bornmann, L., R. Mutz, and D. Hans-Dieter. 2007. Gender differences in grant peer review: A meta-analysis. *Journal of Informetrics* 1: 226–238.

Cacace, M. 2009. *Guidelines for gender equality programs in science. PRAGES – Practising gender equality in science.* Rome: ASDO.

Cacace, M., D. Balahur, I. Bleijenbergh, D. Falcinelli, M. Friedrich, and E. Kalpazidou Schmidt. 2015. *Structural transformations to achieve gender equality in science: Guidelines. Report to the European Commission.* Pontevedra: STAGES.

Cacace, M., L. d'Andrea, and G. Declich. 2016. *Accompanying research on implementation dynamics: Final report of the STAGES (structural change to achieve gender equality in science) project.* Pontevedra: STAGES.

Callerstig, A-Ch., and Müller, J. 2016. *Gender research in GEDII conceptual framework. Project deliverable D1.1.* Gender Diversity Impact.

Castaño, C., J. Müller, A. Gonzales, and R. Palmen. 2010. *Policies towards gender equity in science and research. Meta-analysis of gender and science research – Topic report.* Brussels.

Cole, M.S., S.F. Hubert, and F.G. William. 2004. Interaction of recruiter and applicant gender in resume evaluation: A field study. *Sex Roles* 51: 597–608.

Cullen, J., K. Junge, and C. Ramsden. 2008. *Evaluation of the UK Resource Centre for Women in Science, Engineering and Technology. Final report.* The Tavistock Institute.

Czarniawska, B. 2006. Doing gender unto the other: Fiction as a mode of studying gender discrimination in organizations. *Gender, Work and Organization* 13: 234–253.

Elsevier. 2017. *Gender in the global research landscape: Analysis of research performance through a gender lens across 20 years, 12 geographies, and 27 subject areas.* Amsterdam: Elsevier.

European Commission. 2012. *Structural change in research institutions: Enhancing excellence, gender equality and efficiency in research and innovation.* Luxembourg: Publications Office of the European Union.

———. 2013. *She figures 2012. Gender in research and innovation.* Luxembourg: Publications Office of the European Union.

———. 2016. *She figures 2015. Gender in research and innovation.* Luxembourg: Publications Office of the European Union.

Foschi, M. 2000. Double standards for competence: Theory and research. *Annual Review of Sociology* 26: 21–42.

Gherardi, S., and B. Poggio. 2007. *Gendertelling in organizations: Narratives from male-dominated environments.* Copenhagen: Liber.

Glass, Ch., and K.L. Minnotte. 2010. Recruiting and hiring women in STEM fields. *Journal of Diversity in Higher Education* 3: 218–229.

Graversen, E.K., E. Kalpazidou Schmidt, K. Langberg, and P.S. Lauridsen. 2002. *Dynamik og fornyelse på danske universiteter og sektorforskningsinstitutioner – En analyse af hvad der karakteriserer dynamiske og fornyende forskningsmiljøer. Rapport 2002/1.* Aarhus: Analyseinstitut for Forskning.

Greenwald, A.G., and M.R. Banaji. 1995. Implicit social cognition: Attitudes, self-esteem, and stereotypes. *Psychological Reports* 102: 4–27.

Greenwald, A.G., M.R. Banaji, L.A. Rudman, S.D. Farnham, B.A. Nosek, and D.S. Mellot. 2002. A unified theory of implicit attitudes, stereotypes, self-esteem, and self-concept. *Psychological Review* 109: 3–25.

Kalev, A., K. Erin, and F. Dobbin. 2006. Best practices or best guesses? Assessing the efficacy of corporate affirmative action and diversity policies. *American Sociological Review* 71: 589–617.

Kalpazidou Schmidt, E., and M. Cacace. 2017. Addressing gender inequality in science: The multifaceted challenge of assessing impact. *Research Evaluation* 26: 102–114.

———. 2018. Setting up a dynamic framework to activate gender equality structural transformation in research organizations. *Science and Public Policy.* https://doi.org/10.1093/scipol/scy059.

Meyerson, D.E., and M. Tompkins. 2007. Tempered radicals as institutional change agents: The case of advancing gender equity at the University of Michigan. *Harvard Journal of Law and Gender* 30: 303–322.

Morley, L. 2013. *Women and higher education leadership: Absences and aspiration. Stimulus paper.* London: Leadership Foundation for Higher Education.

Müller, J., S. Klatt, U. Sandström, and A-Ch. Callerstig. 2016. *GEDII conceptual framework. Project deliverable D1.1.* Gender Diversity Impact (GEDII).

Nielsen, M.W. 2015. *New and persistent gender equality challenges in academia.* Aarhus: Politica.

Parsons, E., and V. Priola. 2013. Agents for change and changed agents: The micropolitics of change and feminism in the academy. *Gender, Work and Organization* 20: 580–598.

Priola, V. 2007. Being female doing gender. Narratives of women in education management. *Gender and Education* 19: 21–40.

Rogers, P.J. 2008. Using programme theory to evaluate complicated and complex aspects of interventions. *Evaluation* 14: 29–48.

Schiebinger, L. 2008. *Gendered innovations in science and engineering*. Stanford: Stanford University Press.

Schiebinger, L., and I. Klinge. 2013. *Gendered innovations: How gender analysis contributes to research*. Luxembourg: Publications Office of the European Union.

Timmers, T.M., T.M. Willemsen, and K.G. Tijdens. 2010. Gender diversity policies in universities: A multi-perspective framework of policy measures. *Higher Education* 59: 719–735.

Van den Brink, M., and Y. Benschop. 2012. Slaying the seven-headed dragon: The quest for gender change in academia. *Gender, Work and Organization* 19: 71–92.

Van den Brink, M., and L. Stobbe. 2009. Doing gender in academic education: The paradox of visibility. *Gender, Work and Organization* 16: 451–470.

Van den Brink, M., M. Brouns, and S. Waslander. 2006. Does excellence have a gender? A national research on recruitment and selection procedures for professional appointments in the Netherlands. *Employee Relations* 28: 523–539.

8

Employee Silence and Voice: Addressing Hidden Inequalities at Work

Konstantina Kougiannou

8.1   Introduction

There is a general fear of being labelled a troublemaker or a complainer. The management does not want to get involved with sexual harassment issues. In this kind of industry you can get labels very quickly, so I along with other women do not complain about the sexual harassment stuff. It is a hush, hush kind of a thing.

Milliken et al. (2003, p. 1463) highlight with this quote how employees often are reluctant to voice issues that could be interpreted as negative or threatening to management, with potentially damaging effects on the employment and supervisor-employee relationship. This is especially so when it comes to issues of inequality, even more so when such inequality is not directly visible or legislatively covered. Argyris (1977) notes that organisations have defensive routines and norms that can prevent

K. Kougiannou (✉)
Department of Human Resource Management, Nottingham Business School,
Nottingham Trent University, Nottingham, UK
e-mail: konstantina.kougiannou@ntu.ac.uk

© The Author(s) 2019   **179**
S. Nachmias, V. Caven (eds.), *Inequality and Organizational Practice*, Palgrave
Explorations in Workplace Stigma, https://doi.org/10.1007/978-3-030-11647-7_8

employees from saying what they know, with other scholars finding that organisations can be intolerant of dissent and criticism, and as a result employees might choose to remain silent in order to not create conflict or 'rock the boat' (Redding 1985; Sprague and Ruud 1988).[1]

Issues of equality and discrimination continue to occupy an important focus in human resource management (HRM) and employment relations. The workplace can be an extremely diverse environment of people of different age, gender, social and cultural backgrounds. For example, the United Kingdom's (UK) labour force is becoming increasingly diverse with more women in employment than ever before (Allen 2015) and ethnic minorities making up a larger proportion of the workforce. Product markets are becoming increasingly diverse too, as customers come from diverse ethnic backgrounds (Metcalf and Forth 2000). Yet, people in the workplaces often are the subject of discrimination and inequality because they are different in some way, observable or hidden. Organisations seek to correct this workplace discrimination with the use of diversity management and equal opportunities policies (see Chap. 2 for more information). Equal opportunities policy, practice and legislation is not new in the UK and across the world, gaining more and more importance. Similarly, coming from a different perspective, diversity management, arguing for diverse workforces providing a competitive strength, has also come to the fore. However, discrimination within organisations remains, especially so for any inequality that emanates from non-visible conditions. These are 'grey' or 'hidden' areas of inequality that are not fully legislated for but when used to assign the 'other' stamp to an individual can serve as mechanism of exclusion with a direct negative impact on the individual's dignity and well-being (Nachmias and Caven 2018). Poor recognition of any such inequalities can have a detrimental effect on employees' behaviour including psychological withdrawal, performance issues and turnover (Parzefall and Coyle-Shapiro 2011).

Equal opportunities policies are designed to ensure that all individuals are treated in the same way, advocate a philosophy of 'sameness' (Jewson and Mason 1986) and can be seen as an attempt to eradicate considerations of social differences from organisational decision-making using

---

[1] No real names used in this chapter. They have been replaced with pseudonyms.

bureaucratic means (Liff 1999). In anti-discrimination legislation, 'sameness' is interpreted as people being judged independently of their gender, ethnicity, social background and so on and focusing instead on job-related characteristics (Liff and Wajcman 1996). For example, the Equality Act 2010, in the UK, bans unfair treatment in the workplace by providing access to employment and ensuring fair treatment regardless of age, disability, gender reassignment, marriage and civil partnership, pregnancy and maternity, race, religion or belief, sex and sexual orientation. In practice this means techniques should be developed to ensure that individuals are assessed in the same way and that differences between individuals on characteristics that are not job related should not be considered (Allen 2015).

Nevertheless, legislation differs from actual equal opportunities policies within organisations. For example, the law is not very prescriptive in terms of which areas, such as recruitment, pay and promotional opportunities, need to be legally monitored (Allen 2015). As Daniels and Macdonald (2005) note, it is generally considered good practice for organisations to monitor recruitment processes in order to promote equality. Yet, organisations and workplaces are not legally obliged to collect this information. In addition, legislation does not currently require firms to monitor direct and/or indirect discrimination against those with 'protected characteristics' covered by the 2010 Equality Act, such as gender, disability and ethnicity (Allen 2015). Thus, concerns remain as to whether these policies achieve their stated objectives, especially in the case of addressing hidden inequality. Many of the equal opportunities policies are often based on state regulations on equality and diversity, failing however to cover aspects of perceived inequalities falling out of the regulations' remit. Additionally, evidence suggests that the presence of a written policy does not guarantee successful implementation, impact or intent to address such inequalities (Dundon and Rollinson 2011) and could very well be a 'tick-box' exercise to comply with regulations. The result may be an organisational policy that appears perfect on paper but in practice serves to conceal actual bias and discrimination (Hoque and Noon 2004).

Any inequality in the workplace can lead to separation and isolation from the mainstream workforce, and this can influence affected employees' voice and silence in the workplace (McFadden and Crowley-Henry 2017). Evidence show that employees often do not feel comfortable speaking to their managers about issues that concern them or organisational problems (Milliken et al. 2003). A workplace environment that inadvertently or consciously promotes and/or maintains employee silence would in turn be more likely to sustain and/or enhance inequality at work.

In this chapter we examine when and how employees in organisational settings exercise voice and when and how they opt for silence (Milliken et al. 2003), specifically within the 'grey' areas of equal opportunities policies and the 'hidden' inequalities in a workplace context. The concepts of 'employee silence' and 'employee voice' are used as they can facilitate an understanding of the way in which employees respond to workplace problems, as well as their capacity to respond (Good and Cooper 2014). We consider under what conditions would employees articulate voice, revealing issues of hidden inequalities at work and under what conditions will they opt for silence? Why would employees make the decision to be silent and what types of issues would they be most likely to be silent about? How could organisations overcome this problem? Additionally, we explore the role of managers in structuring employee silence, thus maintaining and/or enhancing 'hidden' inequalities in the workplace.

8.2   Employee Voice and Silence

The phrases 'employee voice', 'employee involvement' and 'employee participation' can be seen as umbrella terms that cover a wide range of definitions and practices (Morgan and Zeffane 2003; Strauss 2006), though with some ambiguity (Bacon and Storey 2000; Tony Dundon et al. 2005). McCabe and Lewin (1992), in their examination of employee voice, include two broad types. First it is the expression, by employees to management, of grievances concerning work issues and second is any kind of employee participation in the decision-making processes of the organisation. Within the same scope, Millward et al. (2000) envisioned voice as comprising three distinctive channels: (1) via representation, recognition and union membership, (2) via participation mechanisms (e.g. joint consultative committees) and (3) via direct employee involvement. Dundon et al. (2004, pp. 1152–53) propose an analytical framework through which voice can be articulated via four principles: (1) articulation of individual satisfaction, (2) expression of collective organisation, (3) contribution to management decision-making and (4) demonstration of mutuality and co-operative relations.

Different conceptualisations of voice come from different disciplines (Mowbray et al. 2015). Within the HRM discipline, we see employee voice as mechanisms used to raise complaints about work-related issues and participation in decision-making processes by employees (McCabe and Lewin 1992). Within organisational behaviour, employee voice is identified as extra-role behaviour where an employee 'proactively challenges the status quo and makes constructive recommendations for change' (Van Dyne et al. 1995, p. 266). Taking account of both perspectives, we consider voice within the equal opportunities and diversity management disciplines as a justice-oriented channel of communication for employees to express concerns and views about possible inequality, hidden and unhidden, in the workplace with a scope to resolve/address them.

On the other hand, the antithesis of voice, employee silence, can potentially lead to or enhance hidden inequality in the workplace. It is defined as an employee's 'motivation to withhold or express ideas, information and opinions about work-related improvements' (Van Dyne et al. 2003, p. 1361). Within this literature, research has focused on when and how employees exercise voice or opt for silence (Milliken et al. 2003), why employees would decide to stay silent, about what types of issues are they likely to be silent and how organisations might address this (Donaghey et al. 2011). In its own right, the literature on employee silence is relatively new, seeking to understand the processes behind an individual's decision to be silent about issues that concern them and what types of issues would those likely be (Donaghey et al. 2011). Specifically, Tangirala and Ramanujam (2008) conceptualise it as information that is held back by employees intentionally, rather than not having anything to say or unintentionally failing to communicate. Focusing on employee perceptions of their co-workers' impressions, a specific strand of the employee silence literature examines how an individual's fear of isolation diverts them from expressing true opinions that might be coming from a minority viewpoint (Milliken et al. 2003). A different interpretation sees silence as a survival strategy, where employees, in an effort to cope with the unpleasant aspects of their work, become detached to the organisation and mentally withdraw (Ezzamel et al. 2001). In sum, silence is seen as the result of employees having insufficient avenues to articulate concerns to the detriment of employee voice and/or as a result of employee disengagement due to cynicism or lack of trust (Donaghey et al. 2011).

8.3 Manager's Role in Structuring Employee Silence

While employee silence has been largely conceived as an individual choice, literature recognises that the choice to remain silent can be influenced by management (Donaghey et al. 2011). Employees' decision to voice or remain silent will be influenced by the target of their speaking up, their expectations about truly being listened to and organisational norms that might encourage or discourage voicing (Donovan et al. 2016; Mowbray et al. 2015). For example, a climate of silence might be created amongst employees in workplaces where speaking up is perceived as dangerous or futile. These perceptions are created when management behaviour discourages bottom-up communication and is seen as intolerant of dissent, as a result employees are disinclined from voicing their concerns (Donaghey et al. 2011). Milliken et al. (2003) argue that silence is chosen by employees that believe their voice falls on 'deaf ears'. Indeed, management, through practices and institutional structures, can perpetuate silence over a range of issues, thereby organising employees out of the voice process (Donaghey et al. 2011). Employee silence may be more pervasive in organisations where top management have long average tenure and there is a high degree of similarity between workers (Donovan et al. 2016; Morrison and Milliken 2000). This can happen as in such environments it would be more difficult for an employee to feel comfortable expressing they are different in some ways from the 'pack'.

Research so far has focused on silence as something which employees choose, thereby overlooking constraints to voice that might be imposed by management in preserving their prerogative (Donaghey et al. 2011). Allen and Tüselmann (2009) argue for the important role of management in identifying what can and cannot be addressed by voice mechanisms. In such a context, management might confine employees' voice when it is perceived to raise issues that might be deemed as conflicting the status quo, for example, hidden inequalities that would disturb the organisation's equal opportunities and diversity management policies, with the result that silence rules over such issues. Thus, even when a voice structure exists but is inhibited by management in terms of its utility, it will become a 'hollow shell' (Charlwood 2003), enforcing silence instead. Overwhelmingly it seems management view voice mechanisms as tools to increase firm efficiency and enhancing firm policy understanding rather than a forum where employees can articulate their diverging interests (Donaghey et al. 2011). For example, Donovan et al. (2016) found management willing to act on employee voice when that concerned workplace problems but were very resistant to it with regard to change in working conditions or a manager's performance. Effectively, management can decide to 'create' silence by reducing voice to non-threatening issues, thus preventing employees from having any concerns raised and addressed.

8.4   The Role of Employee Silence in Sustaining and/or Enhancing Hidden Inequalities at Work

Equality and diversity issues pervade all aspects of employees' working life. The way, and even if employees have a voice, and the methods used to give employees voice in the workplace are bound by issues of equity. On the contrary, employee silence, by its very nature, can contribute to sustained and/or even enhanced inequality in the workplace, especially so when such inequality is 'hidden' and effectively requires employees to come forward and identify it. Effects of such silence can be detrimental not only for the organisation involved but also for the individual as the national scandal of sexual violence in the Canadian military with the accompanied soldiers' silence and silencing highlights (Harlos 2016). Research on discursive practices in organisations suggests that the mechanisms management use to perpetuate silence do not need to be explicit but rather can be embedded in organisational discourse (Donovan et al. 2016). In their study, Brown and Coupland (2005, p. 1062) found the processes by which employees were silenced 'were disguised or, rather, displaced by other discourses, particularly those focused on career advancement' in a way that made these silencing processes mostly concealed. The authors argue that management's capacity to conceal and/or shape discourse can lead to employees rationalising silence, framing it in a positive manner and deeming it as appropriate.

8.4.1   Case Study 1[2]

The UK National Lesbian, Gay, Bisexual and Transgender (LGBT) Survey, published in July 2018, reveals one in five LGBT people still is not 'out' at work. Results reveal that 23 per cent of respondents experienced a negative or mixed reaction from others in the workplace because of being LGBT. A rather worrying majority of 77 per cent of people who had experienced a 'serious' workplace incident related to their sexuality say they did not report it but remained silent because they thought it 'would not be worth it' or that 'nothing would happen or change'. Amongst the most common incidents experienced by LGBT individuals were others disclosing their status without their permission, verbal harassment and exclusion from events and activities. Just over half of the respondents who had experienced serious incidents reported HR departments were unhelpful when handling them or that they were not aware of how to report or had negative experiences when they tried reporting incidents previously and thus choosing silence instead. Claire McCartney, diversity and inclusion adviser at the CIPD, said a culture of underreporting 'will lead to an increase in undesirable behaviours, conflict in

---

[2] Source: Baska (2018), *People Management*.

the workplace and a loss of valuable employees who do not feel supported or included'.

Milliken et al. (2003), in their qualitative study, found that a frequent reason for employees remaining silent was fear of being viewed negatively (e.g. a troublemaker or complainer) and consequently, damaging valued relationships. For example, and taking into consideration the above case study, LGBT employees might think that managers do not take their opinions into consideration or that voicing their views is risky if there is a climate of 'heterosexist' normality within organisations (Colgan and McKearney 2012; Syed 2014). By extension, workers with 'hidden' disabilities may be less likely to express their views and concerns if they perceive the workplace culture as less tolerable. In their investigation of regulation, control and 'silencing' of young English professional footballers, Manley et al. (2016) found silence was perpetuated through surveillance mechanisms and conformity to institutional norms, which in this context led to players withholding information concerning health-related issues and/or personal injury.

8.4.2   Case Study 2

Sexual harassment remains an insidious and very serious workplace problem (Good and Cooper 2014), and despite employees being protected by law, protection does not come to effect until they come forward and report it. However, working conditions, social norms and even the nature of sexual harassment in the workplace can place constraints on employees that can make reporting it difficult, choosing to remain silent instead, thus transforming sexual harassment into a 'hidden' inequality issue and risking perpetuating the problem as it is not examined and addressed at a systemic level.

Consider the following case[3]: Laura is a university student working at a coffee shop in London who has been sexually harassed by customers on more than one occasion. In one of those occasions when she talked to her supervisor about it, she reported the following:

---

[3] Adapted from Good and Cooper (2014, p. 308).

They just told me "Don't go over there". That's the only thing that they actually did to prevent anything from eventuating. They just said, 'Don't serve him'… I actually did my best to avoid serving him. Even when I had to walk past his table, I'd make sure I wouldn't turn my head in any way that would look like I'm making eye contact or about to start some sort of conversation because I didn't want anything to eventuate out of it…but he was still staring and would make comments as I walked past.

Laura did not escalate her complaint, internalising her experience, as she felt unsure of organisational policies and discouraged to complain as 'this is part of the job' that she should be able to cope with. In this context, Laura is led to silence by her supervisor's behaviour but also by the ambiguity of relevant organisational policies. For example, Good and Cooper (2014) report employees' lack of understanding about the definition of sexual harassment and what could be considered inappropriate, with some setting the bar for sexual harassment only on physical touching. Employees remaining silent and internalising inequality can have a serious effect on their stress levels, and general well-being, with consequent negative influence on their workplace relationships, reduced engagement and citizenship behaviour and organisational commitment (Rai and Agarwal 2018), and should be addressed as soon as possible.

8.5   Addressing Hidden Inequalities Through Employee Voice

Similarly to equal opportunities policies, employee voice is justice-oriented. As such, opportunities to exercise voice, with transparent and fair mechanisms, can reveal a range of issues at work, from sexual harassment to any non-declared physical or psychological condition that otherwise can remain hidden. This can be a first step in addressing inequality in the workplace. Evidence show that the implementation of employee voice mechanisms can influence workplace policies (Bryson and Forth 2006). A key finding from Allen's (2015) research using WERS data was that voice is associated with the greater adoption of equal opportunities and diversity management policies in the workplace. Essentially, the more voice a workplace has, the more likely it is to have a range of equality and diversity policies in place. However, this is one of a few studies that examine the influence of employee voice mechanisms on firms' equal opportunities and diversity management policies. Many studies have examined the impact of employee voice and wider human resource (HR) practices on a range of workplace outcomes, such as absenteeism, turnover and performance (e.g. Guest et al. 2003; Wood and Fenton-O'Creevy 2005; Wall and Wood 2005; Wood and Wall 2007); however, relatively little research has focused on the relationship between voice and equal opportunities and diversity management (Noon and Hoque 2001; Forth and Rincon-Aznar 2008).

Contemporary workforces and the changes that occur in them can make traditional voice mechanisms ineffective in capturing the demands of employees from diverse backgrounds (Bell et al. 2011; Syed 2014). In their study of voice and LGBT workers in organisations, Bell et al. (2011) argue for new and transformed mechanisms of voice that use systems and structures relevant to the increasing diversity of the actual and potential workforce. They contend that employers should go beyond the legal requirements in terms of voice and that managers should proactively implement policies and voice practices that support equality. They also argued that policies should go beyond the legal requirement could be perceived as more meaningful and hence more effective to employees. Such policies will signal the firm's level of commitment to equality to employees. In taking a proactive stance towards equality and diversity, leaders can draw on a rich repertoire of specific voice techniques appropriate to promoting equal opportunities (Bell et al. 2011).

More recently, Syed (2014) argued that if traditional voice mechanisms are not supported by inclusive management policies or employer-promoted LGBT networks, they may result in LGBT employees remaining silent rather than voicing their opinions and grievances. Similarly, traditional voice mechanisms may result in women remaining silent about their situations and about the ideas that they have to increase efficiency in organisations (Allen 2015). Women represent at least half of all employees in most developed labour markets, yet their roles as senior decision-makers in organisations are limited (Syed 2014). Their willingness to voice their opinions also differs to that of men, being more likely [women] to voice their views to an internal mediator in order to over-come a disadvantageous situation (Harlos 2010); however, women's will-ingness to do this is moderated by power relationships. In other words, women are less likely than men to voice their concerns when the person who is potentially in the wrong is a supervisor (Harlos 2010). If unions, as an important collective voice mechanism, were able to represent the views of women to a greater extent (Syed 2014), they could help to alter this situation. However, unions have not been able to draw to the full extent on women's insights within work (Allen 2015).

8.6   Implications for Managers

Any kind of inequality in the workplace, hidden and observable, if left 'untreated' can be detrimental for employees' emotions, behaviours and consequent performance and costly for organisations. Therefore, organ-isations should put emphasis on inhibiting inequality of any kind by promoting voice behaviour among employees (Rai and Agarwal 2018) and creating safe spaces for employees to be able to voice their issues. Employees' voice can be significantly influenced by their perceptions of managerial attitudes towards an issue within the workplace (Bowen and Blackmon 2003), especially so for issues that are perceived as sensitive and difficult as is often the case with inequality. Employers need to con-tinually scrutinise their practices and workplace culture to root out dis-crimination and inequality in order to embrace a diverse workforce. Individuals will feel more comfortable to speak up about issues of hidden inequality when they believe that their position has the support of others, and will remain silent when they believe their position is not supported, creating a spiral of silence that can restrict open and honest communica-tion (Bowen and Blackmon 2003). On the contrary, employees' trust in management is an important factor in creating a climate of supportive voice (Farndale et al. 2011), one that could ensure employees feel com-fortable about voicing concerns about inequality in the workplace. Additionally, employees may be more likely to speak up when supportive structures are in place in the organisation along with positive attitudes from supervisors and management (Milliken et al. 2003). In their review of employee voice literature, Mowbray et al. (2015) identified voice climate and leadership as factors influencing employees to voice. Considering management can respond to voice either by acting on it or turning a blind eye and can form opinions about employees that speak up (Burris 2012), it can be expected that management's responses, positive or negative, can influence employees' future decisions on voice and silence (Donovan et al. 2016). Employees may see voice as futile if management and leaders send signals that they are not interested in employee voice (Detert and Burris 2007). There is a need, therefore, to build trust into the process (Kougiannou et al. 2015) and design robust and supportive policies so that employees feel comfortable to raise issues and thus allow hidden inequalities to be uncovered. Inequalities, especially those that are hidden, or not easily observable, cannot be identified and effectively addressed when the organisation, through ambiguous and unclear procedures and unsupportive managerial attitudes, promotes an environment of silence, instead of voice. Managers should be trained and aware of their responsibilities in terms of preventing inequality and supporting employees when they decide to speak up. Additionally, leaving managers handling individually issues of inequality as and when they happen, focusing on coping with particular incidents, can be ineffective in dealing with such issues at a systemic level.

Employers cannot use a 'one size fits all' approach to equality, diversity and inclusion, Darren Towers, the executive director of business development, says (Baska 2018). Practitioners should establish a link between their organisation's equal opportunities and diversity management policies and voice mechanisms in such a way that information feeds from one to the other, making sure there are diverse and *appropriate* ways for all employees to be able and feel comfortable to speak up. For example, McFadden and Crowley-Henry (2017) found that a specific voice mechanism, employee networks, helps mitigate LGBT isolation at work and moderate workplace stigma. However, research on concealable stigmas suggests that while appropriate voice mechanisms represent evidence of active initiative regarding diversity and equality on the part of the employer (Jones and King 2014; Jones et al. 2016), a key difference is the willingness of employees of diverse groups, such as LGBT, to actively engage with employee voice (McNulty et al. 2018). In other words, while voice mechanisms might be in place, the perceived stereotype threat may be so great among employees that they elect to opt-out, choosing a self-selected silence instead (McNulty et al. 2018). To be able to utilise voice mechanisms to the full extent, employees need to believe these provide a strong and genuine opportunity to articulate concerns, especially when such concerns might be highly sensitive and personal as it might be the case when trying to reveal a 'hidden' inequality.

8.7   Conclusion

The popular press is filled with reports of misconduct, misappropriation or mistruths in organisations tolerated, if not enacted, by decision-makers and accompanied by failed or flawed voice systems and employee silence, such as the Volkswagen emissions and General Motors ignition scandals, the France Telecom suicide saga and suppressed child abuse infamy in the Catholic Church most recently detailed by the Australian Royal Commission (Harlos 2016).

With issues of equality and discrimination continuing to occupy an important focus in human resource management and employment relations, in this chapter we offered a discussion on the role of employee silence and voice in perpetuating and addressing, respectively, hidden inequalities in the workplace. The concepts of 'employee silence' and 'employee voice' were used as they can facilitate an understanding of the way in which employees respond to workplace problems, as well as their capacity to respond (Good and Cooper 2014). Additionally, we explored the role of managers in structuring employee silence, thus maintaining and/or enhancing 'hidden' inequalities in the workplace.

The way, and even if employees have a voice, and the methods used to give employees a voice in the workplace are bound by issues of equity. On the contrary, employee silence, by its very nature, can contribute to sustained and/or even enhanced inequality in the workplace, especially so when such inequality is 'hidden' and effectively requires employees to come forward and identify it. Management, through the design of particular institutional arrangements and their approach to voice, can perpetuate a climate of silence over a range of issues (Donaghey et al. 2011) and inadvertently sustain or even enhance hidden inequalities in the workplace.

There are still many voices being unheard in organisations today due to stigmatisation, discrimination and fear of negative career-related consequences to name a few, especially for individuals experiencing concealable stigmas. Providing voice mechanisms allows organisations to move from a reactive managerial perspective to a more encouraging and participative management (Felix et al. 2016). As hidden inequalities are not explicitly covered by equal opportunities policies, organisations need to have processes and mechanisms in place to uncover them in order to address them. A more nuanced consideration of support is required. A prerequisite for that is organisational willingness to extend equal opportunities and diversity management initiatives beyond what is covered by law. This can be done with employee voice mechanisms in place, where employees feel comfortable enough to speak up and identify such inequalities. These mechanisms need to be perceived by employees as trustful and effective so that they can confidently rely on managers to take actions for the effective creation of a climate of voice, one that has the potential to uncover concealed stigmas and hidden inequalities, taking the first step to addressing them.

References

Allen, M.L. 2015. *Employee voice, equal opportunities and workplace outcomes: An analysis of UK workplaces.* Manchester: Manchester Metropolitan University.

Allen, M., and H.-J. Tüselmann. 2009. All powerful voice? The need to include 'exit', 'loyalty' and 'neglect' in empirical studies too. *Employee Relations* 31: 538–552.

Argyris, Ch. 1977. Double loop learning in organizations. *Harvard Business Review* 55: 115–125.

Bacon, N., and J. Storey. 2000. New employee relations strategies in Britain: Towards individualism or partnership? *British Journal of Industrial Relations* 38: 407–427.

Baska, M. 2018. One in five LGBT people still aren't 'out' at work. https://www.peoplemanagement.co.uk/news/articles/one-in-five-lgbt-people-not-out. Accessed 23 May 2018.

Bell, M.P., M.F. Özbilgin, T.A. Beauregard, and O. Sürgevil. 2011. Voice, silence, and diversity in 21st century organizations: Strategies for inclusion of gay, lesbian, bisexual, and transgender employees. *Human Resource Management* 50: 131–146.

Bowen, F., and K. Blackmon. 2003. Spirals of silence: The dynamic effects of diversity on organizational voice. *Journal of Management Studies* 40: 1393–1417.

Brown, A.D., and C. Coupland. 2005. Sounds of silence: Graduate trainees, hegemony and resistance. *Organization Studies* 26: 1049–1069.

Bryson, A., and J. Forth. 2006. Worker voice, managerial response and labour productivity: An empirical investigation. *Industrial Relations Journal* 37: 438–455.

Burris, E.R. 2012. The risks and rewards of speaking up: Managerial responses to employee voice. *Academy of Management Journal* 55: 851–875.

Charlwood, A. 2003. Willingness to unionize amongst non-union workers. In *Representing workers*, ed. H. Gospel and S. Wood, 67–73. London: Routledge.

Colgan, F., and A. McKearney. 2012. Visibility and voice in organisations. *Equality, Diversity and Inclusion: An International Journal* 31: 359–378.

Daniels, K., and L. Macdonald. 2005. *Equality, diversity and discrimination: A student text*. London: CIPD Publishing.

Detert, J.R., and E.R. Burris. 2007. Leadership behavior and employee voice: Is the door really open? *Academy of Management Journal* 50: 869–884.

Donaghey, J., N. Cullinane, T. Dundon, and A. Wilkinson. 2011. Reconceptualising employee silence. *Work, Employment and Society* 25: 51–67.

Donovan, S., M. O'Sullivan, E. Doyle, and J. Garvey. 2016. Employee voice and silence in auditing firms. *Employee Relations* 38: 563–577.

Dundon, T., and D. Rollinson. 2011. *Understanding employment relations*. London: McGraw-Hill Higher Education.

Dundon, T., A. Wilkinson, M. Marchington, and P. Ackers. 2004. The meanings and purpose of employee voice. *International Journal of Human Resource Management* 15: 1149–1170.

———. 2005. The management of voice in non-union organisations: Managers' perspectives. *Employee Relations* 27: 307–319.

Dyne, L., L. Cummings, and J. Parks. 1995. Extra-role behaviors: In pursuit of construct and definitional clarity (a bridge over muddied waters). *Research in Organizational Behavior* 17: 215–285.

Dyne, L., V. Ang, and I.C. Botero. 2003. Conceptualizing employee silence and employee voice as multidimensional constructs. *Journal of Management Studies* 40: 1359–1392.

Ezzamel, M., H. Willmott, and F. Worthington. 2001. Power, control and resistance in 'the factory that time forgot'. *Journal of Management Studies* 38: 1053–1079.

Farndale, E., J. Ruiten, C. Kelliher, and V. Hope-Hailey. 2011. The influence of perceived employee voice on organizational commitment: An exchange perspective. *Human Resource Management* 50: 113–129.

Felix, B., A. Mello, and D. von Borell. 2016. Voices unspoken? Understanding how gay employees co-construct a climate of voice/silence in organisations. *The International Journal of Human Resource Management* Early View: 1–24.

Forth, J., and A. Rincon-Aznar. 2008. *Equal opportunities, employee attitudes and workplace performance.* Employment Relations Research Report. London: Department for Business, Enterprise & Regulatory Reform.

Good, L., and R. Cooper. 2014. Voicing their complaints? The silence of students working in retail and hospitality and sexual harassment from customers. *Labour and Industry: A Journal of the Social and Economic Relations of Work* 24: 302–316.

Guest, D.E., J. Michie, N. Conway, and M. Sheehan. 2003. Human resource management and corporate performance in the UK. *British Journal of Industrial Relations* 41: 291–314.

Harlos, K. 2010. If you build a remedial voice mechanism, will they come? Determinants of voicing interpersonal mistreatment at work. *Human Relations* 63: 311–329.

———. 2016. Employee silence in the context of unethical behavior at work: A commentary. *German Journal of Human Resource Management* 30: 345–355.

Hoque, K., and M. Noon. 2004. Equal opportunities policy and practice in Britain. *Work, Employment and Society* 18: 481–506.

Jewson, N., and D. Mason. 1986. The theory and practice of equal opportunities policies: Liberal and radical approaches. *The Sociological Review* 34: 307–334.

Jones, K.P., and E.B. King. 2014. Managing concealable stigmas at work. *Journal of Management* 40: 1466–1494.

Jones, K.P., E.B. King, V.L. Gilrane, T.C. McCausland, J.C. Cortina, and K. Grimm. 2016. The baby bump. *Journal of Management* 42: 1530–1556.

Kougiannou, K., T. Redman, and G. Dietz. 2015. The outcomes of works councils: The role of trust, justice and industrial relations climate. *Human Resource Management Journal* 25: 458–477.

Liff, S. 1999. Diversity and equal opportunities: Room for a constructive compromise? *Human Resource Management Journal* 9: 65–75.

Liff, S., and J. Wajcman. 1996. 'Sameness' and 'difference' revisited: Which way forward for equal opportunity initiatives? *Journal of Management Studies* 33: 79–94.

Manley, A., M. Roderick, and A. Parker. 2016. Disciplinary mechanisms and the discourse of identity: The creation of 'silence' in an elite sports academy. *Culture and Organization* 22: 221–244.

McCabe, D., and D. Lewin. 1992. Employee voice: A human resource management perspective. *California Management Review* 34: 112–123.

McFadden, C., and M. Crowley-Henry. 2017. 'My people': The potential of LGBT employee networks in reducing stigmatization and providing voice. *The International Journal of Human Resource Management* Early View: 1–26.

McNulty, Y., R. McPhail, C. Inversi, T. Dundon, and E. Nechanska. 2018. Employee voice mechanisms for lesbian, gay, bisexual and transgender expatriation: The role of employee-resource groups (ERGs) and allies. *The International Journal of Human Resource Management* 29(5): 829–856.

Milliken, F.J., E.W. Morrison, and P.F. Hewlin. 2003. An exploratory study of employee silence: Issues that employees don't communicate upward and why. *Journal of Management Studies* 40: 1453–1476.

Millward, N., A. Bryson, and J. Forth. 2000. *All change at work: British employment relations 1980–1998 as portrayed by the workplace industrial relations survey series*. London: Routledge.

Morgan, D.E., and R. Zeffane. 2003. Employee involvement, organizational change and trust in management. *International Journal of Human Resource Management* 14: 55–75.

Morrison, E.W., and F.J. Milliken. 2000. Organizational silence: A barrier to change and development in a pluralistic world. *Academy of Management Review* 25: 706–725.

Mowbray, P.K., A. Wilkinson, and H. Tse. 2015. An integrative review of employee voice: Identifying a common conceptualization and research agenda. *International Journal of Management Reviews* 17(3): 382–400.

Nachmias, S., and V. Caven. 2018. Introduction to 'hidden' inequalities in the workplace. In *Hidden inequalities in the workplace*, ed. V. Caven and S. Nachmias, 1–16. Cham: Springer.

Noon, M., and K. Hoque. 2001. Ethnic minorities and equal treatment: The impact of gender, equal opportunities policies and trade unions. *National Institute Economic Review* 176: 105–116.

Parzefall, M.-R., and J. Coyle-Shapiro. 2011. Making sense of psychological contract breach. *Journal of Managerial Psychology* 26: 12–27.

Rai, A., and U. Agarwal. 2018. Workplace bullying and employee silence. *Personnel Review* 47: 226–256.

Redding, W.C. 1985. Rocking boats, blowing whistles, and teaching speech communication. *Communication Education* 34: 245–258.

Sprague, J., and G. Ruud. 1988. Boat rocking in the high-technology culture. *American Behavioral Scientist* 32: 169–193.

Strauss, G. 2006. Worker participation: Some under-considered issues. *Industrial Relations* 45: 778–803.

Syed, J. 2014. Diversity management and missing voices. In *Handbook of research on employee voice*, ed. A. Wilkinson, J. Donaghey, T. Dundon, and R. Freeman, 34–87. Cheltenham: Edward Elgar.

Tangirala, S., and R. Ramanujam. 2008. Employee silence on critical work issues: The cross level effects of procedural justice climate. *Personnel Psychology* 61: 37–68.

Wall, T.D., and S.J. Wood. 2005. The romance of human resource management and business performance, and the case for big science. *Human Relations* 58: 429–462.

Wood, S.J., and M. Fenton-O'Creevy. 2005. Direct involvement, representation and employee voice in UK multinationals in Europe. *European Journal of Industrial Relations* 11: 27–50.

Wood, S.J., and T.D. Wall. 2007. Work enrichment and employee voice in human resource management-performance studies. *International Journal of Human Resource Management* 18: 1335–1372.

9

Informalisation in Work and Employment: A Permissive Visibility or Another (Hidden) Inequality?

Ian Clark

9.1 Introduction and Purpose

In the first edition of this series, the editors outlined their aim which was to assess how organisations manage hidden inequalities that prevail but do so apparently beyond protections against 'discrimination' in the legislative framework. Moreover Caven and Nachmias (2018, p. 325) suggest that further research on and more detailed specification of hidden inequalities is necessary. This is the case as hidden inequalities stem from organisational practices that appear rational, lawful and therefore beyond the current framework of legal protection against discrimination in the workplace. The contribution of this chapter to the discussion of hidden inequalities builds on what some critics refer to as self-imposed theoretical and empirical limitations that flow from the professionalisation of the human resource function and the associated professionalisation of human resource management (HRM) research. These limitations combine in

I. Clark (✉)
Department of Human Resource Management, Nottingham Business School, Nottingham Trent University, Nottingham, UK
e-mail: ian.clark@ntu.ac.uk

© The Author(s) 2019   **199**
S. Nachmias, V. Caven (eds.), *Inequality and Organizational Practice*, Palgrave
Explorations in Workplace Stigma, https://doi.org/10.1007/978-3-030-11647-7_9

what is termed a 'one standard way for HRM research' where HR(M) ignores the context of substantive data and developments in British employment practice such as the emergence of informalisation within and beyond specific workplaces (Harley 2015; Angrave et al. 2016). At its simplest informalisation of work and employment describes the adoption of business models which enable an organisation to gain competitive advantage, but which also disadvantage labour. Disadvantage can occur within formalised workplaces as employment practice becomes casualised (de Stefano 2016), more pertinently as a hidden inequality informalised work and employment is frequently non-compliant with many aspects of prevailing employment regulation. So beyond the casualisation of formal work and employment, informalisation may witness vulnerable, precarious often migrant workers undertaking work in organisations, which, whilst lawful, is hidden by these employers from regulatory authorities such as HMRC. Therein employers frequently deny the living wage, the minimum wage and evade employer social charges.

As the main body of the chapter reveals, organisations that utilise informal employment practice are often intimately connected to organisations which utilise formalised business and employment practices. Accordingly, the core topic which this chapter examines in detail is the tendency to informalisation in work and employment and is focussed around two research questions; firstly, how does hidden inequality stem from organisational practices that are rational and lawful? Secondly, how do the hidden inequalities that stem from these practices result from vogue organisational practices and strategies which focus not on managing inequality but externalising its presence from a particular organisation?

The chapter is structured as follows; the next section identifies why informalisation and non-compliance inform important hidden inequalities which HRM scholarship and research must address. Section two provides a more detailed discussion of three contexts that inform the tendency to informalisation in work and employment as a hidden inequality. To illustrate these arguments, section three draws on primary source material from studies of informalised employment in hand car washes, garment manufacturing and nail bars. These sources are supplemented by further primary source material reported on at a recent Gangmasters and

Labour Abuse Authority (GLAA) intelligence workshop (Dickens and Meardi 2017). The final section provides a discussion of the research questions raised in this chapter for academics and practitioners and in terms of public policy and is followed by a conclusion.

9.2   The Context of Informalisation

Whilst most work and employment in the British economy supports formalised employment practice, the context of informalisation is important. Estimates suggest that 9–12% of gross domestic product is generated in organisations deploying informalised business and employment practices, an economy that supports two and a half million workers and which generated £6.2 billion in 2013 but which is rife with hidden inequalities (Ipsos Mori 2012; Schneider 2015; Taylor 2017).

Context makes sense of what is happening in organisations that utilise formalised and informalised business and employment practice. Moreover, appreciation of the context within which these practices are diffused necessarily goes beyond professionalism and bureaucratic logic in HRM research (Alvehus 2017). It is likely that the diffusion of business and employment practices which re-skill and professionalise the HR function create the space for informalised work and employment in formal and informal organisations. For example, the Taylor Review (Taylor 2017, p. 6) of modern employment practice suggests that the 'tech' informed pace of change in the British economy diffuses new business models which stimulate informalised employment practice. It is here that a critical contextual development is evident; these employment practices are likely to be adopted, enforced and monitored by re-skilled human resource professionals or those who assume this role under formalised employment practice and those who act as hiring and remuneration managers under informalised employment practice.

The re-skilling of the HR function in large organisations aims to determine a direct contribution from HR to re-focussed organisation performance, that is, enable an organisation to capture value from HR strategies (Sparrow and Makram 2015). Central to this is the segmentation of job roles into different categories where (what become) peripheral categories of classification are casualised and externalised and beyond the ambit of the firm responsible for externalisation possibly become subject to informalisation. It is the architecture of talent management in large organisations, that is, the systems, processes and practices associated with it that re-skills the HR function. Therein the focus is on HR *management* where the segmentation, associated casualisation and potential informalisation of job categories captures value for an organisation. The cost savings created by these measures significantly reduce labour overhead costs which are returned to owners and investors (Appelbaum et al. 2013; Clark 2016).

9.3   Hidden Inequalities Arising from Formalised Employment Practice

Segmentation, externalisation and possible informalisation creates a further contemporary series of inequalities summarised in the term 'non-compliance'. Non-compliance with employment regulation is not only unfair to compliant employers but also reflects the results of three developments which challenge and complicate Labour Market Enforcement in all developed economies. Firstly, the 'fissuring' of the employment relationship refers to the changing structure of organisations and the implications of this for the regulation of employment and the enforcement of employment standards. Fissuring describes the application of business and HR strategies where employers shift the boundary of a firm inwards, reducing the number of workers under its direct control as employees or workers to enable the capture of value for investors and owners within and beyond a particular organisation. Accordingly organisations meet their demand for labour through franchise arrangements, outsourcing and sub-contracting and by heading sometimes globalised value chains. Therein value is concentrated in the brand rather than operations which sustain the brand where separate firms within the chain produce and sell component parts of the goods or services under a particular brand name (Gabriel et al. 2015; Taylor et al. 2015). Following the application of these business and HR strategies, responsibility for labour is sub-contracted beyond the boundary of the firm and diffused between multiple entities. As the recent Carillion case demonstrates, one result of this is that it is often unclear who is a legal employer of an individual and who is responsible for employer legal obligations, both direct and vicarious (also see Weil 2014). The macro-level disintegration of manufacturing and service provider firms into brands at the head of global value chains is now in evidence within organisations but at a micro-level. Take, for example, hotels and hospitality; hotel brands in the contemporary period no longer operate as providers of hotel services but instead merely provide hotel buildings and brands. Therein all hotel services are sourced by secondary providers who are responsible for hotel staff, in-hotel hospitality and food provision and cleaning and housekeeping services. HR and payroll services too may be provided by intermediary shared services and payroll providers. Fissured workers are subject to an array of hidden inequalities that epitomise precariousness; many commentators argue that it is the role of the HR function to protect against this and enforce and codify firm-level compliance with employment regulations (see, e.g. Wills et al. 2009, pp. 3–6). In contrast to this, a current enforcement gap has in part been created by developments in HR practice. Intermediary and umbrella companies (which are often subsidiary companies of what was the employer of now independent contractors or workers) can increase the vulnerability of low paid casual or informalised workers and potentially pass financial burdens on to them. Employers and employment agencies use intermediary companies which effectively pass on costs to workers which would normally be paid by an employer (DLME 2018, p. 108).

A second development which is directly reflective of the professionalisation of HR but has the potential to diffuse inequalities that are hidden from view is the changing composition of the labour force. The use of agency labour, part-time, often casualised workers, and application of 'gig' economy status to work each frequently blur the distinction between the status of employees, workers and the self-employed. In organisations which utilise formalised business and employment practices, the application of these categories and distinctions between them is enforced by the HR function or those who perform these roles but not at all in organisations utilising informalised practices. Estimates suggest that in the British economy up to 1.2 million workers are employed by agencies and that there are 1.3 million gig economy workers (REC 2016; CIPD 2017). What is not known however, is the extent to which these formalised practices are re-produced in the informal economy.

A third medium-term contextual development which resonates with contemporary employment practice is the decline of union membership and the coverage of collective bargaining arrangements; in Britain's private sector beyond former publicly owned services such as railways, fewer than 10% of the labour force are trade union members. Those who work for organisations that utilise informal business and employment practices are unlikely to encounter traditional trade union recognition campaigns. In most liberal market economies, collective bargaining is narrowly representational and not regulatory in nature. Accordingly in archetypical liberal market economies such as Britain, to secure any potential regulatory representation, unions must seek and secure recognition beyond enterprise or bargaining unit level (Ewing 2005). However, recognition drives exhibit bureaucratic and institutional instrumentalism focussed as they are on the likelihood of securing membership which unions then commit to servicing (Holgate 2015). Therefore, these drives are in the main confined to formalised organisations because in the case of employers utilising informalised business and employment practice, it is frequently difficult to identify an employer.

In summary the fissuring of the workplace, the changing composition of the workforce and the decline of trade union membership each inform the contemporary political economy of work and employment which underpins myriad forms of inequality at work. Therein organisations are primarily concerned with investor and shareholder value and informal equivalents for organisations in the hidden or shadow economy and necessarily seek to reduce and squeeze costs to stimulate profits and return monies to investors, shareholders or owners. But what also becomes blurred is who, if anyone, is responsible for providing workers with the written particulars of terms and conditions of employment, associated provision of decent and lawful working conditions and the correct level of pay? Moreover, HR developments in organisations that utilise formal business and employment practice stimulate the development and diffusion of informal business and employment practice both in and beyond what some describe as the formal economy. By association in Britain, Ireland and the United States, the state regulatory regime for work and employment provides a lesser level of protection for workers than in many coordinated market economies. In turn the lesser level of protection derives, shapes and structures the spaces and practices utilised by organisations that deploy precarious and informal business and employment practices (Clark 2018; Ram et al. 2017; O'Sullivan et al. 2017).

9.4   The Tendency to Informalisation in Work and Employment: Another Hidden Inequality

The informal economy is defined as paid activities that are unregulated by, or hidden from, regulatory authorities of the state for tax, social security and/or employment law purposes but are otherwise lawful (Williams 2006, 2014). The informalisation of work and employment creates hidden inequality in three ways. Firstly, an organisation can be formally constituted and registered with regulators and taxation authorities for business purposes but utilise forms of employment practice which are precarious. Precariousness exhibits uncertainty, low income potential and limited or no entitlement to social benefits or statutory entitlements (Vosko 2010; Standing 2014). Precarious HR practices include use of zero hours contracts and other forms of casualisation where agency workers are engaged or where in-company migrant workers are 'posted' from their country of employment origin to another host country where a particular firm has plants or subsidiaries (Adams and Deakin 2014; Lillie 2012; Caro et al. 2015; Tucker 2017). More recently still, contemporary capitalist platforms deny that they are organisations or employers but instead part of the sharing economy. Accordingly, they 'contract with' precarious sometimes (self) employment statuses currently associated with the 'gig' economy or platform capitalism to attempt to completely externalise employment from them other than for key leadership teams, for example, those at Airbnb, Deliveroo and Uber (de Stefano 2016; Srnicek 2017). In the United States, Uber has 160,000 people who are dependent on it for their livelihood; but only 4000 are regular employees (Streeck 2016), a practice which de Stefano (2016) terms 'the informalisation of the formal economy'. Part of the problem is that modern work practices are moving ahead of established patterns of employment regulation and this is where some hidden inequalities arise; for example, whilst online intermediaries and employment agencies source standard employment, they do not consider themselves as operating within the scope of existing regulation such as those that regulate the conduct of employment agencies. That is, they do not consider themselves employment businesses or employment agencies as traditionally defined. The forms of employment and work that are created by these agencies and intermediaries reduce the need for active HR specialists and related policies and procedures within an organisation to cover selection, training, discipline, evaluation and appraisal, supervision of duties, remuneration and integration into business strategies. Therein the role of any in-firm HR (function) is likely to become much more circumspect and atomised (Tucker 2017). This may involve shifting what are otherwise vicarious employer responsibilities (to now externalised workers) such as insurance, delivery of pay into bank accounts, health and safety and pension provision for individual workers to fee-bearing service providers such as payroll companies. More generally HR re-skilling and the professionalisation of HR, in particular the externalisation of job roles, within those organisations which deploy these forms of casualisation reduces the quality of such jobs in terms of employment security, tenure and associated terms and conditions of employment. That is, strategic re-skilling and re-tooling of an HR function exhibits a preference for externalised flexibility which frequently undermines compliance with in-firm regulatory standards (Raess and Bourgoon 2015; Weil 2014).

A second tendency to informalisation of work and employment occurs when a business is formally constituted but employment practice for some workers is informalised where workers make cash payments to secure work, training, uniforms and equipment. Similarly, workers receive cash payments, work for favours or receive other forms of reward such as food and accommodation. In organisations which are otherwise compliant with regulations, employee collusion such as this is a subtle form of inequality which by its very nature is hard to detect. For example, in nail bars those employers who deliberately seek to evade the living wage, national minimum wage and working time regulations regularly exploit compliant workers and impose 'negotiated' inequalities in the workplace (Silverstone and Brickell 2017). Informalised work and employment of this type is indicative of how the casualisation referred to in the first category creates inequality. This is so where casualisation crosses over into informalisation as the externalisation of job roles pushes labour out of the formal labour market into informalised practice where both well-being and productivity are likely to be lessened. In addition to this, informalised practice makes precarious workers much more vulnerable to sustained labour market exploitation centred on charging fees to find work, deducting pay for items such as uniforms, withholding holiday pay and paying workers less than the minimum and living wage.

A third tendency to informalisation occurs when a business is lawful, for example, those in construction, nail bars or hand car washing, but where employment practice is unlawful and criminal. Recent studies of firms in these sectors that utilise informalised business and employment practices found wage theft of between 15% and 46% against the appropriate sector or national minimum wage levels. Wages were frequently paid cash in hand and were often late and excluded holiday pay and grossly underreported hours worked (Vershinina et al. 2018; Clark and Colling 2017; Silverstone and Brickell 2017). Clark and Herman (2017) calculate that unpaid holiday pay and other forms of underpayment totalled £3.1 billion in 2016 where 4.9% of all workers received no holiday pay. A contributory factor to the presence of these hidden inequalities is that only employees but not workers are currently entitled to receive itemised pay slips which distinguish between gross and net pay. An umbrella term to summarise this tendency is the International Labour Organization's (ILO) category 'unacceptable forms of work'. That is work which sustains hidden inequalities, is performed in conditions which deny fundamental rights at work, puts lives at risk and which denies dignity to keep workers in conditions of extreme poverty.

9.5   Practical Importance: Extending the Reach of Hidden Inequalities

To further illustrate the argument developed so far on the scale and scope of hidden inequalities in work and employment, this section places the tendency to informalisation of work and employment in three contemporary empirical contexts: economic re-structuring, the manner in which organisation routines in informal practice derive from and mimic those in formalised practice and the political economy which surrounds the emergence of state-sponsored management of hidden inequalities.

9.5.1   Informalisation Informed by Economic Re-structuring?

Informalisation, beginning with the casualisation of work and employment in formalised organisations, is part of economic re-structuring where it is a proxy for flexibility and innovation. As drivers of casualisation and precocity, deregulation and outsourcing are indicative of the first tendency to informalisation which suppresses wages and related terms and conditions of employment and privileges casualisation; choices are often formulated, enforced and facilitated by re-skilled HR professionals, a development which the one best way to conduct HRM research fails to acknowledge. For example, economic re-structuring in formalised employment practice necessarily re-skills HR practitioners where these dynamics are dominated by and informed by concentrated, large-scale, often multinational, capital across many sectors of the British, Irish and European Union economies. This dominance reflects the success of such firms in securing deregulation, privatisation and outsourcing of work and employment (Carré et al. 2012; Prosser 2016; O'Sullivan et al. 2017). Deregulation and outsourcing are relatively expensive policy options in terms of taxation revenue and associated private capital that pays for it and is usually followed by organisational re-structuring where HR strategies centre on consolidation, associated downsizing, outsourcing and sub-contracting. The recent collapse of BHS and the more recent Carillion case are worst-case examples of the strategic HRM downside of deregulation and outsourcing.

Two examples illustrate how deregulation and outsourcing inform informalisation in what appear as new sectors. Firstly, since 2007 in health care, National Health Service (NHS) modernisation stimulated the entry of new providers into the tertiary care sector, in particular the emergent market for hip and knee replacements but also general surgery, urology and ear, nose and throat procedures. These procedures often take place in independent sector treatment centres (ISTCs), many of which are funded by investors with little or no health care experience, for example, Capio, Carillion and the Partnership Health Care group which are supported by private equity investors. A large number of ISTCs are in place where the deregulation process allows these centres to prefix themselves with the NHS logo and more significantly excused them from HR requirements associated with the procedures they undertake. Specifically, ISTCs were exempted from training and development and employee resourcing in the form of the recruitment of appropriate surgical staff (Player and Leys 2007). Instead of undertaking these requirements, ISTCs are allowed to engage NHS doctors and consultants on a casual basis but receive the same procedure tariff as NHS providers, a portion of which is allocated to HR costs. In effect investors behind ISTCs are allowed to informalise the engagement of highly formalised surgical staff. Some ISTCs employ no surgical staff but help to achieve the government's key objective of breaking up and re-structuring NHS care, encouraging the private sector to provide more secondary and tertiary care.

A second example flows from comparative city studies of hand car washing and illustrates how informal roadside hand car washes have grown from formalised economic re-structuring in alcohol, auto, food and petrol retailing (Clark and Colling 2018). Therein re-structuring and consolidation of supermarkets and the associated move of supermarkets into petrol retailing undercut pump prices charged at independent roadside petrol stations, leading to the closure of many such units during the late 1990s and early 2000s and the abandonment of onsite mechanised car washes. Supermarkets further invested in hypermarket sites in the mid-2000s which often included a 20-pump multi-access (diesel, petrol, higher performance fuels and gas and electricity charging points); this investment put further pressure on independent roadside petrol retailers and oil company-supported sites. They responded by re-structuring which focussed on retail outlets and the scaling back of investment in mechanised car washing where the Petrol Retailer's Association reports that the number of mechanised car washes in use has halved in the last 15 years (PRA 2015). Whilst hand car washing is a lawful area of work and employment, the second tendency to informalisation is manifest as a failure to observe employment regulations. Hand car washes and other areas too deploy informalised practices but operate at an intersection between informalisation and businesses which deploy formal practices.

Stepping beyond the one best way to conduct HRM research, economic re-structuring along brand-headed global value chains and increasingly fissured organisations, flexibility is predominantly one-sided and legitimises inequality for many workers. For example, employers transfer risk to individuals as workers or self-employed contractors and exert control over workers to reduce costs. Therein precarious work systems, casualisation and informalisation of work and employment are the economic linkage between employment management systems and organisational performance (Kroon and Paauwe 2014). This alternative, more critical theorisation of hidden inequality derives informalised practice as originating in formalised HR practices; whilst evidently empirically the case this is unacknowledged by narrow theorising on contemporary HR practice (see Harley 2015, p. 401). Furthermore, this theorisation suggests that in organisations which deploy formalised business and employment practices the trend towards precarious work is part of strategic HRM in a re-skilled HR function. This is evident in the emergence and spread of non-standard work—employment casualisation associated with the use of intermediate agencies, on-call or zero hours working. These developments are mirrored in the informal economy particularly where migrant labour is employed. Intermediaries within formal employment, informalised employment practice or subsistence operations do not employ anyone; rather employment agencies, gangmasters, payroll companies and (informal) country of origin family and kinship networks facilitate work and employment (Joseph Rowntree Foundation 2014; Clark and Colling 2016).

9.5.2   HRM in Formalised Employment Systems and Organisational Routines in Informal Practice?

A particular inequality revealed in the studies which inform this chapter is the theoretical and empirical necessity to move beyond a formal economy-informal economy dichotomy, the former where best way HRM research is conducted and the latter where informalised employment practice is alleged to be confined. Rather than this separation instead there is a symbiotic relationship between approaches to HR in formalised and informalised practice. The two are not separate entities but intimately connected where outlets in the informal economy help re-production of sectors in the formal economy. For example, established business landlords be they supermarkets, breweries or oil companies which own former pub and petrol station sites often lease these premises to roadside hand car washes. Similarly, unoccupied houses may be used for garment manufacturing. Warehouses or small business spaces are also used for food manufacturing or food processing and some parcel delivery workers find themselves effectively operating in the gig economy out of such business spaces whereas peripheral city centre shop spaces house nail bars (Bagwell 2008; Hopkins 2017; Moore and Newsome 2018). In each of these examples, landlords are able to extract revenue from their assets which reside in the formal economy by leasing them to organisations where some of the labour force is engaged informally.

These practices generate inequalities which reflect elements of HR practice such as sub-contracting and outsourcing that reduce wages and erode established conditions of employment in formal employment practice; these reductions are also re-produced in less formal areas of employment to generate hidden inequalities. Again the tendency to informalisation in the formal economy is re-produced and extended in the informal economy but unlawfully. For example, a recent study of garment manufacturing found severe violations of the national minimum wage with many workers paid only £3 per hour when the legal minimum was £6.50. These violations exhibit criminal practice such as use of child labour, wilful breaches of workplace health and safety legislation, refusal to pay agreed wages and/or overtime payments, confiscation of passports and a requirement to reside in premises owned by the employer (Hammer and Plugor 2016).

9.5.3   The Political Economy of Hidden Inequalities: Who Are the New HR Managers?

The tendency to lawful and unlawful informalisation in many of the sectors discussed in this chapter represents a form of sub-contract capitalism. Sub-contract capitalism intersects the formal and informal economy where employers exhibit a preference to employ precarious and vulnerable workers—a so-called precariat (Wills et al. 2009; Standing 2014). In vulnerable and precarious work, erstwhile-formalised forms of external flexibility such as the use of agencies, outsourcing, sub-contracting and HR posting are frequently re-produced by informal intermediaries who choose to ignore labour market regulations.

Central to the contemporary political economy of hidden inequality is the reaction of the state to informalisation in work and employment. The fissuring of the employment relationship, the globalisation of labour supplies, the decline of trade union membership and the associated marginalisation of collective bargaining have for some critical observers created a crisis in employment relations scholarship and its strong problem-solving orientation for practitioners (Tapia et al. 2015). More critically still, as the emergence of casualisation and informalisation in work and employment demonstrates, these developments create a dialectic for the state where solutions (casualisation, deregulation and flexibility) turn into problems. Deregulation, casualisation then informalisation necessitate centralised regulation and enforcement to improve regulatory compliance, measures that only the state action can undertake. Accordingly, there has been a significant expansion in regulatory legislation managed directly by state enforcement bodies. These measures include the living wage, the Modern Slavery Act 2015 and the creation of an Independent Anti-Slavery Commissioner (IASC). Similarly, the GLA has been re-formulated as the Gangmasters and Labour Abuse Authority (GLAA) which has extended powers across the economy in respect of the minimum wage, employment agencies and modern slavery. These measures have been supplemented by the Taylor Review of modern work practices commissioned by the May government, the Watson Independent Commission on the future of work commissioned by the Labour Party and the publication of the Director of Labour Market Enforcement's (DLME) strategy document in May 2018 (DLME 2018).

The individual route to the enforcement of employment rights and the regulatory role of collective bargaining appear to be disconnected from and displaced by these developments. Rather, the state is managing inequalities that were previously delegated to and managed by the HR function and the wider Charted Institute of Personnel and Development (CIPD), employment tribunals and collective bargaining. Therein the director of Labour Market Enforcement (who oversees), the Anti-Slavery Commissioner and the Gangmasters Labour Abuse Authority are becoming new human resource managers responsible for the suppression of hidden inequalities in employment.

In some cases these measures involve monitoring casualisation in formal employment to ensure it is appropriate but more critically may involve undoing elements of non-compliant hidden informalised work and employment and seeking to recover any losses suffered by workers. So, whilst deregulation and labour market flexibility have been the preferred strategies in Britain's neo-liberal state since the Thatcher-Major era through to Blair, Brown, Cameron-Clegg, Cameron and May, the central state has found it necessary to regulate visible and less visible inequalities generated by the extremes of deregulation.

9.6   Discussion and Conclusion

The tendency to informalisation in organisations that deploy formalised business and employment strategies and in those which deploy informalised business and employment strategies are not separate independent developments. The core arguments of this chapter are firstly that both compliant informalisation (casualisation) and non-compliant informalisation centre on in-work exploitation, precariousness and vulnerability. Casualisation and informalisation have developed from a re-skilled HR function focussed on delivering value to business owners and investors. Secondly, the diffusion of both compliant and contested informalisation in organisations that deploy formalised business and employment strategies are re-produced in informalised practice but informally so. Thirdly, by association formalised economic re-structuring stimulates the creation of new socio-economic sectors where hidden inequalities in work practices are dominant. Fourthly, the theoretical and empirical base of these arguments is informed by inescapable contemporary contexts, organisation fissuring, a changing labour market composition and a continued reduction of regulatory standards and practices informed by deregulation, declining trade union membership and associated marginalisation of collective bargaining. There is a spectrum of attitudes and behaviours towards informalisation at work and non-compliance with regulations wherein non-compliance is part of the business model of informalised employers, for example, those in car washes and nail bars, associated intermediaries and other agents. The spectrum ranges from criminal activity to poor practice which requires corrective action.

In terms of economic re-structuring, the trend to casualisation and the permissive visibility of inequalities can be protected in the formal economy however meekly. In contrast to this not only are intermediary relationships that originate in strategic HRM in formalised organisations re-produced and mimicked in informalised organisations but workers subject to informalisation are unprotected because these jobs flow from organisational fissuring; they often disappear as employee jobs and re-appear as self-employed roles or disappear into informalised employment practice. Moreover, developments and new routines in formalised practice inform and are re-produced in informal practice based on the diffusion of (hidden) inequalities.

Accordingly, in terms of the first research question which this chapter addresses—*how informalisation stems from organised practices which are lawful and rational*—it is necessary to place organising concepts such as informalisation more firmly in the wider structural conditions of contemporary British capitalism. These dynamics both create and sustain informal business and employment practice and moreover effectively require the diffusion of inequalities in work. It is necessary to connect firms deploying informal business and employment practices to the mainstream economy. This is so because businesses that deploy informal practices are subject to 'mixed embeddedness' where economic, social and institutional factors must be foregrounded to inform any appreciation of informalisation in the supply and demand for labour in the so-called informal economy.

To achieve such foregrounding of the second research question addressed by the chapter—*how do employers seek to externalise but not manage informalisation*—it is necessary to connect casualisation and informalisation beyond what is characterised as the confines of the informal economy. This is so because it is the wider dynamics of economic re-structuring which enable and facilitate informal business and employment practices. For example, whilst formalised systems and routines inform informal practice regulators such as Acas, employment tribunals and DLME must appreciate that HR practices indicative of the tendency to informalisation are not just that; rather the origin of these work practices lies in the diffusion of formal HR practices such as day labouring, hiring halls and spot contracting. Both regulators and informed public policy must appreciate that the application of hidden inequalities at work cuts across different employee groups; indigenous labour, established embedded migrant labour and new migrant labour and sector categories with differentiated degrees of formalisation. More significantly for practitioners, HR strategies associated with the use of agencies, outsourcing and 'posting' of workers are re-produced in organisations which deploy informalised business and employment practices where parallel informalised intermediary roles are in evidence. The demand and supply of workers who are prepared to accept inequalities that are hidden from the mainstream is not just that; rather it is a demand derived from broader patterns of economic re-structuring, is socially constructed and mimics many HR strategies found in organisations which utilise formalised business and employment practices. The social context of informalisation is informed by formalised national- and firm-level governance regimes; that is, developments in organisations which deploy informalised business and employment practice are not just that; they are likely to have been first developed in and are diffused from formalised organisations frequently under the label of best way strategic HRM.

References

Adams, Z., and S. Deakin. 2014. Institutional solutions to precariousness and inequality in labour markets. *British Journal of Industrial Relations* 54: 779–809.

Alvehus, J. 2017. Conflicting logics? The role of HRM in a professional service firm. *Human Resource Management Journal* 28: 1–17.

Angrave, D., A. Charlwood, I. Kirpatrick, M. Lawrence, and M. Stuart. 2016. HR analytics: Why HR is set to fail the big data challenge. *Human Resource Management Journal* 26: 1–11.

Appelbaum, E., R. Batt, and I. Clark. 2013. Implications for employment relations research: Evidence from breach of trust and implicit contracts in private equity buy-outs. *British Journal of Industrial Relations* 51: 498–518.

Bagwell, P. 2008. Transnational family networks and ethnic minority business development: The case of Vietnamese nail-shops in the UK. *International Journal of Entrepreneurial Behaviour and Research* 14: 377–398.

Caro, E., L. Berntsen, N. Lillie, and I. Wagner. 2015. Posted migration and segregation in the European construction sector. *Journal of Ethnic and Migration Studies* 41: 1600–1620.

Carré, F., P. Findlay, C. Tilly, and C. Warhurst. 2012. Job quality: Scenarios, analysis and interventions. In *Are bad jobs inevitable?* ed. C. Warhurst, F. Carré, P. Findlay, and C. Tilly, 1–25. London: Palgrave Macmillan.

Caven, V., and S. Nachmias. 2018. *Hidden inequalities in the workplace – A guide to current challenges, issues and business solutions.* London: Palgrave Macmillan.

CIPD. 2017. *To gig or not to gig? Stories from the modern economy.* London: CIPD.

Clark, I. 2016. Financialization, ownership and employee interests under private equity at the AA, part two. *Industrial Relations Journal* 47: 238–253.

———. 2018. The political economy of finance-led capitalism: Connecting financialization, private equity and employment outcomes. In *The Routledge companion to management buyouts – Routledge companions in business, management and accounting*, ed. M. Wright, K. Amess, N. Bacon, and D. Siegel, 152–165. London: Routledge.

Clark, I., and T. Colling. 2016. New insights into informal migrant employment: Hand car washes in a mid-sized English city. *Economic and Industrial Democracy.* On-line first. https://doi.org/10.1177/0143831X17740718.

————. 2017. Hand car washes in the East Midlands: Permissive visibility and informal practices in employment. In *Labour market exploitation: Emerging empirical trends*, ed. L. Dickens and G. Meardi. Warwick: IRRU.number 108.

————. 2018. Work in Britain's informal economy: Learning from road-side hand car washes. *British Journal of Industrial Relations* 56 (2): 320–341.

de Stefano, V. 2016. *The rise of the just-in-time workforce: On-demand work, crowd work and labour protection in the gig-economy*. Geneva: ILO.

Dickens, L., and G. Meardi. 2017. *Labour market exploitation: Emerging empirical evidence*. Warwick papers in industrial relations, number 108. Warwick: IRRU.

Director of Labour Market Enforcement. 2018. *UK labour market enforcement strategy, 2018–2019*. London: BEIS.

Ewing, K. 2005. The function of trade unions. *Industrial Law Journal* 34: 1–22.

Gabriel, Y., M. Korczynski, and K. Reider. 2015. Organisations and their consumers: Bridging work and consumption. *The Organ* 22: 629–643.

Hammer, N., and R. Plugor. 2016. Near-sourcing UK apparel: Value chain restructuring, productivity, and the informal economy. *Industrial Relations Journal* 47: 402–416.

Harley, B. 2015. "The one best way? Scientific" research on HRM and the threat to critical scholarship. *Human Resource Management Journal* 25: 399–407.

Holgate, J. 2015. An international study of trade union involvement in community organising: Same model different outcomes. *British Journal of Industrial Relations* 53: 460–483.

Hopkins, B. 2017. Analysing the 'migrant work ethic' – Comparing managers' perceptions of local workers and central and eastern European migrants in the United Kingdom. *European Urban and Regional Studies* 24: 442–452.

Ipsos Mori. 2012. *Non-compliance with the national minimum wage*. London: Ipsos mori.

Joseph Rowntree Foundation. 2014. *Forced labour in the UK*. York: JRF.

Kroon, B., and J. Paauwe. 2014. Structuration of precarious employment in economically constrained firms: The case of Dutch agriculture. *Human Resource Management Journal* 24: 19–37.

Lillie, N. 2012. Subcontracting, posted migrants and labour market segmentation in Finland. *British Journal of Industrial Relations* 40: 87–103.

Moore, S., and K. Newsome. 2018. Paying for free delivery: Dependent self-employment as a measure of precarity in parcel delivery. *Work, Employment and Society* 32: 475–492.

O'Sullivan, M., T. Turner, J. Lavelle, J. MacMahon, C. Murphy, L. Ryan, P. Gunnigle, and M. O'Brien. 2017. The role of the state in shaping zero hours work in an atypical liberal market economy. *Economic and Industrial Democracy.* On-line first. https://doi.org/10.1177/0143831X17735181.

Player, S., and C. Leys. 2007. *Confuse and conceal: NHS and Independent Sector treatment Centres.* Monmouth: Merlin.

PRA (Petrol Retailer's Association). 2015. *Automatic car washes are dying out.* London: PRA.

Prosser, T. 2016. Dualization or liberalization? Investigating precarious work in eight European countries. *Work, Employment and Society* 30: 949–965.

Raess, D., and B. Bourgoon. 2015. Flexible working and immigration in Europe. *British Journal of Industrial Relations* 53: 94–111.

Ram, M., T. Jones, and M. Villaares-Varela. 2017. Migrant entrepreneurship: Reflections on research and practice. *International Small Business Journal* 35: 3–18.

REC (Recruitment and employment confederation). 2016. *Recruitment industry trends.* London: REC.

Schneider, F. 2015. The size and development of the shadow economy of 31 European and five other OECD countries from 2003 to 2015: Different development. http://www.econ.jku.at/schneider1. Accessed 12 May 2018.

Silverstone, D., and D. Brickell 2017. *Combating Modern Slavery experienced.* Vietnamese nationals en route to and within the UK. IASC: HMSO.

Sparrow, P., and H. Makram. 2015. What is the value of talent management? Building value-driven processes within a talent management architecture. *Human Resource Management Review* 22: 249–263.

Srnicek, N. 2017. *Platform capitalism.* London: Verso.

Standing, G. 2014. *The precariat – The new dangerous class.* London: Bloomsbury.

Streeck, W. 2016. *How will capitalism end?* London: Verso.

Tapia, M., C. Ibsen, and T. Kochan. 2015. Mapping the frontier of theory in industrial relations: The contested role of worker representation. *Socio-Economic Review* 13: 157–184.

Taylor, M. 2017. *Good work: The Taylor review of modern working practices.* London: BEIS.

Taylor, P., K. Newsome, J. Bair, and A. Rainnie. 2015. Putting labour in its place: Labour process analysis and global value chain. In *Putting labour in its place: Labour process analysis and global value chains,* ed. N. Taylor and B. Rainnie. Basingstoke: Palgrave Macmillan.

Tucker, E. 2017. Migrant workers and fissured workforces: CS wind and the dilemmas of organising intra-company transfers in Canada. *Economic and Industrial Democracy.* On-line first. https://journals.sagepub.com/doi/full/10.1177/0143831X17707822.

Vershinina, N., P. Rodgers, M. Ram, N. Thodorakopoulos, and Y. Rodionova. 2018. False self-employment: The case of Ukrainian migrants in London's construction sector. *Industrial Relations Journal* 49: 2–18.

Vosko, L. 2010. *Managing the margins: Gender, citizenship and the international regulation of precarious employment.* Oxford: Oxford University Press.

Weil, D. 2014. *The fissured workplace.* Cambridge: Harvard University Press.

Williams, C. 2006. *The hidden enterprise culture: Entrepreneurship in the underground economy.* Cheltenham: Edward Elgar.

———. 2014. Explaining cross-national variations in the prevalence of envelope wages: Some lessons from a 2013 Eurobarometer survey. *Industrial Relations Journal* 45: 524–542.

Wills, J., K. Datta, Y. Evans, J. Herbert, J. May, and C. McIlwaine. 2009. *Global cities at work new migrant divisions of labour.* London: Pluto Press.

10

Hidden Inequalities Amongst the International Workforce

Gaye Özçelik, Washika Haak-Saheem, Chris Brewster, and Yvonne McNulty

10.1 Introduction

There are, as this volume shows, hidden inequalities in many workplaces. These issues are magnified when we take a detailed look at internationally mobile workers. The focus of most of the international human resource management (IHRM) literature has been on high-status, high-skilled expatriates assigned by their companies to important positions in foreign

G. Özçelik (✉)
Faculty of Communication, İstanbul Bilgi University, İstanbul, Turkey
e-mail: gaye.ozcelik@bilgi.edu.tr

W. Haak-Saheem • C. Brewster
Henley Business School, University of Reading, Reading, UK
e-mail: w.haak-saheem@henley.ac.uk; c.j.brewster@henley.ac.uk

Y. McNulty
SR Nathan School of Human Development, Singapore University of Social Sciences, Singapore, Singapore
e-mail: yvonnemcnulty@suss.edu.sg

© The Author(s) 2019
S. Nachmias, V. Caven (eds.), *Inequality and Organizational Practice*, Palgrave Explorations in Workplace Stigma, https://doi.org/10.1007/978-3-030-11647-7_10

subsidiaries for a temporary period. This has provided rich insights into the management of internationally mobile workers at the 'top of the pyramid' (e.g. Hechanova et al. 2003; McNulty and Selmer 2017). Being assigned from their company headquarters, which are usually located in countries with high standards of living, these expatriates are for the most part the beneficiaries of enhanced and generous terms and conditions of employment (Andresen et al. 2012), significantly better than those earned by most of their local contemporaries. However, there are other kinds of expatriates. There are self-initiated expatriates (SIEs) who take their own initiative to find the opportunity to work, for a temporary period, in the global workforce, usually on the same kind of contractual terms as locally employed people (Suutari and Brewster 2000; Andresen et al. 2012; Cerdin and Selmer 2014).

There are other internationally mobile members of the workforce, such as migrants (Al Ariss and Crowley-Henry 2013). They are mostly from less developed or developing countries and are either obliged to leave their home countries due to some natural disaster, war or political upheaval, in which case they are usually referred to as 'refugees'; or they may be seeking to escape high unemployment, or just looking for a better life, in which case they are usually referred to as 'economic migrants'. Migrants, economic migrants especially, intend to settle in the new country, having expectations of permanent residency and/or citizenship. Some migrants may be highly qualified (Cerdin et al. 2014) and many of them will earn good salaries in their new country, often much higher than might have been possible in their original home. We note, though, that because of failure to recognise qualifications or perhaps because of straightforward prejudice, migrants often end up in jobs that do not equate to their qualifications (Fullin and Reyneri 2011; Harvey 2012; Al Ariss et al. 2014). Many migrants of course are unfortunately exposed to more inferior if not exploitative conditions of employment (Alberti et al. 2013; Platt et al. 2017).

One group of internationally mobile workers—low-status expatriates—have largely been hidden from business and management research (Haak-Saheem and Brewster 2017). Though recent research has aimed to put emphasis on vulnerable workers (Connell and Burgess 2013) and has started to examine the 'bottom of the pyramid', usually in terms of countries rather than individuals (Simanis 2012; Simanis and Milstein 2012), these workers remain hidden because they have been, until recently, overlooked by policymakers in the industries and countries in which they work; and they have been ignored by the business and management literature (Haak-Saheem and Brewster 2017). They fall between the migration literature, which looks at people trying to have a permanent residence in their new society, and the expatriation literature—which is almost entirely concerned with 'top talent' and has turned a blind eye to the larger numbers of low-status expatriates, a substantial part of the workforce in many countries.

We begin this chapter by defining hidden expatriates and then outlining the extent of hidden expatriation and its location and characteristics. Then we adopt an Organisational Justice theory lens to examine the way hidden expatriates are managed. To bring some reality to the picture, we examine the situation of hidden expatriates in three specific countries: Turkey, the United Arab Emirates, and Singapore. Lastly, we draw some conclusions and suggest recommendations for policymakers, practitioners, and scholars.

10.2 Hidden Expatriation: Extent, Location, and Characteristics

McNulty and Brewster (2017) provide some construct clarity around the 'expatriate' concept. They argue that there are four distinguishing characteristics: (1) they are working individuals, (2) legally, and (3) temporarily living in a country, (4) other than the one of which they are a citizen. This definition includes assigned expatriates and self-initiated expatriates but excludes retirees and students (who are not working in the local labour market) and migrants (who are seeking citizenship). It does not, however, restrict the term to only high-status expatriates, even though almost the entire literature on expatriates makes that assumption. Hidden expatriates are low-status workers who otherwise meet all the criteria of being 'expatriates'. These people are SIEs in the sense that have chosen to seek temporary work in another country, but they work in menial or manual occupations with very limited legal rights, often hidden from the sight of other members of the host society as well as from academic study. They are, however, far more numerous than any other form of expatriation.

In adopting the above definition of expatriates as our focus in this chapter, we note that an important issue in relation to the international workforce (whether high- or low-status expatriates, qualified immigrants, economic migrants, or refugees) is the high number of *illegal* workers in host countries. This is a global issue concerning 'irregular migration', found to some extent in all countries including developed and first-world nations (Geddes 2005). Syrian refugees in Turkey, for instance, have often had to flee with nothing, and that includes any official papers or approval for their border crossing (Ekmekçi 2017). There are other examples, including people staying beyond their work permits, and cases of people-smuggling and modern slavery (Crane 2013). Penalties can be severe: even when these workers manage to stay in the country, they are often in a vulnerable position. For example, in the Gulf Cooperation Council,[1] such workers are subject to labour abuse, with the loss or withholding of income, long hours of work, insufficient nutrition, and unequal status. It is impossible for them to speak up against their employer (Malit and Naufal 2016).

Hidden expatriates account for approximately 150 million individuals with no, or limited, educational background who live and work outside their country of origin, of whom 11.5 million are domestic workers, with half of the world's male domestic workers located in the Arab Gulf States (ILO 2015). In 2015, the East Asia and Pacific region hosted nine million low-paid foreign workers, 69% of whom were from within the region, mainly from Thailand, Malaysia, China, Indonesia, and the Philippines (World Bank Group 2016). Turkey, the United Arab Emirates, and Singapore represent countries with large numbers of hidden expatriates,[2] where their presence is an important factor in the host coun-

---

[1] Formally known as the *Cooperation Council for the Arab States of the Gulf* (or colloquially as GCC), a regional intergovernmental political and economic union consisting of all Arab states of the Persian Gulf (Bahrain, Kuwait, Oman, Qatar, Saudi Arabia, and the UAE) except for Iraq.

[2] In contrast to, for example, Malaysia at 9.5% (World Bank Group 2013), South Korea at 3% (Roh 2014), and Australia at 1% (Australian Government 2016). Across the EU countries, foreign workers made up 7.4% of persons in employment in 2015 (Eurostat 2016).

try's economic development. The GCC has the highest proportion of low-skilled workers as a share of all workers, at 35.6%. About 75% of all expatriate domestic workers are women. Male migrant workers are much less likely to be domestic workers, with noteworthy regional differences (ILO 2015).

Hidden expatriates come mainly from developing countries and suffer from the low educational levels and skill base typical of such countries. They find (nearly always low-paid) jobs in manual and menial roles across industries in richer countries, working as security staff, building site labourers, drivers, and maids. They are expatriates (not migrants) because their stay in the country is temporary—in many countries they will either be expressly forbidden from permanent residency, or they will find it almost impossible to meet the requirements for citizenship. Hidden expatriates have few social rights (Frantz 2013). Like some migrants, many of them earn low wages, live in poor conditions, and see no opportunity to advance their expertise and career. At the end of their work contract, they will either have to find ways to extend the contract or to get another one (Au 2017a, b), or they will be required, legally, to go home.

These hidden expatriates, at the bottom of the employment pyramid as well as coming from 'bottom of the pyramid' countries, are motived to work abroad in order to improve the standards of living for themselves and their families. Many of them are geographically separated from their families over long distances, living in their employer's premises or in compounds or in shared apartments, often many to a room (Loh 2016; Chong 2017c). They do this in order to send money back to their families. Despite the fact that they earn very low sums in the host country, they still manage to remit substantial amounts back home (see Table 10.1 and 10.2). Developing ('bottom of the pyramid') countries received two-thirds of that, nearly three times the amount of official development assistance. The true size of remittances, including unrecorded flows

Table 10.1 Remittance outward flows

	Worldwide	Turkey	Arab Gulf States	Singapore
Remittances flow in billion USD	601	24	98	5.9

Source: World Bank (2015)

Table 10.2 Remittance inward flows (leading countries)

	Developing countries	India	Philippines	Bangladesh
Remittances flow in billion USD	441	72.2	29.7	15.8

Source: World Bank (2016)

through formal and informal channels, is believed to be significantly larger. There were substantial outward remittances from the Gulf States; Turkey, notably to the Russian Federation; and proportionately from Singapore. For a number of poor countries such as India, the Philippines, and Bangladesh, such remittances are a substantial element of the gross national product (World Bank Group 2016).

These financial gains for the family come at a price—children growing up separately from their parents and the worker's parents dying without their own children in attendance. Hidden expatriates also pay a price; their work is frequently in menial, exhausting jobs (Chia and Zaccheus 2012)—more than a few, indeed, are assaulted or killed (Alkhatib 2017a; Chong 2017a). Many of them are subject to varying degrees of deception, injustice, and unfairness (Haak-Saheem and Brewster 2017).

Job security for hidden expatriates is typically low. This arises from *how* they are employed. Many are hired via local employment agencies or subcontractors in the countries they come from, leaving them with low or no levels of voice and union representation (Fillinger et al. 2017). Often their passports are held by their employer, or in some cases by an agency, giving third parties considerable control over them. Nearly all are institutionally disempowered to deal with workplace violations.

While the above is true of many hidden expatriates, some have different motives: their main aim is simply to stay alive. There are, as we write, people fleeing Syria and neighbouring countries (UNHCR 2017): fleeing from civil war and the violence of ISIS (Islamic State of Iraq and al-Sham) to Turkey but hoping to 'go home' once (and if) the situation in their home country is resolved. They are perhaps the most vulnerable hidden expatriates, facing many burdens and hardships, often situated in dangerous or unregulated work environments, facing long-term unemployment or under-employment (Geddes 2005).

10.3   The Context of Hidden Expatriates in Organisational Justice Theory

Some hidden expatriates (probably more than is ever reported) suffer varying degrees of injustice and unfairness at the hands of agents or employers. Such vulnerability manifests in Organisational Justice issues related to compensation, work conditions, exploitation, discrimination, and abuse (Justice Without Borders 2017). Organisational Justice examines whether employees feel they have been treated fairly in their jobs and the ways in which those determinations influence other work-related variables such as work behaviour and motivation (Hassan and Hashim 2011, p. 83). It is a relevant framework for hidden expatriates who routinely tolerate poor working conditions rather than express dissatisfaction. In the sections that follow, we explain the link between Organisational Justice and hidden inequality using four justice dimensions: distributive, procedural, informational, and interpersonal justice. Our analysis by country is informed by these four dimensions illustrating that current management practice is not in line with the principles and perspectives of workplace justice. Further, there is a lack of a generic framework that explains, illustrates, or supports workplace justice for hidden expatriates to the extent that our adaptation of Organisational Justice in the current context is able to do.

Uncertainty is a powerful source of stress (Monat et al. 1972), where the anticipation of facing an unknown, possibly threatening situation is more stressful for some individuals than for others (Greco and Roger 2003). Hidden expatriates face continual uncertainties. Accordingly, feelings of loss, helplessness, anxiety, and anger are normal experiences during their time abroad (Ashford 1988, Hausman and Reed 1991). Ambiguity is pervasive, leading to feelings of little ability to control the external environment and feelings of inequality. In such situations, fair treatment can have a powerful effect (van den Bos and Miedema 2000; van den Bos 2001; Diekmann et al. 2004). Unfairness creates doubt for people regarding their capacity to cope, leading to emotional exhaustion and organisational withdrawal (Cole et al. 2010).

Of fundamental importance to the study of Organisational Justice is Deutsch's (1975) principles pertaining to equity (whether perceived outcomes reflect the receivers' respective input), equality (whether received outcomes are equal across individuals within the same group), and need (whether received outcomes satisfy the receivers' relative needs). Four dimensions of Organisational Justice have been conceptualised and empirically confirmed, and measures have been psychometrically validated (Bies and Moag 1986; Greenberg 1993; Colquitt 2001). These dimensions are: (1) *distributive justice*, the fairness of decision outcomes affecting employees such as pay, reward, or performance ratings; (2) *procedural justice*, the fairness of the process and procedures used to determine allocation decisions including employee outcomes; (3) *informational justice*, the fairness of information provided to employees by decision makers regarding organisational issues that affect them in terms of specificity, completeness, and timeliness; and (4) *interpersonal justice*, the fairness of interpersonal treatment of employees by decision makers with regard to politeness, respect, sensitivity, and dignity (e.g. whether they explain decisions thoroughly).

10.3.1 Distributive Justice

Distributive justice assesses the perceived fairness of outcomes received in comparison to one's input, education, and what others receive (Adams 1965). Perceptions of distributive justice have been shown to impact positively on individuals' attitudes to work, work outcomes, and supervisors (Moorman 1991). In contrast, violations increase the desire to punish and impose harmful consequences on a putative wrongdoer (Skarlicki and Folger 1997). In the hidden expatriate context, the effects of unfair distributive justice are most frequently seen in workplace violations related to pay. Bangladeshi workers, for example, pay the highest agency fees to relocate to Singapore (circa SG$5000–$15,000) but earn the lowest salaries (SG$350–$800 a month) (TWC2 2017), and take an average of 16.5 months to repay their recruitment fees (Baey and Yeoh 2015). Relatedly, when domestic workers physically harm or steal from their employers or purposefully damage the employer's property, the most common explanation given is retaliation for abuses of distributive justice (Chia 2016; Chong 2017b).

10.3.2 Procedural Justice

Procedural justice includes opportunities for control of a process and its related outcomes, the ability to voice one's viewpoints (Folger and Cropanzano 1998), consistency, lack of bias, availability of appeal mechanisms, accuracy, and following ethical and moral norms (Leventhal 1980). Past studies show that procedural justice has a positive relationship with stress (Judge and Colquitt 2004), organisational commitment (Cohen-Charash and Spector 2001; Colquitt et al. 2001), motivation, performance, and turnover intentions (Williams et al. 2002). One of the principal tenets of procedural justice is voice, meaning the opportunity for individuals to put forward their points of view during the process of making decisions that will affect them (Judge and Colquitt 2004). Hidden expatriates, because they are foreigners, usually do not speak the host country language, and work in positions with little authority, thus having virtually no opportunity to voice their questions and concerns. In Bangladesh, it is common for licensed and unlicensed intermediaries to be involved in linking foreign workers with training centres and agents. At each stage of the process, additional payments are demanded and collected through a banking system called *hundi*, but with little or no official documentation detailing what these payments are for and no opportunity to question the arrangements (Bal 2016). This example (among many) illustrates an increasing need to know more about hidden expatriates' position in, and views of, procedural justice (Aleksynska et al. 2017; Justice Without Borders 2017).

10.3.3 Informational Justice

It has been established that people respond to uncertainty in their work lives by seeking information (Ashford and Cummings 1985). Not being sufficiently informed about upcoming changes, especially if they affect a person directly, can cause perceptions of injustice (Bies 2013). Information needs to be timely (Sapienza and Korsgaard 1996) and from an appropriate source and phrased in a way that can be understood by the recipient (Marschan-Piekkari et al. 1999). Hidden expatriates have expressed dissatisfaction about delays in receiving crucial information from employers that is often 'funnelled' through agents (Fillinger et al. 2017). Ideally, information should be delivered through the most direct medium possible and, if necessary, through other avenues altogether if collusion between agencies and employers is suspected (Justice Without Borders 2017). In Singapore, for example, a recent report (Fillinger et al. 2017) shows that hidden expatriates face considerable obstacles in furnishing evidence to substantiate wage-theft claims due to a lack of access to documentation such as contracts, timesheets, and salary slips; many workers report not having seen or signed employment contracts, in some cases deliberately withheld by their employer to ensure there is no paper trail or proof of employment. Many of these workers lack the knowhow and 'positional power' to circumvent established channels when negotiating fees and obtaining needed documentation (Aleksynska et al. 2017).

10.3.4   Interpersonal Justice

Interpersonal justice, whether people are treated with respect in interactions, has been found to have a significant negative relationship with stress (Judge and Colquitt 2004; Takeuchi et al. 2007). Four different facets of interpersonal justice have been proposed (Bies 2005): (1) derogatory judgments when not true; (2) deception, such as feeling lied to in recruitment; (3) invasion of privacy and unwarranted disclosure of personal information; and (4) disrespect, being ignored. All of these categories have relevance for hidden expatriates. For instance, it is common for them to live in cramped and crowded dormitories with no opportunity for privacy (Loh 2016), and for employers or agencies to retain their passports, employment contracts, and pay slips, thus denying them the evidence needed to file legitimate grievances (Fillinger et al. 2017). Despite legal agreements about pay being made in their home country before relocating, hidden expatriates are frequently deceived and coerced into signing lower-wage contracts upon arrival in the host society or simply paid less than what was originally promised (Justice Without Borders 2017). When wage-theft or injury claims are made, many find themselves accused of lying because witnesses are coerced by employers to tell a different version of events under threat of repatriation or being blacklisted from future entry into the country (Fillinger et al. 2017).

The above four areas of Organisational Justice illustrate that at issue for hidden expatriates and their employers is often the (lack of) agreement as to what constitutes 'fairness'. We suggest that for hidden expatriates, high job demands coupled with perceived low control and, too often, unjust treatment impact their job satisfaction and motivation and can be linked to counterproductive work behaviours such as running away from employers, faking illness/injury, leaving before contract completion, theft, or physically harming the employer (Chong 2017b).

10.4   Hidden Expatriates in Turkey

Over the last three decades, Turkey has hosted a great number of hidden expatriates. Sectors such as textile, tourism, entertainment, domestic help, and construction benefit from these temporary, low-status foreign workers, who mostly come from Turkmenistan, Uzbekistan, Azerbaijan, Armenia, Kyrgyzstan, Moldova, Russia, and Ukraine. They choose to come to Turkey because there are more job opportunities than in their home countries and because those from Azerbaijan, Turkmenistan, and Uzbekistan share similar religious beliefs, cultural values, and aspects of language with Turkish people (Şanlıer-Yüksel and İçduygu 2018), thus finding it relatively easy to integrate (Ekmekçi 2017).

Since the 1990s, Turkey has hosted a large cohort of foreign female domestic workers (maids and child-minders) originating from these former socialist countries. There is an increasing demand for such help among local middle- to upper-class women in professional fields whose work takes them away from the home (Akalın 2010; Cheung and Lui 2017). Wages in Turkey are higher than in their home country. For instance, an Uzbek domestic worker earns a salary of US$600–800 per month, nearly four times the amount they would earn back in their home country for a similar job. Most hidden expatriates send remittances home to their families to buy a house and/or car and to subsidise their family and children's household costs (Kaska 2006). Some, but not all, intend to save enough money to eventually return to their home country (Erdoğdu and Toksöz 2013). It is common for domestic workers to take a day off per week for which they receive 'pocket money' from their employers (usually US$15–20) and which is typically the only money they spend on themselves.

These hidden expatriates are subject to certain inequalities and sometimes exploitation. Those whose status is undocumented and irregular are a particular target for human rights violations. There have been recent systematic procedural reforms to enable foreign workers to get a work permit in Turkey, via application by the employer (Ministry of Interior Directorate General of Migration Management 2014). However, some employers prefer not to get work permits, which can be expensive (they then have to pay social security payments of around US$100 per month, for example), or deduct these costs from the workers' salaries. The result is many hidden expatriates agree to work under difficult conditions without objection, such as working for more hours for lower wages, sometimes being left unpaid, and bad behaviour by their employers.

Other hidden expatriates in Turkey are not economic migrants but, especially since 2011, are refugees and asylum seekers from Syria and neighbouring countries (UNHCR 2017). Turkey signed the 1951 Geneva Refugee Convention, defining standards for the treatment of refugees. The extreme flow of asylum seekers during the last few years led Turkey to adopt a comprehensive new law, the 'Law on Foreigners and International Protection, No. 6458', in April 2014. Under this law, refugees from Syria benefit from a group-based 'temporary protection' regime, which grants them the right to stay, protection from forcible repatriation, and access to a set of basic rights and services, including free healthcare, primary and secondary education, and work permits. Nearly all gain access into Turkey through its open-door policy, concentrating in big cities such as İstanbul, İzmir, and the southern cities of Şanlıurfa, Hatay, Gaziantep, Mersin, Adana, and Kilis (Ministry of Internal Directorate General of Migration Management 2018), although some get stuck in government-run sheltered camps (Baban et al. 2017). Officially there were 3.56 million such refugees in Turkey by mid-March 2018 (UNHCR

2018), making it one of the largest immigrant flows of the past century.[3] However, the real number, including those who arrive in 'irregular' ways, is considered to be much higher. Their motives for relocating to Turkey are to protect themselves and their families from violence (Yıldız and Uzgören 2016), to find employment (usually low-paid), and/or to transit through the country to Europe.

These hidden expatriates have to be legally registered in order to have access to health and education services. Around 30% of the Syrians are illiterate with no schooling, and young women and teenage girls have more difficulty integrating into the Turkish education system because of language, cultural issues, and years of absence from schooling (Woods et al. 2016).

Work raises lots of difficulties for this hidden expatriate community. They are entitled to social assistance and access to the labour market, but the majority of them work illegally because they do not want to pay the expenses of getting a work permit or having tax deducted from their wages. Their irregular position drags them into working under very poor conditions (Woods et al. 2016). In many Syrian families, the norm is that women stay home as caregivers and men go out to work. Women who do work find jobs in the garment and textile industries. Some men also work in textiles but most work in the food, tourism, cement, metal, and leather industries (İçduygu 2016).

10.5 Hidden Expatriates in the Arabian Gulf States

The Arab Gulf region attracts a large number of hidden expatriates. For example, in the UAE low-paid expatriates account for 51% of the work-force in industries such as construction or services (Haak-Saheem and Brewster 2017; Ministry of Human Resources and Emiratization 2015). For example, over 95% of construction and domestic workers in the Gulf

---

[3] Approximately 84% of refugees are hosted by developing countries, led by Turkey, Pakistan, and Lebanon. Turkey hosted the largest number of refugees worldwide, with 3,561,707 people as of 22 March 2018. The Syrian Arab Republic was the top source country of refugees worldwide in 2016 (World Bank Group 2017).

States are hidden expatriates, mainly coming from the Indian Subcontinent, the Philippines, and other poor Asian and African countries. The attractiveness of the Gulf States lies in its economic status and the geographical and cultural, and in some cases religious, proximity to their home states.

Word of mouth about the experiences of hidden expatriates, shared with their families and friends back home, is an important source of information for potential moves, particularly because many hidden expatriates are illiterate and have limited access to information. They have to rely on information provided by previous expatriates or agencies. Therefore, the level of uncertainty remains high and people often move to the Gulf without any clear understanding of the implications of expatriation. Recently, the government of the UAE has issued a set of new laws and regulations to ensure the protection of domestic workers in key areas such as terms of contract, nature of work, workplace, remuneration, and the period of daily and weekly rest. Respective agencies involved in the relocation should inform workers about the legal framework of the UAE before they cross their national border, but these illiterate workers often do not get the information. In addition to the national legal system, the UAE has signed bilateral agreements and memoranda of understanding with various labour supplying countries to (1) promote regional integration, (2) control irregular migration, (3) ensure temporariness and (4) protect rights and encourage just and fair treatment of hidden expatriates. In reality, despite these efforts, most of these individuals are either not able to comprehend the complex legal system of the foreign country or their desperate financial situation leaves them with no other alternative than moving under high level of uncertainty and risk. Often, agencies and employers misuse their situation by treating them unfairly.

While unfair treatment remains somewhat gender independent, in that it applies to both sexes, the landscape of low-skilled and paid expatriates changes as the number of female workers increases (ILO 2015). For instance, in the UAE, these women work in traditionally female-dominated jobs, such as maids or nannies in private households or beauty technicians in salons. Private households prefer to employ female maids and cooks rather than males, viewing them as a safer choice, especially if children are involved. Additionally, cultural and religious restrictions among men and women has increased the drive to employ low-paid female expatriates; female family members can move freely in their houses if their servants are female, whereas the principles of Islam require them, for example, to cover their hair when interacting with men. Hidden expatriates are 'sorted' into male and female occupations based on stereotypes and prejudices (Darity and Mason 2004) and/or family and societal structures (Jacobs 1989; Platt et al. 2017).

Haak-Saheem and Brewster (2017) found that hidden expatriates in the UAE are exposed to poorer working conditions than other groups of expatriates, which impacts on their work outcomes. For example, often they do only what they are asked to do, being unlikely (nor expected) to act beyond their specific duties. The classification of hidden expatriates as manual workers often neglects their capacity to do other work than providing household services or working on construction sites. Their social and personal lives are impacted by their status of being low-paid expatriates. If not in the private households of their employers, hidden expatriates live in communities designed for them. So male workers may live in labour camps carefully separated from better districts of the cities. As their families remain in the home countries, they share the accommodation with other male hidden expatriates. Any sexual interaction outside marriage is unlawful in the United Arab Emirates (UAE) and can result in jail sentences and deportation. There is no or very limited interaction between male and female hidden expatriates.

10.6   Hidden Expatriates in Singapore

Singapore relies heavily on hidden expatriates, with the highest foreign-to-local labour ratio in the world after the Arabian Gulf States (Fillinger et al. 2017). Approximately 1.67 m people (38% of the total population of 5.61 m) are classified as 'non-residents' and legally entitled to reside and/or work there, of which the two largest categories are low-skilled 'work permit holders' in the construction, cleaning, security, and retail sectors (44%) and 'foreign domestic workers' (14%) (Yong 2016; Ministry of Manpower 2017). Work permit holders, the lowest wage category of foreign workers in Singapore, comprise nearly a third of the total workforce (Fillinger et al. 2017). Male foreign workers from Bangladesh, China, and India make up the majority of the workforce in Singapore's construction and marine sectors, with the highest concentration of low-status foreign workers being 75% in construction (Ministry of Manpower 2016). Hidden expatriates are drawn to Singapore because it is relatively safe, low on corruption, and provides a comparatively 'decent' wage (Yeoh 2006). The employment of foreign workers in Singapore is regulated by the Employment of Foreign Manpower Act, which was established to protect their legal rights (Justice Without Borders 2017).

Hidden expatriates in Singapore work in well-defined, segregated jobs, separated according to nationality, race, and gender. For example, maids have mandatory medicals every six months as a condition of continued employment, including pregnancy and HIV tests. Those who become pregnant will lose their jobs and be repatriated. Homosexual acts are illegal and lead (if discovered) to jail sentences and deportation. These restrictions are often more than just practical; for example, maids are forbidden from marrying a local citizen without approval from the Ministry of Manpower.

Understandably, financial incentives are critical to these individuals. The value of the financial benefits they receive must, however, be viewed through the lens of their referent context (see Heine et al. 2002): a Filipina domestic worker earning a salary of SG$700 per month in Singapore would earn no more than 10% of that amount doing the same job in the Philippines.

There are numerous cases of criminal conviction in Singapore for employers guilty of workplace violations involving hidden expatriates; for instance, of failing to pay workers (Seow 2016; Toh 2017a, b), of blackmailing construction workers by demanding kick-backs to guarantee their continued employment (Lee 2017), and of hiring workers illegally (Alkhatib 2017b). In similar cases, hidden expatriates (predominantly women) can be physically ill-treated, sometimes viciously so, being starved, beaten, sexually harassed, and verbally abused (Alkhatib 2017a; Chong 2017a; Kerr 2007). The government acts swiftly, in the cases that come to light, to prosecute offenders, who are dealt with harshly in the zero-tolerance legal environment. Many workplace violations for hidden expatriates involve pay. In most cases, an employer has the power to terminate and repatriate the worker and may do so without returning 'savings' money,[4] especially if the amounts are undocumented. The reporting of 'wage-theft', while historically low, is slowly rising (Humanitarian Organisation for Migration Economics 2017; Salleh 2017). It has also, as noted above, been linked to counterproductive work behaviours among hidden expatriates. This is a particular concern for female domestic workers such as maids and caregivers, as they interact with minors and elderly people (Wong 2016). Their dissatisfaction and frustration has resulted in serious and harmful actions against their employers (Chong 2017b; Yong and Sim 2012).

In Singapore, a growing debate is centred around whether there is enough 'justice-oriented' help to resolve wage-theft and injury claim disputes among hidden expatriate construction workers (Au 2017a; Cheong 2017; Lam 2017; Tan 2017a, b), and the job demands stress of domestic workers (Seow 2017), where in many instances the majority of support is offered by charities and non-governmental organisations (NGOs) (Humanitarian Organisation for Migration Economics 2010; TWC2 2015; Justice Without Borders and National University of Singapore 2014). Table 10.3 summarises the key issues of hidden expatriates in the context of the three selected countries.

10.7   Cultural Aspects of Hidden Expatriation in Turkey, Arabian Gulf States, and Singapore

The inequalities faced by low-skilled expatriates in all three countries have some potential to be explained in a cultural context. Using Hofstede's cultural dimensions, *Power Distance* and *Individualism-Collectivism* are the most relevant for differentiating nations and cultures (Basabe and Ros 2005). All three countries (Turkey, Arabian Gulf

---

[4] Savings money is an illegal practice where employers make salary deductions of SG$50–100 a month for the purposes of ensuring workers' 'good behaviour' and helping them to save for their eventual return to their home country (see Chan 2011; Humanitarian Organisation for Migration Economics 2011).

Table 10.3 Key issues of hidden expatriates in selected countries

Organisational justice dimension	Organisational justice in selected countries			
	General	Turkey	United Arab Emirates	Singapore
Distributive	Unfair distributive justice frequently seen in workplace violations related to pay and treatment	Subject to certain inequalities and exploitation Illegal status results in higher vulnerability Bad behaviour by employers	Labour laws often violated due to workers' inability to read and comprehend national rules and regulations Limited impact of changes in legal framework to improve living and working conditions	Work in well-defined, segregated jobs Separated according to nationality, race and gender Numerous cases of criminal for employers guilty of workplace violations (e.g. failing to pay workers)
Procedural	Typically, do not speak the host country language because they are foreigners Work in positions with little authority Have few opportunities to voice questions and concerns	Agree to work under difficult conditions without objection, such as working for more hours	Agency placements without providing detailed information about employment terms and conditions Exposed to poorer working conditions than other groups of expatriates, which impacts on work outcomes	Dissatisfaction may lead to counterproductive work behaviours Lack of possibilities to voice concerns and ill treatment can result in serious and harmful actions against employers

(continued)

Table 10.3 (continued)

Organisational justice dimension	Organisational justice in selected countries			
	General	Turkey	United Arab Emirates	Singapore
Informational	Many lack know-how and 'positional power' to circumvent established channels when negotiating fees and obtaining needed documentation	Inability to understand local knowledge and norms Residency status often remains undocumented	Word of mouth about experiences of hidden expatriates, shared with families and friends back home, is important source of information	Incorrect and incomplete information provided about contracts Limited access to information due to language barriers Some restricted access to respective agency support due to uneven working hours
Interpersonal	Frequently deceived and coerced into signing lower wage contracts upon arrival in host country Paid less than what was originally promised	Majority work illegally because they do not want to pay the expense of getting work permit or having tax deducted from wages	No possibility to become equal member of society Due to low status often subject of discrimination	Physically ill-treated, sometimes viciously so, being starved, beaten, sexually harassed, and verbally abused Authorities swift to act when abuse is known

States, and Singapore) demonstrate high power distance with acceptance of a hierarchical order including inherent inequalities (Hofstede
2001). Inequalities of power, which coincide with strongly hierarchical
societies, are evident through the higher incidence, for example, of
human rights violations (Basabe and Ros 2005). Hidden expatriates in
Turkey pursue cultural patterns similar to the Turkish culture (Şanlıer-
Yüksel and İçduygu 2018), particularly related to the Islamic religion,
which supports a hierarchical culture (Basabe and Ros 2005) that may
leave people unpaid or lower paid, unprotected, and exposed to inequalities and sometimes exploitation. In a similar way, high power distance
of the UAE is shared by hidden expatriates originating from India, the
Philippines, Bangladesh, and other poor Asian and African countries,
who are used to accepting a steeply hierarchical order and conforming
to the diktats of their 'superiors'. Singapore, on the other hand, hosts
low-status workers from countries such as China, India, and Bangladesh
(Ministry of Manpower 2016; Yue 2011), many of whom share the
Confucian background of Singapore, which is reliant on unequal relationships between people and is positively related to hierarchy (Basabe
and Ros 2005).

On the individualism-collectivism dimension, the three countries are
all considered collectivist societies (Hofstede 2001). Islam, dominating
the majority of societies in Turkey and the Arabian Gulf States, is a collectivist religion, as is the Confucianism of Singapore. For instance,
Syrian refugees in Turkey often fail to express their demands or raise concerns through bureaucratic channels as they do not want to appear too
demanding and to go against the authorities (ORSAM 2016). The language problem is another important cultural issue that hidden expatriates
have to bear (Salleh et al. 2012; Woods et al. 2016), making it difficult
for many to achieve informational justice.

10.8   Conclusion and Implications

As ever more low-skilled expatriates relocate to work and live (temporarily) in a country other than their home, the management literature, and
particularly the human resource management (HRM) literature, will

have to more fully develop in order to create space for accommodating the reality of global labour mobility. As current research on IHRM has started recently to examine non-traditional expatriates, more scholarly discussion is needed to examine the working conditions of low-status expatriates. We have used the Organisational Justice theory to discuss workplace-related inequalities. Turkey, the Arab Gulf States, and Singapore show the unequal practices hidden expatriates face while working and living in a host country, but we stress that hidden expatriates can be found in almost all developed countries, and many less developed ones, even if in those countries they represent a smaller percentage of the workforce. These are vulnerable people in unequal circumstances and they are often exploited.

Prior studies indicate that perceptions of justice related to a number of human resource management (HRM) practices have been studied and found to be positively related to organisational outcomes such as commitment, outcome satisfaction, job satisfaction, evaluation of authority, organisational citizenship behaviours, and performance (Colquitt et al. 2001; Podsakoff et al. 2006). However, there has been very little investigation of perceptions of justice regarding management policies and practices for low-status global workers or even high-status expatriates. This is an area, as we have indicated, where there are large numbers of very practical research questions to which we simply do not have the answers. We suggest that the 'justice' literature provides a valuable theoretical framework for extending knowledge in the fields of work and occupations, IHRM, and migration relating to the circumstances of these many millions of members of the international workforce. This feeds into a growing debate about whether employers and government agencies are providing enough 'justice-oriented HRM' to help resolve wage-theft and injury claim disputes among large populations of hidden expatriates, which in many instances is handled instead by charities and non-governmental organisations.

We know, for example, that while fairer, more equal treatment for hidden expatriates is only beginning to be addressed by policymakers, NGOs, and researchers (Bal 2016; Ekmekçi 2017; Gleeson 2015a, b; İçduygu 2016; İçduygu and Diker 2017; Justice Without Borders and

National University of Singapore 2014; Khatir 2017; TWC2 2015), so much more is needed given the extent of the problem (as outlined in this chapter) and the widespread implications for the workers involved. We call for scholars' attention to be directed towards the extensive numbers of these hidden and vulnerable global workers, most particularly because the issues these workers face are not typically associated with the modern economies in which they work, often falling below the standards deemed 'decent work' (Arnold 2010; Wettstein 2012).

As the number of these low-status expatriates grows, managers and policymakers have to direct more attention towards their management. In particular, the emergence of practices and policies tailored to organisational and individual needs is of significant importance. Specific policies and practices are required that enable refugees to access education, training, and employment. Vocational training programmes can provide qualifications to the standards expected by the institutions in the host country (İçduygu 2016). Acquiring new skills or adapting their knowledge to the economy will give hidden expatriates the opportunity to work in just and favourable conditions and enable them to enjoy a better standard of living with sustained physical and mental health.

For economically driven expatriates, these same objectives require not just fair laws and regulations but effective enforcement of them. The moves to extend such legislation to the 'recruiting' countries are welcome, but need to be backed up by local enforcement. Employers need to understand that almost all hidden expatriates have, like all other human beings, the capacity, with care and attention, to do much more than they are often allowed to do, to the benefit of the society, the employer, and the individual. Providing such care and attention, and such opportunities, would go a long way to alleviating the failures of Organisational Justice that so plague these workers at present. Whilst there remains a major research demand to fill many of our basic knowledge gaps, and to develop theoretical understanding of the role of hidden expatriates within organisations, we believe that awareness is the first step, and we hope that in the future such expatriates will be considerably less 'hidden' from the view of scholars than they have been hitherto.

References

Adams, S.J. 1965. Inequity in social exchange. *Advances in Experimental Social Psychology* 2: 267–299.

Akalın, A. 2010. 'Yukarıdakiler-Aşağıdakiler': İstanbul'daki Güvenlikli Sitelerde Göçmen Ev Hizmetlisi İstihdamı. In *Türkiye'ye Uluslararası Göç içinde*, ed. B. Pusch and T. Wilkoszewski. İstanbul: Kitap Yayınevi.

Al Ariss, A., and M. Crowley-Henry. 2013. Self-initiated expatriation and migration in the management literature: Present theorizations and future research directions. *Career Development International* 18: 78–96.

Al Ariss, A., J. Vassilopoulou, M. Özbilgin, and A. Game. 2014. Understanding career experiences of skilled minority ethnic workers in France and Germany. *The International Journal of Human Resource Management* 24: 1236–1256.

Alberti, G., J. Holgate, and M. Tapia. 2013. Organising migrants as workers or as migrant workers? Intersectionality, trade unions and precarious work. *The International Journal of Human Resource Management* 24: 4132–4148.

Aleksynska, M., S. Aoul, and V. Petrencu. 2017. Deficiencies in conditions of work as a cost to labor migration: Concepts, extent, and implications. The Global Knowledge Partnership on Migration and Development (KNOMAD), KNOMAD Working Paper 28.

Alkhatib, S. 2017a. Couple who starved maid jailed. *The Straits Times*. Singapore: Singapore Press Holdings.

———. 2017b. Labour scam mastermind jailed 5 years, fined $144k. *The Straits Times*. Singapore: Singapore Press Holdings.

Andresen, M., F. Bergdolt, and J. Margenfel. 2012. What distinguishes self-initiated expatriates from assigned expatriates and migrants? In *Self-initiated expatriation: Individual, organisational and national perspectives*, ed. M. Andresen, A. Al Ariss, M. Walther, and K. Wolff, 166–194. London: Routledge.

Arnold, D. 2010. Transnational corporations and the duty to respect basic human rights. *Business Ethics Quarterly* 30: 371–399.

Ashford, S. 1988. Individual strategies for coping with stress during organisational transitions. *The Journal of Applied Behavioral Science* 24: 19–36.

Ashford, S., and L. Cummings. 1985. Proactive feedback seeking: The instrumental use of the information environment. *Journal of Occupational Psychology* 58: 67–79.

Au, A. 2017a. MOM's advice out of step with reality. *The Straits Times*. Singapore: Singapore Press Holdings.

————. 2017b. Set up portal for employers to hire foreign workers. *The Straits Times*. Singapore: Singapore Press Holdings.

Australian Government. 2016. A national disgrace: The exploitation of temporary work visa holders. Senate Enquiry, Australian Government, March.

Baban, F., S. Ilcan, and K. Rygiel. 2017. Syrian refugees in Turkey: Pathways to precarity, differential inclusion, and negotiated citizenship rights. *Journal of Ethnic and Migration Studies* 43: 41–57.

Baey, G., and B. Yeoh 2015. *Migration and precarious work: Negotiating debt, employment, and livelihood strategies amongst Bangladeshi migrant men working in Singapore's construction industry*. Working paper, University of Sussex and Migrating Out of Poverty Research Programme Consortium.

Bal, C. 2016. *Production politics and migrant labour regimes: Guest workers in Asia and the Gulf*. London: Palgrave Macmillan.

Basabe, N., and M. Ros. 2005. Cultural dimensions and social behavior correlates: Individualism-collectivism and power distance. *Revue Internationale de Psychologie Sociale* 1: 189–226.

Bies, R. 2005. Are procedural and interactional justice conceptually distinct? In *Handbook of organisational justice*, ed. J. Greenberg and J.A. Colquitt, 85–112. Mahwah: Erlbaum.

————. 2013. *The manager as intuitive politician: Blame management in the delivery of bad news*. Working paper no. 10–108, Washington, DC: Georgetown University, McDonough School of Business.

Bies, R., and J. Moag. 1986. Interactional justice: Communication criteria of fairness. In *Research on negotiations in organisations*, ed. R. Lewicki, B. Sheppard, and M. Bazerman, 43–55. Greenwich: JAI Press.

Cerdin, J.-L.E., and J. Selmer. 2014. Who is a self-initiated expatriate? Towards conceptual clarity of a common notion. *The International Journal of Human Resource Management* 25: 1281–1301.

Cerdin, J.-L., M. Abdeljalil-Diné, and C. Brewster. 2014. Qualified immigrants' success: Exploring the motivation to migrate and to adjust. *Journal of International Business Studies* 45: 151–168.

Chan, A. 2011. *Hired on sufferance - China's migrant workers in Singapore*. Hong Kong: China Labour Bulletin.

Cheong, D. 2017. App makes foreigners' work-pass checks easier. *The Straits Times*. Singapore: Singapore Press Holdings.

Cheung, A.-L., and L. Lui. 2017. Hiring domestic help in Hong Kong: The role of gender attitude and wives' income. *Journal of Family Issues* 38 (1): 73–99.

Chia, R. 2016. Maid gets 18 years' jail for killing employer, socialite Nancy Gan. http://www.straitstimes.com/singapore/maid-gets-18-years-jail-for-killing-employer. Accessed 18 Mar 2018.

Chia, Y. and M. Zaccheus 2012. Hard life, but foreign workers labour on. http://www.asiaone.com/News/Latest%2BNews/Singapore/Story/A1Story20121209-388579/5.html. Accessed 17 Sept 2017.

Chong, E. 2017a. Couple jailed over years of maid abuse. *The Straits Times*. Singapore: Singapore Press Holdings.

———. 2017b. Myanmar maid jailed for mixing disinfectant into cereal drink of employer's mother-in-law. http://www.straitstimes.com/singapore/courts-crime/myanmar-maid-jailed-for-mixing-disinfectant-into-cereal-drink-of-employers. Accessed 15 Aug 2018.

———. 2017c. Safety, hygiene lapses at worker dorms. *The Straits Times*. Singapore: Singapore Press Holdings.

Cohen-Charash, Y., and P. Spector. 2001. The role of justice in organisations: A meta-analysis. *Organisational Behavior and Human Decision Processes* 86: 278–321.

Cole, M., J. Bernerth, F. Walter, and D. Holt. 2010. Organisational justice and individual's withdrawal: Unlocking the influence of emotional exhaustion. *Journal of Management Studies* 47: 367–390.

Colquitt, J. 2001. On the dimensionality of organisational justice: A construct validation of a measure. *Journal of Applied Psychology* 86: 386–400.

Colquitt, J., D. Conlon, M. Wesson, C. Porter, and K. Ng. 2001. Justice at the millennium: A meta-analytic review of 25 years of organisational justice research. *Journal of Applied Psychology* 86: 425–445.

Connell, J., and J. Burgess. 2013. Vulnerable workers in an emerging Middle Eastern economy: What are the implications for HRM? *The International Journal of Human Resource Management* 24: 4166–4184.

Crane, A. 2013. Modern slavery as a management practice: Exploring the conditions and capabilities for human exploitation. *Academy of Management Review* 38: 49–69.

Darity, W., and P. Mason. 2004. Evidence on discrimination in employment: Codes of color, codes of gender. *The Journal of Economic Perspectives* 12 (12): 63–90.

Deutsch, M. 1975. Equity, equality, and need: What determines which value will be used as the basis for distributive justice? *Journal of Social Issues* 31: 137–149.

Diekmann, K., Z. Barsness, and H. Sondak. 2004. Uncertainty, fairness perceptions, and job satisfaction: A field study. *Social Justice Research* 17: 237–255.

Ekmekçi, P. 2017. Syrian refugees, health and migration legislation in Turkey. *Journal of Immigrant Minority Health* 19: 1434–1441.

Erdoğdu, S., and G. Toksöz 2013. The invisible face of women's invisible labour, conditions of work and employment. http://digitalcommons.ilr.cornell.edu/cgi/viewcontent.cgi?article=1302&context=intl. Accessed 17 Feb 2018.

Eurostat. 2016. European union labour force survey – Annual results 2015. European Union, Luxembourg. Retrieved from http://ec.europa.eu/eurostat/statistics-explained/index.php/EU_labour_force_survey. Accessed 16 Sept 2017.

Fillinger, T., N. Harrigan, S. Chok, A. Amirrudin, P. Meyer, M. Rajah, and D. Fordyce. 2017. Labour protection for the vulnerable: An evaluation of the salary and injury claims system for migrant workers in Singapore. Transient Workers Count Too and Chen Su Lan Trust. Singapore.

Folger, R., and R. Cropanzano. 1998. *Organisational justice and human resource management*. Thousand Oaks: Sage.

Frantz, E. 2013. Jordan's unfree workforce: State-sponsored bonded labour in the Arab region. *The Journal of Development Studies* 49: 1072–1087.

Fullin, G., and E. Reyneri. 2011. Low unemployment and bad jobs for new immigrants in Italy. *International Migration* 49: 118–147.

Geddes, A. 2005. Chronicle of a crisis foretold: The politics of irregular migration, human trafficking and people smuggling in the UK. *The British Journal of Politics and International Relations* 7: 324–339.

Gleeson, S. 2015a. 'They come here to work': An evaluation of the economic argument in favor of immigrant rights. Cornell University, Industrial and Labour Relations School. Retrieved from http://digitalcommons.ilr.cornell.edu/articles/1226. Accessed 20 Mar 2018.

———. 2015b. Between support and shame: The impacts of workplace violations for immigrant families. In *Research in the sociology of work: Immigration and work*, ed. J. Agius Vallejo, vol. 27, 29–52. Bingley: Emerald Publishing.

Greco, V., and D. Roger. 2003. Uncertainty, stress, and health. *Personality and Individual Differences* 34: 1057–1068.

Greenberg, J. 1993. The social side of fairness: Interpersonal and informational classes of organisational justice. In *Justice in the workplace: Approaching fairness in human resource management*, ed. R. Cropanzano, 79–103. Hillsdale: Erlbaum.

Haak-Saheem, W., and C. Brewster. 2017. 'Hidden' expatriates: International mobility in the United Arab Emirates as a challenge to current understanding of expatriation. *Human Resource Management Journal* 27: 423–439.

Harvey, W. 2012. Labour market experiences of skilled British migrants in Vancouver. *Employee Relations* 34: 658–669.

Hassan, A., and J. Hashim. 2011. Role of organisational justice in determining work outcomes of national and expatriate academic staff in Malaysia. *International Journal of Commerce and Management* 21: 82–93.

Hausman, M., and J. Reed. 1991. Psychological issues in relocation: Response to change. *Journal of Career Development* 17: 247–258.

Hechanova, R., T. Beehr, and N. Christiansen. 2003. Antecedents and consequences of employees' adjustment to overseas assignment: A meta-analytic review. *Applied Psychology. An International Review* 52: 213–236.

Heine, S., D. Lehman, K. Peng, and J. Greenholz. 2002. What's wrong with cross-cultural comparisons of subjective Likert scales? The reference-group effect. *Journal of Personality and Social Psychology* 82: 903–918.

Hofstede, G. 2001. *Culture's consequences: Comparing values, behaviors, institutions, and organisations across nations.* 2nd ed. Thousand Oaks: Sage.

Humanitarian Organisation for Migration Economics. 2011. The exploitation of migrant Chinese construction workers in Singapore. Research Report. Retrieved from http://web.archive.org/web/20160902064532/http://www.home.org.sg/wp-content/uploads/2015/07/PRC_MCW_Report_nal_2011.pdf. Accessed 17 Sept 2017.

Humanitarian Organisation for Migration Economics. 2017. Wage theft and exploitation among Singapore's migrant workers. https://tinyurl.com/HOMEwagetheft. Accessed 16 May 2018.

Humanitarian Organisation for Migration Economics and TWC2. 2010. Justice delayed, justice denied: The experiences of migrant workers in Singapore. http://twc2.org.sg/2010/12/15/justice-delayed-justice-denied/. Accessed 17 Apr 2018.

İçduygu, A. 2016. Turkey: Labour market integration and social inclusion of refugees. http://www.europarl.europa.eu/RegData/etudes/STUD/2016/595328/IPOL_STU(2016)595328_EN.pdf. Accessed 29 Mar 2018.

İçduygu, A., and E. Diker 2017. Labor market integration of Syrian refugees in Turkey: From refugees to settlers. *The Journal of Migration Studies*, [Göç Araştırmaları Dergisi] 3: 12–35.

ILO. 2015. ILO global estimates on migrant workers. http://www.ilo.org/global/topics/labour-migration/publications/WCMS_436343/lang%2D%2Den/index.htm. Accessed 16 Aug 2018.

Jacobs, J. 1989. *Revolving doors: Sex segregation and Women's careers.* Stanford: Stanford University Press.

Judge, T., and J. Colquitt. 2004. Organisational justice and stress: The mediating role of work-family conflict. *Journal of Applied Psychology* 89: 395–404.

Justice Without Borders. 2017. *Protecting low-wage foreign workers in Singapore from bait-and-switch contracts*. Washington, DC: Justice Without Borders.

Justice Without Borders and National University of Singapore. 2014. *A practitioner's manual for migrant workers – Singapore: Helping victims of exploitation and human trafficking seek just compensation*. Washington, DC: Justice Without Borders.

Kaska, S. 2006. *The new international migration and migrant women in Turkey: The case of Moldovan domestic workers*. Turkey: Migration Research Program, Koç University.

Kerr, S. 2007. Gulf states 'fail to curb abuse of maids'. https://www.ft.com/content/f2b0d252-9299-11dc-b9e6-0000779fd2ac. Accessed 21 May 2018.

Khatir, S. 2017. All Qatar workers are entitled to at least one day off a week. https://dohanews.co/reminder-all-qatar-workers-are-entitled-to-at-least-one-day-off-a-week/. Accessed 17 May 2018.

Lam, K.H. 2017. Contractors' association portal helps foreign workers find new employer. *The Straits Times*. Singapore: Singapore Press Holdings.

Lee, M.K. 2017. Director charged with collecting kickbacks from foreign workers. *The Straits Times*. Singapore: Singapore Press Holdings.

Leventhal, G. 1980. What should be done with equity theory? New approaches to the study of fairness in social relationships. In *Social exchange: Advances in theory and research*, ed. K. Gergen, M. Greenberg, and R. Willis, 27–55. New York: Plenum Press.

Loh, R. 2016. Inside a foreign workers' dormitory. http://www.tnp.sg/news/singapore/inside-foreign-workers-dormitory. Accessed 19 May 2018.

Malit, F., and G. Naufal. 2016. Asymmetric information under the Kafala Sponsorship System: Impacts on foreign domestic workers' income and employment status in the GCC countries. *International Migration* 54: 76–90.

Marschan-Piekkari, R., D. Welch, and L. Welch. 1999. In the shadow: The impact of language on structure, power and communication in the multinational. *International Business Review* 8: 421–440.

McNulty, Y., and C. Brewster. 2017. Theorising the meaning(s) of 'expatriate': Establishing boundary conditions for business expatriates. *The International Journal of Human Resource Management* 28: 27–61.

McNulty, Y., and J. Selmer. 2017. *Research handbook of expatriates*. London: Edward Elgar.

Ministry of Human Resources and Emiratization. 2015. United Arab Emirates Ministry of Human Resources and Emiratization. https://www.mohre.gov.ae/en/home.aspx. Accessed 12 May 2018.

Ministry of Interior Directorate General of Migration Management. 2014. Law on foreigners and international protection. http://www.goc.gov.tr/files/files/eng_minikanun_5_son.pdf. Accessed 21 Mar 2018.

Ministry of Internal Directorate General of Migration Management. 2018. Geçici Koruma Kapsamındaki Suriyelilerin İllere Göre Dağılımı, the distribution of Syrian refugees under temporary protection on the basis of cities, Republic of Turkey. http://www.goc.gov.tr/icerik3/gecici-koruma_363_378_4713. Accessed 22 Mar 2018.

Ministry of Manpower. 2016. Annual employment change by industry and residential status. Administrative Records and Labour Force Survey, Manpower Research & Statistics Department. http://stats.mom.gov.sg/Pages/EmploymentTimeSeries.aspx. Accessed 15 Apr 2018.

———. 2017. Foreign workforce numbers. http://www.mom.gov.sg/documents-and-publications/foreign-workforce-numbers. Accessed 17 Apr 2018.

Monat, A., J. Averill, and R. Lazarus. 1972. Anticipatory stress and coping reactions under various conditions of uncertainty. *Journal of Personality and Social Psychology* 24: 237–253.

Moorman, R. 1991. Relationship between organisational justice and organisational citizenship behaviors: Do fairness perceptions influence employee citizenship? *Journal of Applied Psychology* 76: 845.

ORSAM (Centre for Middle Eastern Strategic Studies). 2016. Syrian refugees in Turkey: Challenges and opportunities for longer term integration. http://www.orsam.org.tr/files/T_Degerlendirme/1/1eng.pdf. Accessed 10 May 2018.

Platt, M., G. Baey, B. Yeoh, C. Khoo, and T. Lam. 2017. Debt, precarity and gender: Male and female temporary labour migrants in Singapore. *Journal of Ethnic and Migration Studies* 43: 119–136.

Podsakoff, P., W. Bommer, N. Podsakoff, and S. MacKenzie. 2006. Relationships between leader reward and punishment behavior and subordinate attitudes, perceptions, and behaviors: A meta-analytic review of existing and new research. *Organisational Behavior and Human Decision Processes* 99: 113–142.

Roh, J. 2014. Korea's employment permit system and wage development of foreign workers. *Public Policy and Administration Review* 2 (3): 41–63.

Salleh, A. 2017. Wage theft' leaves workers in distress. *The Straits Times*. Singapore: Singapore Press Holdings.

Salleh, N.A., N.M. Nordin, and A.K. Rashid. 2012. The language problem issue among foreign workers in the Malaysian construction industry. *International Journal of Business and Social Science* 3: 97–99.

Şanlıer-Yüksel, İ., and A. İçduygu. 2018. Flexibility and ambiguity: Impacts of temporariness of transnational mobility in the case of Turkey. In *Characteristics of temporary migration in European-Asian transnational social spaces*, ed. P. Pitkänen, M. Korpela, M. Aksakal, and K. Schmidt, 99–119. Cham: Springer.

Sapienza, H., and M. Korsgaard. 1996. Procedural justice in entrepreneur-investor relations. *Academy of Management Journal* 39: 544–574.

Seow, J. 2016. 50 workers say firm owes at least 2 months' wages. *The Straits Times*. Singapore: Singapore Press Holdings.

———. 2017. NGOs – Need to protect Cambodian maids better. *The Straits Times*. Singapore: Singapore Press Holdings.

Simanis, E. 2012. Reality check at the bottom of the pyramid. *Harvard Business Review* 90: 120–125.

Simanis, E., and M. Milstein 2012. Back to business fundamentals: Making "bottom of the pyramid" relevant to core business. http://factsreports.revues.org/1581. Accessed 19 Apr 2018.

Skarlicki, D., and R. Folger. 1997. Retaliation in the workplace: The roles of distributive, procedural, and interactional justice. *Journal of Applied Psychology* 82: 434–443.

Suutari, V., and C. Brewster. 2000. Making their own way: International experience through self-initiated foreign assignments. *Journal of World Business* 35: 417–436.

Takeuchi, R., D. Lepak, S. Marinova, and S. Yun. 2007. Nonlinear influences of stressors on general adjustment: The case of Japanese expatriates and their spouses. *Journal of International Business Studies* 38: 928–943.

Tan, FQ. 2017a. Foreign workers should lodge complaints without delay. *The Straits Times*. Singapore: Singapore Press Holdings.

———. 2017b. MOM – Early reporting of errant employers sees better outcomes. *The Straits Times*. Singapore: Singapore Press Holdings.

Toh, YC. 2017a. 158 employers convicted in last 3 years of not paying workers. *The Straits Times*. Singapore: Singapore Press Holdings.

———. 2017b. Ministry looking into 31 labourers' unpaid wages. *The Straits Times*. Singapore: Singapore Press Holdings.

TWC2. 2015. Wage protection system in UAE and Qatar. http://twc2.org.sg/2015/06/17/wage-protection-system-in-uae-and-qatar/. Accessed 17 May 2018.

———. 2017. Average recruitment cost hit $15,000 in 2015 for first-time Bangladeshi construction workers. http://twc2.org.sg/2017/02/05/average-recruitment-cost-hit-15000-in-2015-for-first-time-bangladeshi-construction-workers/. Accessed 14 May 2018.

UNHCR. 2017. UNHCR Turkey: Key facts and figures. https://data2.unhcr. org/en/documents/download/54623. Accessed 12 Aug 2018.

―――. 2018. Syria regional refugee response. http://data.unhcr.org/syrianref- ugees/country.php?id=224. Accessed 22 Mar 2018.

van den Bos, K. 2001. Uncertainty management: The influence of uncertainty salience on reactions to perceived procedural unfairness. *Journal of Personality and Social Psychology* 80: 931–941.

van den Bos, K., and J. Miedema. 2000. Toward understanding why fairness matters: The influence of mortality salience on reactions to procedural fair- ness. *Journal of Personality and Social Psychology* 79: 355–366.

Wettstein, F. 2012. CSR and the debate on business and human rights: Bridging the great divide. *Business Ethics Quarterly* 22: 739–770.

Williams, S., R. Pitre, and M. Zainuba. 2002. Justice and organisational citizen- ship behavior intentions: Fair rewards versus fair treatment. *The Journal of Social Psychology* 142: 33–44.

Wong, L. 2016. Elderly sick turn to foreign, live-in caregivers. *The Straits Times*. Singapore: Singapore Press Holdings.

Woods, A., B. Benvenuti, and N. Kayalı 2016. Workshop report: Syrian refu- gees in Istanbul. ["Çalıştay raporu: İstanbul'daki Suriyeli sığınmacılar"]. Istanbul Policy Center, Sabancı University, Stiftung Mercator Initiative.

World Bank Group. 2013. *Immigration in Malaysia: Assessment of its economic effects, and a review of the policy and system*. Washington, DC: World Bank Group.

―――. 2016. *Migration and remittances factbook. International Bank for Reconstruction and Development*. Washington, DC: World Bank Group.

―――. 2017. The world bank in Syrian Arad Republic. https://www.world- bank.org/en/country/syria

Yeoh, B. 2006. Bifurcated labour: The unequal incorporation of transmigrants in Singapore. *Tijdschrift voor Economische en Sociale Geografie* 97: 26–37.

Yıldız, A., and E. Uzgören. 2016. Limits to temporary protection: Non-camp Syrian refugees in İzmir, Turkey. *Southeast European and Black Sea Studies* 16: 195–211.

Yong, C. 2016. Singapore's population grows 1.3% to 5.61 million. *The Straits Times*. Singapore: Singapore Press Holdings.

Yong, A. and Sim, B. 2012. Maid, 16, gets 10 years for killing 'demanding' boss. http://www.asiaone.com/print/News/Latest%2BNews/Singapore/Story/ A1Story20120308-332337.html. Accessed 18 Mar 2018.

Yue, C. 2011. Foreign labor in Singapore: Trends, policies, impacts and challenges. https://dirp3.pids.gov.ph/ris/dps/pidsdps1124.pdf. Accessed May 9 2018.

11

Hidden Inequalities of Globally Mobile Workforce: A Cross-Cultural and Trust Perspective

Konstantina Kougiannou and Maranda Ridgway

11.1 Introduction

The profile of migration and global mobility literature has grown in prominence in recent years as organizations continue to expand into the global marketplace (Guo and Al Ariss 2015). International expansion requires the mobility of skilled professionals around the world and thus greater importance and emphasis is being placed on the global talent pool. Due to the importance that skilled migrant workers play in facilitating organizational success, it is essential to understand the challenges of inequality, both visible and hidden, that this group might face and how it might affect their international work experience. Trust and expatriation are respectively well-established and researched topics, yet

K. Kougiannou (✉) • M. Ridgway
Department of Human Resource Management, Nottingham Business School, Nottingham Trent University, Nottingham, UK
e-mail: konstantina.kougiannou@ntu.ac.uk; maranda.ridgway@ntu.ac.uk

© The Author(s) 2019
S. Nachmias, V. Caven (eds.), *Inequality and Organizational Practice*, Palgrave Explorations in Workplace Stigma, https://doi.org/10.1007/978-3-030-11647-7_11

the intersection of these two areas is under-researched. Existing studies have focused on cross-national supervisory relationships (Banai and Reisel 1999), procedural justice and job satisfaction (Hon and Lu Lin 2010), information sharing (Toh and Srinivas 2012) and interpersonal interactions between expatriate workers and host country nationals (HCNs) (Shimoda 2013). The dearth of studies in this area indicates that the way trust unfolds and affects the expatriation experience is under-theorized.

There are even fewer studies, with the notable exception of the work of Oltra, Bonache and Brewster (2013), that have examined inequality from the perspective of cultural differences and trust. As a consequence, it is unclear how inequalities, both hidden and visible, may emerge from a lack of trust born from cultural dissimilarity. Furthermore, we have a scant understanding about the organizational and managerial practices that expatriate workers attribute as trustworthy and those that they do not.

As organizations continue to expand internationally so will the need for a globally mobile workforce. In parallel to the ethical imperative, expatriate workers are noted as a very costly staff model (Nowak and Linder 2016), thus to maximize return-on-investment there is a need to, at worst, minimize and, at best, eradicate workplace inequality. The ethical imperative becomes more important in light of political uncertainty manifested through the UK's vote to leave the European Union (referred to as Brexit) and Donald Trump's successful presidential election. Concerns about increasing xenophobia (Elliott and Stewart 2017) present an opportunity to extend our knowledge and understanding to inform policy makers who are well positioned to reduce inequality within the increasingly globally mobile workforce.

This chapter is structured as follows: firstly, the notion of trust is presented through a succinct discussion of the extant literature. Secondly, cultural differences and their prevalence in literature pertaining to global mobility are explored. The third section considers how trust develops across cultures. The fourth part of the chapter draws on the preceding sections to debate how hidden inequalities may emerge from mistrust between different cultures. In the final section, the importance at the micro-, meso and macro-levels are argued and avenues for future research are identified to promote the success of expatriate employment.

11.2 Defining Trust

Trust plays a fundamental role in the decision to relocate globally and the mutual cultural acceptance between expatriates and HCNs. The presence of trust creates a willingness to accept and embrace cultural differences, whereas a lack of trust can lead to parties failing to reach insight into individual differences and become incapable of reconciliation, thus hindering efforts for diversity promotion. Despite the apparent importance of trust and global mobility, the interconnection remains under-researched. This section of the chapter defines the notion of trust and identifies models which are helpful to explore trust in the context of the globally mobile workforce, with particular focus on how a lack of trust can cause hidden inequalities.

Throughout trust literature, the existence of diverse approaches and definitions is noticed, while at the same time the multidimensional character of the term is recognized (Rousseau et al. 1998; Whitener 1997; Kramer 1999; Costa 2003).

Most definitions of trust entail a three-stage process (McEvily et al. 2003): trust as a *belief*, where one party assesses the other party's trustworthiness (Lewicki et al. 1998); trust as a *decision*, where one party, based on its previous beliefs, has 'the intention to accept vulnerability based upon positive expectations of the intentions or behaviour of another' (Rousseau et al. 1998); and trust as an *action*, where, the parties engage in risk-taking activities after having evaluated their target's trustworthiness (Mayer et al. 1995). Whitener et al. (1998, 513) use a three-faceted definition: (a) 'trust in another party reflects an expectation or belief that the other party will act benevolently', (b) 'trust involves a willingness to be vulnerable and risk that the other party may not fulfil that expectation' and (c) 'trust involves some level of dependency on the other party'. Similarly, Robinson (1996, 576) defined trust as a person's 'expectations, assumptions or beliefs about the likelihood that another's future action will be beneficial, favourable or at least not detrimental'. In a slightly different conceptualization, Barney and Hansen (1994) portray trust as mutual confidence that there will be no exploitation of each other's vulnerabilities and continue to describe trustworthiness as an idea that characterizes someone who will not exploit the other party and is worthy of the others' trust.

In the above definitions positive expectations, vulnerability and risk appear central to all. According to Luhman (1979) risk is a prerequisite when one chooses to trust, while Rousseau et al. (1998) believe that it creates an opportunity for trust. Mayer et al. (1995, 724) state that 'there is no risk taken in the willingness to be vulnerable, but risk is inherent in the behavioural manifestation of the willingness to be vulnerable. One does not need to risk anything in order to trust; however, one must take a risk in order to engage in a trusting action'. The fundamental difference between trust and trusting behaviors is between a 'willingness' to assume risk and actually 'assuming risk'. Gambetta (1988, 217) proposes that risk taking involves 'engaging in some form of cooperation' with the other party and Lewicki and Bunker (1996) argue that trust is not only positive expectations about the intentions of others, but also considerations concerning the potential risks involved. Two dominant categories of trusting behavior have been identified in work contexts: *reliance*—on another party's knowledge, skills, judgments or actions, and *disclosure*—sharing sensitive personal or work-related information with another party (Gillespie 2003).

McEvily et al. (2003) distinguish trust and trustworthiness commenting that because we define trust as an expectation, the distinction between trustworthiness and trust is based on the actual versus perceived intentions, motives and competencies of a trustee—the former being trustworthiness and the latter being trust. Without trustworthiness trust is not sustainable.

A widely acknowledged and commonly used model is that proposed by Mayer et al. (1995, 717–19). They suggest three characteristics of another's trustworthiness: *ability*—set of skills and competencies that will enable a party to perform reliably, *benevolence*—suggests attachment to the other party, the extent to which the other party is believed to be concerned for the trustor, and *integrity*—the trustee's adherence to certain principles acceptable by the trustor. They propose that the level of perceived trustworthiness depends on the existence of these three factors and emphasize that a lack of any of them would weaken trust. The model focuses on the trusting relationship between two parties in an organizational setting—a trusting party [trustor] and the one to be trusted [trustee]. Within this kind of relationship, the two parties will evaluate evidence about the other party's ability, benevolence and integrity and reach a decision to trust or not the trustee. This belief about the other party's trustworthiness will also be influenced by the trustor's propensity to trust. That is, his or her 'general willingness to trust others' (Mayer et al. 1995, 715). Once the evidence has been gathered, the trustor will assess the risk involved in deciding to trust the other party [the authors are comparing the level of trust with the level of perceived risk in the situation (ibid. 726)]; if the trust level is bigger than that of perceived risk, then the trustor will engage in an action of trust, in other words, in the 'risk taking in the relationship' (ibid. 726). Accepting an overseas assignment or deciding to become a self-initiated expatriate entails a certain amount of risk (e.g. unknown environments, adapting to different cultures and working with new people); therefore, trust is required for such a decision.

In a similar vein, focusing on managerial trustworthy behavior, Whitener et al. (1998) propose a five factor model that influences the employees' perceived trustworthiness of their managers: (a) behavioral consistency, which means positive and predictable behavior enhancing trust level: 'If managers behave consistently over time and across situations, employees can better predict managers' future behavior, and their confidence in their ability to make such prediction should increase' (ibid. 516); (b) behavioral integrity, referring to consistency between the party's words and actions; (c) sharing and delegation of control, which has to do with whether the other party feels involved. This is very important because 'when managers share control they demonstrate significant trust in and respect for their employees' (ibid. 517); (d) communication, as having a positive effect on trust when it is accurate and true. Emphasis on the effect of communication on the level of perceived trustworthiness is also given by Becerra and Gupta (2003). Specifically, they comment that the frequency of communication between the involving parties moderates the impact of the other factors on trustworthiness; (e) demonstration of concern, which consists of actions that demonstrate sensitivity and interest to the other party's needs. Benevolence itself consists of three actions: '(1) showing consideration and sensitivity for employees' needs and interests, (2) acting in a way that protects employees' interests, and (3) refraining from exploiting others for the benefit of one's own interest' (ibid. 517).

In addition to the trustor's perceptions of the trustee's trustworthiness, their decision to trust will be influenced by their propensity to trust (Colquitt et al. 2007), especially unfamiliar actors and organizations, which are a notable feature of the globally mobile context. Rotter (1967) defines propensity to trust as a person's predisposition toward trusting other people. Colquitt et al. (2007), in their meta-analysis of trust, trustworthiness and trust propensity, identify trust propensity and trustworthiness as trust antecedents and find that all three components of trustworthiness (ability, benevolence and integrity) have a unique and significant positive relationship with trust.

Trust is a very dynamic phenomenon that develops through time and can be violated at any time. It is based on evidence about the other party's character and motives, from which a future judgment is derived about the party's future behavior (Dietz et al. 2010). This judgment is adjusted based on subsequent evidence and/or the outcomes of their trust toward the other party (Mayer et al. 1995). Central to this development of trust is the quality and interpretation of evidence gathered, which are distinguished between direct and presumptive. Direct evidence comes from first-hand knowledge and interaction with that party and presumptive relies on indirect sources of evidence, such as the person's social or organizational membership (e.g. profession, nationality), information from third parties (e.g. gossip), role expectations (e.g. expectation of abiding to responsibilities and obligations attached to one's role) and institutions and regulations (e.g. equal opportunities policies) (Dietz and Den Hartog 2006). Moreover, trust is based not only on relational bonds, strengthened by direct and/or presumptive evidence but also on institutional support. With repeated cycles of successful reciprocation and expectation fulfillment, trust is strengthened with parties demonstrating more reliance on, and disclosure to, each other (Dietz et al. 2010).

11.3   Cultural Differences and the Globally Mobile Workforce

To understand how culture and trust can influence perceptions of inequality as experienced by expatriates it is necessary to explore the notion of cultural differences and, for the purpose of this chapter, who the globally mobile workforce are. The research pertaining to national culture is well established, yet scholars cannot agree on a single definition for culture, as noted by Vaiman and Brewster (2015, 152):

> There are numerous definitions of culture, and taking into consideration different proxies used in social science literature (e.g. country of origin, world outlook, philosophy of life) to equate to culture, it is becoming increasingly difficult to come up with one definition that would satisfy everyone.

Despite a lack of agreement as to what culture definitively is, culture has played a central role in global mobility studies; for example, research has examined the role it plays in selecting host destinations (Ridgway and Robson 2018), how it influences organizational practices (Yao 2013), how it affects adjustment (Jackson and Manderscheid 2015) and the impact it has on expatriate success (Kartar Singh and Nik Mahmood 2017). There are mixed views about how cultural distance affects international experience and whether culturally distant or similar nations help or hinder expatriate adjustment (Koveshnikov et al. 2014).

In his seminal studies, Hofstede (1978, 1980, 1983a, b) identified four dimensions to profile national cultures: 'Power Distance', the acceptance of unequal power distribution; 'Uncertainty Avoidance', the aversion toward ambiguity; 'Individualism versus Collectivism', a continuum between focusing on the self or the group; and, 'Masculinity versus Femininity', the focus on which society places value (Hofstede and Bond 1984). A fifth dimension 'Long versus Short Term Orientation' (Hofstede 1991) and a sixth dimension 'Indulgence versus Restraint' (Hofstede et al. 2010) were later added. Hofstede's work remains among the most widely cited, yet it is now considered dated and was only ever limited to one organization. Furthermore, as Vaiman and Brewster (Vaiman and

Brewster 2015) highlight, Hofstede focuses his work on countries as opposed to national cultures; a narrow but important distinction. Inspired by Hofstede's foundation, the work on culture has continued to evolve, notable studies include, but are not limited to, Schwartz (1994), Trompenaars (1993) and the work of House et al. (2004) known as the GLOBE studies (Global Leadership and Organizational Behavior Effectiveness). How culture has evolved in recent years, in light of the rise of social media and other forms of communication, has not been explored.

The intersection of culture and global mobility literature is prevalent and continues to be a focal topic in social sciences. The question of who constitutes the globally mobile workforce, however, remains a point of contention. Expatriates have been demarcated from migrant workers according to the following characteristics: firstly, that they originate from a developed country and relocate to a developing country. Secondly, their sojourn is for a finite and predetermined period. Finally, the reason to relocate is through desire and subsequent career prospects are perceived as positive (Al Ariss 2010). Expatriate workers have been further delineated into those whose relocation is facilitated and directed by their home country employer, termed company-backed expatriates and those who pursue foreign work experience on their own initiative, otherwise known as self-initiated expatriates (Suutari and Brewster 2000). Further studies (e.g. Andresen et al. 2014; Haak-Saheem and Brewster 2017) have sought to identify and theorize expatriate typologies. The focus of this chapter is expatriate workers, considered broadly as skilled workers who choose to relocate internationally regardless of whether their relocation is self-initiated or facilitated by their home country employer.

Recent studies into culture and global mobility have taken a more nuanced view than Hofstede's earlier work, for example Jackson and Manderscheid (2015) use culture to express a difference of priorities to explain the lack of desire to integrate between Western expatriates and HCNs in Saudi Arabia. Syed, George, Hazboun and Murray (2014) examined the different perceptions between HCN and expatriate workers into the organizational justification for 'foreign management', their study suggests that the resilience by HCNs to expatriate managers can be overcome by expatriate managers demonstrating respect for local cultures and business contexts. Other studies, for example Ridgway and Robson

(Ridgway and Robson 2018), have noted that the desire to experience different cultures can drive the pursuit of foreign work experience, in tandem however, it can act as a deterrent if there is a perception that individuals cannot project their own cultural background in the host country. The world views and values that individuals accumulate through working in a multicultural context come together to form individual cultural resources, which are used to deal with different situations (Rindova et al. 2011). Culturally diverse networks have been noted as a mechanism for changing cultural identity, allowing expatriate workers to relinquish or dilute national identities in reaction to multiculturalism (Mao and Shen 2015). A critical view, offered by Anthias (2015), suggests that cultural differences are perceived as discordant with Western society and this is manifested through notions such as the war on terror driving greater divides between people of different origin.

An alternative approach to examining country characteristics is through an institutional view. An institutional perspective focuses on the physical environment, such as country demography and geographical characteristics, alongside the socio-political structure (Vaiman and Brewster 2015). While the institutional perspective gives credence to the more tangible characteristics, the focus tends to be on countries within the Global North; as such, the cultural perspective in the psychological sense has been used for the purpose of this chapter.

11.4   Trust Across Cultural Boundaries

In a globalized world of business, organizations and employees, expatriates and HCNs are increasingly involved in complex interaction across borders, having to manage unfamiliar relationships with a variety of different parties with diverse national, professional and organizational backgrounds. In such uncertain and ambiguous contexts, trust plays a vital role in building and maintaining relationships (Dietz et al. 2010). By way of example, Dirks and Ferrin (2001) explore two models that explain the positive role of trust within organizational settings. The first is the model that presents trust as having a direct effect on attitudes, behaviors, perceptions and performance outcomes and is the prevailing one in the existing literature. The authors imply that this model does not represent the only way that trust might have positive consequences and propose a second model which suggests that trust moderates the effects of other determinants on the above outcomes via two processes: firstly, by affecting the assessment of another party's future behavior and secondly, by affecting the interpretation of past (and present) actions and the motives underlying them. In this way, trust is acting as a moderator and 'by impacting the assessment of the other party's future or prior actions, it reduces some of the concomitant uncertainty and ambiguity' (ibid. 456). In contrast, people with different cultural backgrounds bring different values and beliefs, behaviors, judgments and assumptions to their work, all of which could undermine the role trust plays to create beneficial cooperation and successful interactions. Indeed, national cultural traits and norms influence people's perceptions, values, beliefs and behaviors is enduring (Pothukuchi et al. 2002) and especially problematic for trust building (Johnson and Cullen 2002). This highlights the challenge of building and maintaining trust between different cultures.

Drawing upon insights from trust literature, Dietz et al. (2010, 28–30) propose a staged model of trust development across cultural boundaries that can be extremely useful when discussing the importance of trust in minimizing the emergence of hidden and unhidden inequalities faced by expatriates.

11.4.1   Stage 1: Context

The authors identify 'context' as the first stage, where prior to first encounters, parties arrive with their own cultural preconceptions (varying in complexity and compatibility), a set level of cross-cultural awareness, capabilities and motivation to adapt, all shaping the likelihood of trust. Examples of this stage could include predeparture training to enhance cross-cultural awareness, facilitating internal networking groups to share cultural knowledge and mentoring. It is important to note that some of these activities are typically only offered to senior-level company-backed expatriates.

11.4.2   Stage 2: Opening Stance

In the second stage, the 'opening stance', parties will either arrive with a willingness to trust or distrust each other. The authors suggest that this stance will be culturally determined to some extent, by immediate assessments of the other party's values and by each party's cultural receptiveness to unfamiliar situations. A distrust scenario at this stage would leave the parties prone to confirmation bias. At the second stage, to embed local allies (McNulty et al. 2017) activities such as induction and buddy systems are some examples of good practice that are more prevalent in expatriate reliant regions, the cultural element of these activities however is often omitted in regions with fewer expatriate workers.

11.4.3   Stage 3: Early Encounters

In 'early encounters', the third stage, communication is initiated where parties gather trust-relevant information, interpret cues and test their assumptions while potentially modifying their expectations. There is reliance on supervisors to manage expatriate workers' expectations and assumptions during the 'early encounters' stage; good practice would allow discussion to prevent inequalities from emerging but too often the need to examine possible issues is neglected. An example of how organizations may facilitate communication at this stage could be through internal enterprise social networking tools to allow relationships to be established and reinforced between home and host country colleagues during the early stages of relocation.

11.4.4   Stage 4: Breakthrough or Breakdown

Depending on how trust building efforts fare, parties move to the fourth stage: (a) the 'breakthrough', where positive relationships have developed (e.g. parties recognize commonalities, reconcile differences and accept the other party despite cultural differences) that lead to trust; or, (b) the 'breakdown', where parties are not able to reconcile differences and fail to accept the other party's culture, maintaining suspicion of the other party because of irreconcilable cultural differences, which results in distrust. The importance of ensuring expatriates' families are supported and engaged is a useful example of how trust can help to prevent a breakdown of trust among expatriate workers. A practical example of preventing breakdown may be to facilitate networking groups for the families of expatriate workers. This allows support networks for families to be established through sharing reconciliation experiences and advice.

11.4.5   Stage 5: Consequences

The fifth and final stage, 'consequences', will be different depending on whether the parties have had a 'breakthrough' (i.e. maturing trust relationship) or a 'breakdown' (i.e. dissolution, or decline/violation) in their relationship. We suggest that the more evident equal opportunities and diversity management policies are in the first three stages of the model the more likely it is for expatriates to experience a breakthrough (Howe-Walsh and Schyns 2010).

11.5   Hidden Inequalities Emerging from Mistrust Between Different Cultures

Inequality remains a prominent feature within the globally mobile workforce. While some inequalities are visible, such as the challenges faced by the queer community, for example relocation packages not reflecting different forms of sexuality, or additional safety and security considerations being required for certain country destinations (Gedro et al. 2013; Paisley and Tayar 2016), some inequalities are hidden. In some cases, inequalities which are visible in the home country such as disability or sexuality may become hidden to allow the individual to integrate into the host country setting (Ridgway 2018). The necessity of hiding one's true self in a different culture immediately raises the notion of trust as expatriate workers, in some cases, may not trust HCNs or expatriate colleagues from different cultural backgrounds with their true self. The perspective from HCNs regarding trust raises concerns about expatriate workers not being able to assimilate in to host country culture (Syed et al. 2014).

Culture can be seen as socially constructed boundaries and hierarchies resulting in assumptions being made about perceived homogenous characteristics of different groups; the danger is that we treat individuals based on predisposed ideas that we have about different cultures (Anthias 2015). This idea emerges in a global setting as HCNs may negatively stereotype expatriate workers based on cultural characteristics (Bonache et al. 2016). Further complexity is created as ethnicity can be substituted for culture in terms of assumptions about different groups (Baruch and Forstenlechner 2017). It has been noted that nationality and ethnicity form barriers between different communities in an expatriate setting (ibid.); however, cultural differences can evolve into racism; Anthias (2015, 180–81) identified four constructs that can overlap. These constructs are underlying antecedents of inequalities experienced by expatriate workers in a global setting. Furthermore, if left unaddressed, these constructs can contribute to increasing and sustaining hidden inequalities.

- **Danger:** Anthias (2015) refers to danger as the perceptions of culture and identity that may be associated with threat. In a workplace setting this could emerge as different expectations regarding safe working practices because health and safety standards vary around the world. Perceived lack of safety at work can generate distrust between employee and employer.
- **Deviance:** Deviance draws focus to the differences in beliefs that are embedded in society (Anthias 2015), for example, views on homosexuality. Depending on the socio-cultural context, employees may be forced to 're-closet' (Paisley and Tayar 2016) to avoid social rejection, thus not trusting their employer with their 'whole self' (i.e. disclosure).
- **Deficit:** Standards and measures within society such as citizenship tests, informal hierarchies and workplace cultural etiquette can create the notion of deficit (Anthias 2015). In the workplace this may be noticeable as different performance and reward expectations between expatriate workers of different nationalities and HCNs, reinforcing inequitable treatment (Al-Waqfi and Al-Faki 2015).

- **Disgust:** Anthias (2015) positions disgust and, by contrast, desire as the cultural embodiment of different countries, for example smells, style of dress and food. Disgust or disdain for surface-level cultural differences can hinder workplace integration and reinforce already apparent barriers between different homogenous groups. In some societal contexts, institutionalized structures, such as gender segregation prevent expatriate integration and thus reinforcing 'otherness' (Jackson and Manderscheid 2015).

The four constructs that have been discussed can unfold in the workplace to reinforce 'otherness', cause suspicion and break down trust thus giving rise to hidden inequalities. Preconceived notions of 'otherness' personified by cultural differences fosters a lack of inclusivity, such stereotyping affects behaviors leading to inequality and unconscious bias. Skovgaard-Smith and Poulfelt (2018, 147) draw an interesting argument that even cosmopolitanism which seeks to neutralize external demarcations is itself creating 'otherness' by excluding those who are not deemed to be cosmopolitan; succinctly, 'it is thus also bounded and characterized by its own specific kind of parochialism – despite being imagined as the opposite'.

11.6   Conclusion

In this chapter, we have argued how culture and trust can influence perceptions of inequality as experienced by expatriates. Globalization is unlikely to diminish (Toh and Srinivas 2012); however, recent events such as Brexit have highlighted increased levels of xenophobia (Elliott and Stewart 2017), and this presents situations in which hidden inequalities may occur. To conclude this chapter, we present three levels of analysis to advance knowledge on the interconnectivity between trust, global mobility and hidden inequality: firstly, the micro-level which emphasizes the trust that individuals place upon organizations. Secondly, the meso level, which demonstrates the trust, placed upon individuals by management. Finally, the macro-level, which articulates the trust that organizations place upon management in relation to the globally mobile workforce. The three levels are depicted in Fig. 11.1 to illustrate the trust relation-

Fig. 11.1   Tripartite trust relationship

ship in an expatriate context and between the different parties. The figure provides an organizational tool to show the actors in the trust relationship within the global mobility context. To explore how trust is developed among the globally mobile workforce in these different levels we use the cross-cultural trust development model by Dietz et al. (2010).

11.6.1   Micro-Level: Trust Experienced by Individuals

Relocating to a different country is a significant life event and can be the cause for anxiety for individuals. Company-backed expatriates place significant trust in organizations to protect and support them during integrational assignments. Trust is developed based on evidence such as the safeguards that organizations put in place (Gillespie 2003). Company-backed expatriates have established relationships with their employing organizations thus relational trust is more likely to exist.

Equal opportunities offered by organizations and effective diversity management would enhance trust. Absence of these on the other hand would hinder trust development and even potentially lead to distrust. Such policies provide evidence of organizational trustworthiness and can lead to the individual's reliance on the organization. These policies can also provide enough evidence to individuals to make them confident about disclosing sensitive information, which may help to minimize or address any perceived inequalities. A lack of organizational commitment toward equality and diversity, portrayed through policies and practices, may lead to an individual sense of deviance (Anthias 2015) and a subsequent reluctance to disclose sensitive information. This initial barrier in the trust between employee and employer could manifest into hidden inequalities if organizations treat individuals differently on the basis of characteristics that they do not realize are present.

The 'Early Encounters' stage of the model by Dietz et al. (2010) is most prominent at the micro-level as preconceived ideas of culture might modify the initial desire to relocate based on the support and protection that is offered by the organization. While the support and protection are typically a feature of assignment packages for company-backed expatriates, providing direct evidence of trustworthiness, such support is often absent for self-initiated expatriates, who rely more on presumptive evidence (e.g. third-party information about host country) about the organization's trustworthiness. In the absence of direct evidence and/or relational bonds trust may not be established as effectively for SIEs when compared to company-backed counterparts.

Mistrust between individuals leads to discord subsequently affecting organizational productivity (Syed et al. 2014). Expatriates will be supported by HNCs if they demonstrate commitment and collaboration (Toh and Srinivas 2012). Expatriates are, however, at risk of experiencing hidden inequalities when modifying their behavior to avoid deviance from social norms (Anthias 2015).

11.6.2   Meso Level: Trust and Management

At the meso level, managers are entrusted by organizations to select the right people to work in international settings. Simultaneously, individuals trust that managers are acting in their best interests to facilitate the support offered by organizations. In turn, managers must trust that individuals will fully engage with HCNs to overcome cultural differences. It is concerning, however, where cultural distance is too great, less effort is made by individuals to assimilate in the local culture (Baruch and Forstenlechner 2017). The employee-supervisor role may also be important as expatriate workers are likely to rely on the host country supervisor to understand local norms and customs (Nolan and Morley 2014), demonstrating reliance on their knowledge, skills, judgments or actions (Gillespie 2003).

This level of trust aligns most with the 'Context' and 'Opening Stance' level of the model put forward by Dietz et al. (2010). Biases and preconceived notions of culture are often confirmed by managers. There is also an expectation that managers will provide cross-cultural adjustment training. While such training is a common feature of assignment packages for company-backed expatriates, it is often ignored for self-initiated expatriates. In this context of trust, managers have higher expectations of self-initiated expatriates in terms of their cultural intelligence. Trust can be developed and reinforced with effective cross-cultural training and identifying expatriates with high emotional intelligence (Bonache et al. 2016). Arguably, cross-cultural training should also be extended to HCNs who will be working with expatriates.

11.6.3   Macro-Level: Organizational Trust

At the organizational level a lack of trust, emerging from negative stereotypes, can affect expatriate performance (Bonache et al. 2016). As expatriation remains a very costly staffing model (Nowak and Linder 2016), yet very popular, there is an organizational imperative that international work is successful. Furthermore, if organizations engage cultural resources they are well positioned to diversify and differentiate themselves (Rindova et al. 2011) from the competition. Similarly, trust is seen as an important contributor to organizational competitiveness as it is difficult to replicate (Barney and Hansen 1994). Thus reaching the 'breakthrough' stage between organization and expatriates is important. This can be achieved through carefully designed selection methods, ensuring right people are identified for international work, provided the support and protection to allow them to be successful. Selection methods can create commonalities, leading to acceptance of the other party despite any cultural differences.

The 'consequences' of achieving a 'breakthrough' means that the differences of culture recede in terms of significance, thus allowing expatriates to be embedded within the organization and potentially minimizing hidden inequalities. While the existing literature considers hostile environments as those in which expatriates, and arguably HCNs, are faced with immediate physical danger (Dickmann and Watson 2017), there is a case to explore how cultural distance may also constitute a hostile environment in which hidden inequalities may be allowed to arise. There is an opportunity to extend our knowledge and understanding to reduce inequality within the increasingly globally mobile workforce through an exploration of the role of trust in minimizing perceived inequalities and preventing a 'breakdown'. If trust is not established then the expatriate would not feel confident disclosing characteristics which then may lead to hidden inequalities and inevitably, leading to a disillusion and dissolution of the entire relationship.

11.6.4   Practical Implications for Organizations

In this chapter we have offered a tool that organizations can utilize to enable the relational actors that have a role to play in identifying and addressing hidden inequalities within the globally mobile workforce. While organizations may implement policies to address inequalities, if employees are not engaging with such policies or place trust in them, they will not come forward with hidden inequalities. There is a need, therefore, to build trust into the process (Kougiannou et al. 2015) so that employees feel comfortable to raise issues and thus allow hidden inequalities to be uncovered. Inequalities, both visible and hidden, cannot be addressed if they are not identified; however, they cannot be identified without the trust of employees in the organization and management practices.

11.6.5   Future Research

Expatriation will not diminish in the foreseeable future despite the new challenges emerging, for example xenophobia amplified by Brexit. It is important, therefore, to increase our understanding of how inequalities can be mitigated to ensure successful international work. Future research is required to explore how trust can be developed across cultures and what its role is in addressing potential inequalities in the expatriate workforce. This can be investigated at different levels, that is, organizational, managerial and individual. Furthermore, we have a scant understanding about the organizational and managerial practices that expatriate workers attribute as trustworthy and those that they do not, which warrants further examination.

References

Al Ariss, Akram. 2010. Modes of engagement: Migration, self-initiated expatriation, and career development. *Career Development International* 15 (4): 338–358.

Al-Waqfi, Mohammed A., and Ibrahim Abdalla Al-Faki. 2015. Gender-based differences in employment conditions of local and expatriate workers in the GCC context: Empirical evidence from the United Arab Emirates. *International Journal of Manpower* 36 (3): 397–415.

Andresen, Maike, Franziska Bergdolt, Jil Margenfeld, and Michael Dickmann. 2014. Addressing international mobility confusion – developing definitions and differentiations for self-initiated and assigned expatriates as well as migrants. *The International Journal of Human Resource Management* 25 (16): 2295–2318.

Anthias, Floya. 2015. Interconnecting boundaries of identity and belonging and hierarchy-making within transnational mobility studies: Framing inequalities. *Current Sociology* 64 (2): 172–190.

Banai, Moshe, and William D. Reisel. 1999. Would you trust your foreign manager? An empirical investigation. *International Journal of Human Resource Management* 10 (3): 477–487.

Barney, Jay B., and Mark H. Hansen. 1994. Trustworthiness as a source of competitive advantage. *Strategic Management Journal* 15: 175–190.

Baruch, Yehuda, and Ingo Forstenlechner. 2017. Global careers in the Arabian Gulf: Understanding motives for self-initiated expatriation of the highly skilled, globally mobile professionals. *Career Development International* 22 (1): 3–22.

Becerra, Manuel, and Anil K. Gupta. 2003. Perceived trustworthiness within the organization: The moderating impact of communication frequency on trustor and trustee effects. *Organization Science* 14 (1): 32–44.

Bonache, Jaime, Hélène Langinier, and Celia Zárraga-Oberty. 2016. Antecedents and effects of host country nationals negative stereotyping of corporate expatriates. A social identity analysis. *Human Resource Management Review* 26 (1): 59–68.

Colquitt, J.A., B.A. Scott, and J.A. LePine. 2007. Trust, trustworthiness, and trust propensity: A meta-analytic test of their unique relationships with risk taking and job performance. *Journal of Applied Psychology* 92 (4): 909–927.

Costa, Ana Cristina. 2003. Work team trust and effectiveness. *Personnel Review* 32 (5): 605–622.

Dickmann, Michael, and Ashley Helen Watson. 2017. 'I might be shot at!' Exploring the drivers to work in hostile environments using an intelligent careers perspective. *Journal of Global Mobility* 5 (4): 348–373.

Dietz, G., and D. Den Hartog. 2006. Measuring trust inside organisations. *Personnel Review* 35 (5): 557–588.

Dietz, G., N. Gillespie, and G.T. Chao. 2010. Unravelling the complexities of trust and culture. In *Organizational trust: A cultural perspective*, ed. Mark N.K. Saunders, Denise Skinner, G. Dietz, N. Gillespie, and R.J. Lewicki, 3–41. Cambridge: Cambridge University Press.

Dirks, Kurt T., and Donald L. Ferrin. 2001. The role of trust in organizational settings. *Organization Science* 12 (4): 450–467.

Elliott, Carole, and Jim Stewart. 2017. What are the (C)HRD implications of Brexit? A personal reflection? *Human Resource Development International* 20 (1): 1–8.

Gambetta, D. 1988. *Trust : Making and breaking cooperative relations*. Oxford: Basil Blackwell.

Gedro, J., Robert C. Mizzi, Tonette S. Rocco, and Jasper van Loo. 2013. Going global: Professional mobility and concerns for LGBT workers. *Human Resource Development International* 16 (3): 282–297.

Gillespie, Nicole. 2003. *Measuring trust in the work relationships: The behavioral trust inventory*. Annual Meeting of the Academy of Management. Seattle.

Guo, Chun, and Akram Al Ariss. 2015. Human resource management of international migrants: Current theories and future research. *The International Journal of Human Resource Management* 26 (10): 1287–1297.

Haak-Saheem, Washika, and Chris Brewster. 2017. 'Hidden' expatriates: International mobility in the United Arab Emirates as a challenge to current understanding of expatriation. *Human Resource Management Journal* 27 (3): 423–439.

Hofstede, Geert. 1978. *Value systems in forty countries: Interpretation, validation and consequence for theory*. Bruxelles: European Institute for Advanced Studies in Management.

———. 1980. Culture and organizations. *International Studies of Management and Organization* 10 (4): 15–41.

———. 1983a. Dimensions of national cultures in fifty countries and three regions. In *Expiscations in cross-cultural psychology*, ed. J.B. Deregowski, S. Dziurawiec, and R.C. Annis, 335–355. Lisse: Swets and Zeitlinger.

———. 1983b. National cultures in four dimensions. *International Studies of Management and Organization* 13 (1–2): 46–74.

———. 1991. *Cultures and organizations: Software of the mind*. London: McGraw-Hill.

Hofstede, Geert, and Michael H. Bond. 1984. Hofstede's cultural dimensions. *Journal of Cross-Cultural Psychology* 15 (4): 417–433.

Hofstede, Geert, G.J. Hofstede, and M. Minkov. 2010. *Cultures and organizations: Software of the mind*. 3rd ed. New York: McGraw-Hill.

Hon, Alice H.Y., and L. Lu Lin. 2010. The mediating role of trust between expatriate procedural justice and employee outcomes in Chinese hotel industry. *International Journal of Hospitality Management* 29 (4): 669–676.

House, R.J., P.J. Hanges, M. Javidan, P.W. Dorfman, and V. Gupta. 2004. *Culture, leadership, and organizations: The GLOBE study of 62 societies*. Thousand Oaks: SAGE Publications.

Howe-Walsh, Liza, and Birgit Schyns. 2010. Self-initiated expatriation: Implications for HRM. *The International Journal of Human Resource Management* 21 (2): 260–273.

Jackson, Derrick, and Steven V. Manderscheid. 2015. A phenomenological study of western expatriates' adjustment to Saudi Arabia. *Human Resource Development International* 18 (2): 131–152.

Johnson, J.L., and J.B. Cullen. 2002. The bases and dynamics of trust in cross-cultural exchange relationships. In *The Blackwell handbook of cross-cultural management*, ed. M.J. Gannon and K.L. Newman, 335–360. Oxford: Blackwell.

Kougiannou, Konstantina, Tom Redman, and Graham Dietz. 2015. The outcomes of works councils: The role of trust, justice and industrial relations climate. *Human Resource Management Journal* 25 (4): 458–477.

Koveshnikov, Alexei, Heidi Wechtler, and Cecile Dejoux. 2014. Cross-cultural adjustment of expatriates: The role of emotional intelligence and gender. *Journal of World Business* 49 (3): 362–371.

Kramer, Roderick M. 1999. Trust and distrust in organizations: Emerging perspectives, enduring questions. *Annual Review of Psychology* 50 (1): 569–598.

Lewicki, Roy J., and Barbara Benedikt Bunker. 1996. Developing and maintaining trust in work relationships. In *Trust in organizations: Frontiers of theory and research*, ed. Roderick M. Kramer and Tom R. Tyler, 114–139. Thousand Oaks: Sage.

Lewicki, Roy J., Daniel J. McAllister, and Robert J. Bies. 1998. Trust and distrust: New relationships and realities. *Academy of Management Review* 23 (3): 438–458.

Luhman, N. 1979. *Trust and power*. Chichester: Wiley.

Mao, Jina, and Yan Shen. 2015. Cultural identity change in expatriates: A social network perspective. *Human Relations* 68 (10): 1533–1556.

Mayer, Roger C., James H. Davis, and F. David Schoorman. 1995. An integrative model of organizational trust. *Academy of Management Review* 20 (3): 709–734.

McEvily, Bill, Vincenzo Perrone, and Akbar Zaheer. 2003. Trust as an organizing principle. *Organization Science* 14 (1): 91–103.

McNulty, Yvonne, Ruth McPhail, Cristina Inversi, Tony Dundon, and Eva Nechanska. 2017. Employee voice mechanisms for lesbian, gay, bisexual and transgender expatriation: The role of Employee-Resource Groups (ERGs) and allies. *The International Journal of Human Resource Management* 29 (5): 829–856.

Nolan, Eimear Marie, and Michael J. Morley. 2014. A test of the relationship between person–environment fit and cross-cultural adjustment among self-initiated expatriates. *The International Journal of Human Resource Management* 25 (11): 1631–1649.

Nowak, Christian, and Christian Linder. 2016. Do you know how much your expatriate costs? An activity-based cost analysis of expatriation. *Journal of Global Mobility* 4 (3): 88–107.

Oltra, Victor, Jaime Bonache, and Chris Brewster. 2013. A new framework for understanding inequalities between expatriates and host country nationals. *Journal of Business Ethics* 115 (2): 291–310.

Paisley, Varina, and Mark Tayar. 2016. Lesbian, gay, bisexual and transgender (LGBT) expatriates: An intersectionality perspective. *The International Journal of Human Resource Management* 27 (7): 766–780.

Pothukuchi, Vijay, Fariborz Damanpour, Jaepil Choi, Chao C. Chen, and Seung Ho Park. 2002. National and organizational culture differences and international joint venture performance. *Journal of International Business Studies* 33 (2): 243–265.

Ridgway, Maranda. 2018. Hidden inequalities of the expatriate workforce. In *Hidden inequalities in the workplace: A guide to the current challenges, issues and business solutions*, ed. Valerie Caven and Stefanos Nachmias, 303–330. Cham: Palgrave Macmillan.

Ridgway, Maranda, and Fiona Robson. 2018. Exploring the motivation and willingness of self-initiated expatriates, in the civil engineering industry, when considering employment opportunities in Qatar. *Human Resource Development International* 21 (1): 24–45.

Rindova, Violina, Elena Dalpiaz, and Davide Ravasi. 2011. A cultural quest: A study of organizational use of new cultural resources in strategy formation. *Organization Science* 22 (2): 413–431.

Robinson, Sandra L. 1996. Trust and breach of the psychological contract. *Administrative Science Quarterly* 41 (4): 574–599.

Rotter, Julian B. 1967. A new scale for the measurement of interpersonal trust. *Journal of Personality* 35 (4): 651–665.

Rousseau, D.M., S.B. Sitkin, S.R. Burt, and C. Camerer. 1998. Not so different after all: A cross-discipline view of trust. *Academy of Management Review* 23 (3): 393–404.

Schwartz, S. 1994. Individualism and collectivism: Theory, method and application. In *Cross-cultural research and methodology series, Vol. 18. Individualism and collectivism: Theory, method, and applications*, ed. H.C. Kim, C. Triandis, S.-C. Choi Kagitcibasi, and G. Yoon, 85–119. Thousand Oaks: SAGE Publications.

Shimoda, Yukimi. 2013. Talk, trust and information flow: Work relationships between Japanese expatriate and host national employees in Indonesia. *The International Journal of Human Resource Management* 24 (20): 3853–3871.

Kartar Singh, Jugindar Singh, and Nik Hasnaa Nik Mahmood. 2017. Managing successful overseas assignments in Malaysia: Social competencies, emotional competencies, job performance and cultural adjustment. *International Journal of Business and Management* 12 (11): 174.

Skovgaard-Smith, Irene, and Flemming Poulfelt. 2018. Imagining 'Non-nationality': Cosmopolitanism as a source of identity and belonging. *Human Relations* 71 (2): 1–26.

Suutari, Vesa, and Chris Brewster. 2000. Making their own way: International experience through self-initiated foreign assignments. *Journal of World Business* 20 (4): 417–436.

Syed, Jawad, Nour George Hazboun, and Peter A. Murray. 2014. What locals want: Jordanian employees' views on expatriate managers. *The International Journal of Human Resource Management* 25 (2): 212–233.

Toh, Soo Min, and Ekkirala S. Srinivas. 2012. Perceptions of task cohesiveness and organizational support increase trust and information sharing between host country nationals and expatriate coworkers in Oman. *Journal of World Business* 47 (4): 696–705.

Trompenaars, F. 1993. *Riding the waves of culture: Understanding diversity in global business.* Chicago: Irwin.

Vaiman, Vlad, and Chris Brewster. 2015. How far do cultural differences explain the differences between nations? implications for HRM. *The International Journal of Human Resource Management* 26 (2): 151–164.

Whitener, Ellen M. 1997. The impact of human resource activities on employee trust. *Human Resource Management Review* 7 (4): 389–404.

Whitener, Ellen M., Susan E. Brodt, M. Audrey Korsgaard, and Jon M. Werner. 1998. Managers as initiators of trust: An exchange relationship framework for understanding managerial trustworthy behavior. *Academy of Management Review* 23 (3): 513–530.

Yao, Christian. 2013. The impact of cultural dimensions on Chinese expatriates' career capital. *The International Journal of Human Resource Management* 25 (5): 609–630.

12

Expatriation and Incapacity Created by a Multitude of Hidden Equalities

Christine Mortimer

12.1 Introduction

Whilst preparing for my own expatriate adventure, I researched journal articles concerning the experiences of expatriates. The research primarily focused on why these experiences are not always as positive as hoped, often leading to shortened assignments (Tharenou and Caulfield 2010; Wang and Varma 2017). What is often missing from these articles is the lived experiences of those for whom the assignment finished before expected. Caligiuri and Bonache (2016) have identified a lack of research into the individual-level issues of working abroad, and Ng and Earley (2006) suggest that the failed experiences offer an opportunity to reflect and learn increasing self-efficacy and cultural intelligence (Ramalu et al. 2012). This chapter begins the process of addressing this

C. Mortimer (✉)
Department of Organisational, Work and Technology, Lancaster University Management School, Lancaster, UK
e-mail: c.mortimer1@lancaster.ac.uk

© The Author(s) 2019
S. Nachmias, V. Caven (eds.), *Inequality and Organizational Practice*, Palgrave Explorations in Workplace Stigma, https://doi.org/10.1007/978-3-030-11647-7_12

gap by offering a personal narrative (Denzin 2000) of life as an academic expatriate working in China through a period of intense change.

In order to address research at the individual level, the chosen methodology is reflexive auto-ethnography. The narrative style of auto-ethnography forms and reforms as it progresses into socially mediated discourse (Schembri and Boyle 2013), and has two objectives. The first is to address and mediate between various constructed realities, including the researcher's own constructs (Wolcott 2009). The second is to enable the researcher/practitioner to consciously embed personal experiences within theory and practice surrounding the study (McIlveen 2008).

When developing qualitative and personal research, there is an issue of how to write the study, so that it may develop constructive conclusions (Southgate 2003; Tosh 2013). Within business management research, Humphreys and Watson (2009) make a case for a more creative writing style to develop authenticity and reader engagement. The use of ethnographic and auto-ethnographic research can bridge the gap between the assumed and demanded readily style of text within social sciences, as opposed to the writerly text more often found in humanities. The distinction between these two writing styles is important in the writing of this auto-ethnographic study. Barthes (1983) initially identified the distinction. Within a readily text, the author 'authorises' the experiences of the reader. Highlighted experiences in the chapter are pre-determined by the author within a text that is usually linear with clear explanations of events and subjects. There are clear signposts, and the reader does not have to include or consider their own thoughts when reading the text in order to make sense. The writerly text, on the other hand, requires the reader to make connections between images and events within the text and their own experiences. It requires a reflexive style of writing and reading. In many ways, it represents the real world more accurately in terms of the open, ambiguous and unpredictable nature of life, allowing the wisdom of the reader to add depth of understanding or action to the text (Sumara and Luce-Kapler 1993).

Auto-ethnographic writing is therefore a writerly text, leaving the reader to empathise with the researcher/practitioner in order to understand the more subjective areas of human life coming from a first-person voice. There are various formats used for writerly texts, Humphreys

(2005) uses Vignettes to illustrate certain experiences in his academic life. Misiaszek (2018) uses a series of mediations including poetry to develop a view of her experiences in Chinese higher education. The auto-ethnographic study of Gant (2017) takes direct diary quotations to explore the challenges of bringing up a disabled child. From a business perspective, Vickers (2008) tells a story from a personal perspective of changes happening within his company during a takeover by an American firm. All of these texts offer a subjective insight into the challenges and reactions of the practitioner/researcher. However, these texts also articulate and anticipate the author's vulnerability in writing this type of text.

Buzard (2003, p. 1608) suggests that the researcher should 'Treat any auto-ethnographic text as an inked tattoo', something that will be permanently there. The idea of vulnerability and how others might interpret the text is a concern (Humphreys 2005; Misiaszek 2018), and I particularly identify with the notion of 'not commodifying out China experience' (2018, p. 90). Although I also admit that part of this exercise is to enable a development of my own multicultural identity (Mao and Shen 2015), there is also truth in the fact that this type of writing is an 'uncomfortable experience' one that is fraught with protecting others and oneself whilst attempting to articulate the experience in a meaningful way. The issue of protecting others becomes more problematic in a small institution. The institution concerned in this auto-ethnographic account is a small, hierarchical Sino-Foreign College part of a larger Chinese University. This makes anonymising other actors, whilst enabling a fair representation of the interactions, problematic. It is a small international academic culture within the larger cultures of a big University, large city and China more generally (Moosa 2013). On the other hand, auto-ethnographic writing should not be tamed (Ellis and Bochner 2006, p. 433) because of these considerations. If it is not a truthful reflexive piece, there is little value and it has little purpose. Therefore, the decision centres on what experiences to write, and how to safeguard other actors and myself, whilst keeping faith with the stories chosen.

The data comes from an extensive diary kept over the year. It includes impressions and reflections of meetings, notes taken at meetings, engagement with various academic report writing and new curriculum developments. My reflective writings at the time where an attempt to take the opportunity to learn from tensions between differences and diversity that I knew and expected would exist (Suransky and Alma 2018). This was one of the reasons I accepted the role, I wanted to learn and I was in China to learn. The reflexive practice that I am now engaging in (Johnson and Duberley 2003; Alvesson and Willmott 2003), is an attempt to surface the hidden inequalities that contributed to the experiences I had and to enable some sort of sense-making (Weick 1995). In light of the above discussion, I have chosen to explore my interaction with specific Chinese policies, the practices created and the resultant hidden inequalities engendered. The choice of something inanimate links to Non-Representational Theory (Thrift 2008) where there is a focus on the material dimensions of life and how practices inform the enactment and performance of human life, so seems an ethical way to proceed.

12.2   From Small Beginnings

Reading my materials, there are five events that I would like to share, linking policies with subsequent performance, practice, action and reaction. Entry 1 reflects on my arrival and first few weeks in China. Entry 2 considers my first annual Learning and Teaching meeting with Chinese and international academic staff. Entry 3 details a formal meeting with the Ministry of Education and the Department of International Cooperation and Partnerships. Entry 4 relates an initial preparation meeting for a quality audit from the local municipal education department, which started in April 2017. The thread through these events was the government policy of 'Cultivation of Talent and the underlying Internationalisation agenda'. These policies created a series of actions and reactions within the College academic group, highlighting a range of hidden inequalities embedded within the College's small academic culture. The concluding Entry focuses on preparations to leave China and contains the conclusion, summary and recommendations.

12.2.1 Entry 1: Arrival in China

Arriving in China was a mind-blowing experience, the noise, the smells, the people all of it was deafening to all senses. Along the way, I had also accrued two new descriptions of myself. The first was a self-initiated expatriate (McNulty and Brewster 2017), defined as 'Legally working individuals who reside temporarily in a country of which they are not a citizen in order to accomplish a career-related goal, being relocated abroad either by an organisation, by self-initiation or directly employed within the host country' (McNulty and Brewster 2017, p. 21). The second was that of Foreign Expert/ Foreign Talent, these two phrases are interchangeable depending on which Ministerial Office is being dealt with. These terms did cause me difficulty, as I was neither an expert nor a talent according to the Oxford Dictionary definitions: Expert: Noun – A person who is very knowledgeable about or skilful in a particular area (oxforddictionaries.com). Talent: Noun – Natural aptitude or skill (oxforddictionaries.com). I am a 'non-standard academic' (Humphreys 2005), having spent 12 years in manufacturing and a similar number of years as a mother and part-time worker. As a late academic, I felt that I had to some extent developed my own academic identity, understood what I felt was important and had managed to overcome the 'imposter' syndrome that I experienced following the award of my PhD (Knights and Clarke 2014; Hutchins and Rainbolt 2017; Breeze 2007). However, I had never viewed myself as a 'Talent' or 'Expert'. In my diary, I noted 'so, not only am I a member of the College Senior Management Team, I am also an expert and a foreigner! Amazing what a trip across the world can do!' I just considered these bureaucratic terms as part of the immigration policy in China.

Within three weeks, I had an apartment, registered at the local police station, undergone my medical examination, acquired my 'Foreign Expert Certification' transferred my Z visa to a visa of residency. I had acquired a Chinese mobile phone, two Chinese bank accounts and managed to furnish my apartment, including the acquisition of a European mattress from Ikea. I enjoyed the daily life in China, sorted out Chinese lessons and looked forward to my new job. My role had College wide responsibility for academic quality of the UK degree courses and was threefold. The first was to embed a re-structure that occurred prior to my arrival. Second, to start off the process of developing a Higher Education culture of scholarship and research into an institution that ran a UK foundation degree and four separate undergraduate programmes from UK Universities. The third was to develop a coherent quality structure that fulfilled the requirements of all four Universities but gave the College its own Quality Assurance identity. I was very comfortable with these objectives. I had spent 12 years in manufacturing introducing cultural change and felt that my knowledge of UK Higher Education quality assurance systems was up to date following the writing and validation of several programmes, together with ensuring the quality of a range of international partnerships within Asia. The role and the challenges were exciting, and I could not wait to start, and was excited by the task.

At the time, I had not reflected fully on the effect of the titles, labels and names that I had acquired during my 6000-mile flight. Language is never neutral and there is always a surface and a socially embedded meaning to any word (Derrida 1976). Foucault (1979) defines statements such as 'Foreign Talent or Foreign Expert' as a discursive formation, embedded within the culture. They are statements that generate and to some extent demand particular actions from individuals in order for the individual to 'own' that statement. It also demands actions from others in terms of the cultural significance of the statement. From a reflexive position, I cannot help but wonder whether these labels not only affected me but also affected the actions and reactions of those around me. In China, titles and names are very important in the social hierarchical structure of the society at all levels. Names and titles provide the information required for social engagement and etiquette. Looking back, I should have recognised that the term was more than a bureaucratic convenience, that it did also have social meaning (Blum 1997; Edwards 2006; Scollon et al. 2011).

Recalling my frame of mind subsequent to receiving the title of Doctor, I felt a return of the 'imposter syndrome' (Knights and Clarke 2014; Hutchins and Rainbolt 2017; Breeze 2007), creating a feeling of low-level anxiety and uncertainty. This is one key area that can affect expatriate performance (Shaffer et al. 2006) and have a damaging effect on the ability to engage with cross-cultural adjustment and access cultural intelligence (Ramalu et al. 2012; Ang et al. 2006, 2007). There is a link between Foreign Expert and the government policy 'Cultivation of Talent' together with the underlying internationalisation policy. This is particularly relevant to the aspirations of achieving globally ranked universities (Deem et al. 2008). This policy also has a negative aspect, with Chinese academics concerned that the foreign interventions would result in the loss of academic and educational sovereignty (Qin 2014). This is an aspect I have only considered having returned to the UK and perhaps justified my feelings of anxiety at the time. It is not a cultural issue, as such, it is more of a 'small culture issue' (Moosa 2013) that of academia and in particularly the 'small culture' within the Sino-Foreign College.

The second point of consideration in relation to the title Foreign Expert was the fact that I had the money to acquire a two-bedroom apartment in a downtown area of a Tier 1 city. I had the money to purchase a mobile phone, a European mattress and all the other items that I needed to feel comfortable. In other words, I had everything I needed from international health care to a lovely apartment enabling a rapid psychological adjustment to the new culture (Ramalu et al. 2012). This is one of the advantages of being a Foreign Expert; the pay was substantially more than a Chinese National (Caligiuri and Bonache 2016; Wang and Varma 2017), together with a range of additional tax benefits. I also remember talking to a Chinese colleague about it and feeling the need to justifying it.

It was easy to justify, back in the UK, there are things like mortgages to repay, pension funds to pay into, and the salary to some extent compensates for lost academic opportunities, for example, access to all the high-quality resources we have in a UK institution, the opportunities to apply for and receive grants and the time to write papers for publishing. However, Koh (2003) does offer an alternative idea, suggesting it comes down to who is grateful to whom. I suppose it is a mutual gratitude. I was very pleased and grateful for having the opportunity to go and work in this particular institution. The more problematic question was 'were they grateful to have me, or did my Chinese colleagues perceive me as a threat to their academic sovereignty due to my role and brief?' My second reflexive question concerns gratitude to the government and the Ministry of Education. Should I have in some way demonstrated gratitude to the government for the privileged position I held? I will return to these two initial questions as the answers become clearer.

12.2.2 Entry 2: The First Learning and Teaching Meeting—January

My Chinese counterpart, who had overview of the Chinese arrangements at the College, arranged a meeting with one day's notice. My initial reaction was annoyance. I had planned meetings with some of the academic staff for that day, duly logged in my outlook calendar together with meeting requests and an agenda. That evening I wrote in my diary, 'really... no notice, no agenda, and no papers for discussion...how do I prepare...why only 1 days' notice???' I later found out it was a regular annual meeting with Chinese colleagues to discuss the forthcoming year. The meeting was about four hours and the agenda and any papers made available at the meeting. If anything, I was more annoyed as it was my first major meeting with Chinese colleagues and I could not prepare. However, I also thought it would give me the opportunity to start networks with our Chinese counterparts and to find out a bit more about the quality assurance processes at the College and within the Chinese University. At this meeting the College team was informed of the introduction of a new module to demonstrate entrepreneurial and innovative activities.

The one thing I had so far identified within the College was the large workload that students had. Although students completed a foundation course which included English Language courses. These courses were designed for students moving to an English-speaking environment for the second and subsequent years. Our students, however, continued their studies in English within China, so did not have the benefit of an immersive language experience. They also had to complete a series of Chinese modules in order to graduate. I voiced my concerns about workload and the possibility that this could be detrimental to the grades reached by students in their UK degrees. A colleague pointed out that across all the courses we ran, creativity, innovation and entrepreneurship were embedded within key modules. After discussion, it was agreed that we would develop a table demonstrating the embedded nature of these activities and that the Chinese QA would check whether that was fulfilling their module requirements. In a discussion, it was also mentioned that it might be productive to introduce a student portfolio of their educational journey that could also include engagement with the activities mentioned. There the conversation was left. I felt that I was in control of the situation, gained confidence from the support from the UK staff and the acknowledgment from Chinese colleagues and a way forward to mitigate the additional module. In my diary, I wrote 'All good, the end of a long but productive meeting'.

I also put a note into my outlook calendar for December 2017 to check out when the annual meeting was going to be and to ensure the UK voice within the meeting. The Heads of School duly completed the mapping exercise and it was submitted to the University. Job Done! I decided that over the course of my duties I would gradually introduce a system of using outlook-meeting invitations and start to create an academic meetings calendar where meetings of a reoccurring nature could be set in advance and logged into diaries as would happen in a UK institution. Lead by example! Bachelor.

From a reflexive perspective, I realise there were several opportunities here for me to engage with difference and diversity and engage with learning (Suransky and Alma 2018). The first was around the setting of meetings. It did not occur to me that there might be cultural significance in the way meetings were organised, and I should have taken the time out to understand from a cultural perspective what was happening and why. Instead, I considered that there is only one acceptable set of academic and ethical values attached to this situation (Qin 2014; Wilkins 2017). I was viewing the setting of meetings from an individualistic perspective; everyone's time is important and therefore planning for regular meetings should take place out of respect. What I did not appreciate was that within that University there was a meeting each week with the Chinese management team to set meetings for the following week. However, the discovery of this knowledge creates further reflexivity. Why were my colleagues and myself excluded from this planning meeting?

I felt at the time it was about power and it felt that I was losing a power struggle. It felt as if my time and therefore I was not important. However, if I focus on policies rather than feelings, a different view comes into focus, one that is more in line with Suransky and Alma's (2018) suggestion that learning is only possible in tension. The aim is not to fully integrate or assimilate differences but to engage in dialogue. This is because actions and motives require, but do not always receive, 'a patient effort of interpretation' (Nussbaum 1997, p. 63). The development of networks both socially and in the workplace is important in helping with cultural adjustment and developing trust (Wang and Varma 2017). The weekly planning meeting in the main University campus would have been an ideal opportunity to start this process. However, this never transpired. My main question is why? There seemed to be a roadblock between myself and my Chinese counterpart, and I was increasingly uncertain as to how this dynamic could be changed. As each week went by, the opportunities to build trust and develop reciprocity between us, an important part of cultural integration, moved further out of reach. Unfortunately, it was going to be several months before the reason behind this inability to build a relationship became clearer.

12.2.3   Entry 3: The Meeting—March

The inability to understand the exclusion I felt left me feeling at odds with the academic world I found myself in. This feeling continued into a meeting that was held with the local municipal Department of Education, the Ministry of Education and the Department of International Cooperation and Exchanges. It was a very formal meeting; participants were sat in a very specific order, according to ranking (or perhaps perceived ranking). Prior to the meeting, however, some really engaging informal conversations took place in English, giving an insight into the political world of academia, not much different to the UK, expect I probably will never get the opportunity of having an informal conversation with the Minister for Education! What surprised me was that the formal event took place in Chinese. This meant that all the English-speaking participants had to have an interpreter whispering the translation.

However, the most important message of the meeting was delivered in English. We were told in no uncertain terms that the internationalisation agenda was a top priority for all Higher Education institutions. Bringing international students into the classroom and developing academic relationships and programme provision with the top-ranking Universities in the UK was our main purpose. In my journal I noted that this was not something we had succeeded in. It was a difficult situation. Until we gained the trust of the UK Universities in terms of quality assurance and delivered top performances from students, it would be difficult to engage with the top universities in the

UK. In my diary, I noted that the term 'Foreign Expert' could be viewed as a Utility term, one which could provide a distinct service and then disposed of, either after delivering the service or not being able to deliver that service.

Looking back on this meeting, from a safe distance of several thousand miles, I can identify a range of hidden inequalities beginning to materialise. There seemed to be a connection between names and titles, the notion of Face, *Guanxi* and the use of language. The first comes down to the importance of names and titles in China and a connection with the notion of Face and *Guanxi* (Blum 1997; Fang and Faure 2011; Li et al. 2016). Face concerns the desire to present a positive image of one's self or to confirm a positive image of another in a social interaction. *Guanxi* refers to the use of networks and connections to secure favours and to gain competitive advantage (Li et al. 2016).

I can understand the pragmatic logic at work. My colleagues and I on the UK management team were employed as foreign academic experts. From the University perspective, the Sino-Foreign College was a perfect vehicle for bringing in International students and providing programmes from top UK Institutions. Logically, through Guanxi, we were in a perfect position to leverage contacts in the UK and enable the Chinese University to fulfil its obligations within the Internationalisation agenda. Having not delivered that requirement, irrespective of the time frame, did we deserve the title of 'Foreign Expert'? Secondly, could it possibly be that my Chinese colleague felt that I was being ungrateful for not employing my Guanxi in order to help the University in their obligations. Or worse, was I deliberately engineering a position where 'Face' was being lost by my colleague because I had made no commitment to deliver 'top UK University programmes or international students' to the University. Was the use of Chinese in the meeting, rather than a mixture of Chinese and English which was normally the case, a particular point being made?

Within this Higher Education context, a tension develops between internationalisation, world-class University status and the concern of losing academic sovereignty (Qin 2014). There is a complex interaction here between policy, that of internationalisation and the tensions inherent in China's wish to stand independently in the global academic world and us as the 'Experts' of internationalisation. This idea of the importance of academic sovereignty is recognisable in the structural charts of Sino-foreign collaborations. Although on the structural chart there was an equivalency between the UK senior management team members and the corresponding Chinese colleagues, this was not necessarily out of an understanding of mutual respect or true partnership. It was part of the Chinese legislation governing Sino-foreign collaborations. The principal position must also be a Chinese national (Qin 2014). So in effect, the Chinese colleagues were more senior. Over the last few years, this oversight has been intensified. Universities have set up Communist Party departments to oversee political teaching and thinking at University level (Times Higher Education 2017/8/30).

This emphasises the academic seniority of the Chinese colleagues with the Sino-foreign partnerships. Was the use of language in the high-level meeting an attempt to clarify that boundary? Even through this reflexive piece of work, I have not found an answer to this question; however, it brings into perspective the idea of cultural intelligence and cultural knowledge (Ang et al. 2006, 2007). From an academic perspective, I am a reasonably culturally aware person. I teach diversity and have always felt that I embrace diversity. One of the reasons I chose to work abroad was to learn more about living in a culturally different society. What happens though, when you are comfortable with the external realities, the day-to-day living in a different culture, but the 'small culture' of your workplace is suddenly going through a political change of emphasis? How do you catch up and understand the intricate details of what is changing when your language ability is limited?

12.2.4   Entry 4: Audit Preparation Meeting—April/May

Following the visit, strange things started to happen in the College, which were not reported in the Management meetings. The first was signage, all the signage in the campus was being changed from just English into Chinese Characters and English underneath. A whole floor was taken out of use and was 'refurbished' to create an Entrepreneurial, Innovation and Creative space. Teaching space had to be reallocated at short notice, it was hard to find out what was going on, Staff were confused and the UK management team were in the dark with no answers.

One morning, in amongst the chaos and confusion, a message came through that an important preliminary audit meeting was being held that afternoon. It was this first meeting and the subsequent workload that led me to understand more about the context in which I had been working. The meeting did bring lightness to the dark! The meeting was once again called at very short notice, being informed in the morning that the meeting was to take place in the afternoon. In my diary I had made no note of being annoyed, either there was too much else happening for me to find time to be annoyed, or I have acclimatised to the issue.

At the meeting, I learned that I had responsibility for six sections of the audit document. I was given a piece of paper written in Chinese with some handwritten annotations in English, giving titles of the various sections. The meeting was conducted in Chinese with only the sections relevant to me being translated. I could feel my anxiety rising as I did not understand the context of the audit or what the perimeters were. I was even confused about what I was supposed to write. When asking for a translation I was told there was no time in the group to translate the document and I would have to find a secretary to do it for me. This meant asking someone who could speak English well and was already overworked. I was also aware by this point at the very small salary that the administrative staff received.

In my reflections of this meeting I noted that I felt very uneasy about asking the academic administrators to translate the document at a time when the academic side was preparing for examination boards, but I needed to get the document translated. My 'Foreign Expert' title was in perspective; I certainly was no expert in Chinese. I was also informed that my writing had to be translated into Chinese before being submitted. The document was in total 10 chapters and I asked about word count and was told the document in total should be over 500 pages. Once the audit requirements document had been translated, I was actually more confused, probably because I did not understand the context. The first heading was 'The Cultivation of Talent'. I asked my international colleagues if they knew what this meant, and how to write about it within what was happening in the College. There was no answer, the Chinese academic staff were also unsure. Therefore, I started to research.

My Chinese counterpart had responsibility for the audit. I thought this might be an opportunity to shift the dynamics between us. It was also an area that I had experience of in the UK. I completed the document ahead of schedule, in spite of the problems with translation. I had added photographs, which my Chinese counterpart loved. It was not long before other colleagues were taking photographs to add to their sections of the report. However, to this day I have no idea what the final version of the report said. I requested a copy, now in Chinese with no English translation. I could not guarantee that what I had written was in the report following the review process. I asked for a track-changed Chinese version, but that was unavailable. It was a difficult position and quite worrying. If I continued to challenge, I would be seen as causing my colleague to lose 'face' (Scollon et al. 2011; Hwang 1987). My feelings of anxiety were rapidly increasing, my Chinese was developing slowly but not of a quality to undertake such complex communication. Overall, I felt that something was happening within the cultural context that I was operating but which I did not understand.

From a reflexive process, so much has become clearer. The meeting that happened in January laid the ground for some of the challenges I was facing in what appeared to be a rapidly changing cultural context. My research for the audit paper revealed a primary objective of the Chinese Education system and the relationship with the meeting in January. I discovered an academic tension between cultivating innovative and creative talent and the conflict this creates. There is recognition that thinking is normalised and that knowledge is non-dynamic within the Chinese system (Xiao-dong 2004) and the need to produce a generation of students who can 'think outside the box'. There were also papers from Chinese Universities commenting on the changes needed to UK curriculums in some subject areas to cover the 'Cultivation of Talent' agenda (Yuqi 2006), implying that the UK Higher Education system also needs amendment. This coincides with the discourse of academic sovereignty and almost a battle for which is correct.

I mentioned earlier about the setting up of Party Offices in Universities to oversee the curriculum teaching, and the tension between creativity and innovation and control of education becomes clearer. My whole perspective of what was happening and how this particular policy of Cultivation of Talent, which encompasses internationalisation, had set up a chain of actions and reactions since the start of the year had changed. These were heavy issues to be negotiated through, when the responsibility for UK academic quality standards is an ultimate performance measure.

Language is all-powerful, and in the main, in a professional environment, it is usually a hidden inequality, as people patiently try to understand each other. However, looking back at Entry 3 and now considering this chapter, there appears to be an escalation in the negative use of language, almost a micro-aggressive act of power (Misiaszek 2018). The use of Chinese and the need to engage in multiple translations in an environment that was short of those skills created additional pressure and feelings of worthlessness. The pay discrepancy exacerbated the situation questioning the term 'Foreign Expert' and bringing my worthiness of the title into question. My failure was not appreciating that along with a very different social culture there was also a very different academic culture, which was in itself changing rapidly. This appeared to leave less space within the institution for the two cultures to merge into a peaceful harmony.

The policy of Cultivation of Talent also links back to Entry 2 and the Learning and Teaching meeting. In retrospect, I had created a situation where my Chinese counterpart had lost 'face' (Blum 1997; Li et al. 2016). The meeting was a 'community and institutional' event. In this particular circumstance, my Chinese counterpart had put forward a University-level agreed solution to implement the government policy of developing innovation and creativity, a new module that demonstrated requirements. My comments had disrespected my colleague, by pointing out the issues students were facing. It could also be viewed as disrespecting the larger University community, who had quality assured the module, a lack of giving Face at an institutional level (Fang and Faure 2011). Although from my perspective, not realising the context, I had treated the recommendation of including the module as a proposal rather than as an action. If the wider context were clearer, the negotiations over the issue would have been different (Nussbaum 1997).

12.3   From Small Beginnings Come Bigger Endings, or Not...

The final chapter, how does it all end? Come September I had to decide whether to renew my residency permit. There was a part of me that really did not want to fail. It was a pride thing more than anything was. It meant having to tell people that I was coming home. I did not want to disappoint my family or my friends, all of whom had given so much support and encouragement. I started the new semester, did the large introductory lecture to seven hundred and fifty students. After the lecture, based on Avatar, I received a round of applause, which is always lovely and students coming up to talk to me. One of our new colleagues was not able to start at the beginning of the term, so I took over the teaching. I really enjoyed being back in the classroom. It always reminds one of what is important about academia as a career. It is the engagement of the students. However, from a management perspective, many things were rapidly changing within the College, all driven by the external political process, very similar to what had also happened in UK Higher Education. Eventually, I decided not to renew my visa and handed in my letter of resignation. I genuinely felt that I was unable to perform my role and that I was creating anxiety within myself and not enjoying my job because of it. The day I handed in my notice, I felt a massive burden falling away from my shoulders. I started the planning for repatriation, whilst hoping that I would find a job somewhere. In my diary, I wrote.... I am relieved! The final chapter, how does it all end?

Within this entry, the consequences of hidden inequalities become clear, that of my decision not to renew my visa. From current research, anxiety, inability to adjust and not developing networks are the key reasons for expatriation failure (Liu and Shaffer 2005; Ramalu et al. 2012; Tharenou and Caulfield 2010). However, my reflections generated a series of questions, which form three distinct, but related areas of learning. The first is concerned with the use of titles and names, and the cultural expectations of those designations. The second is the lived experience of dealing with cultural concepts such as 'Face' and 'Guanxi' and, finally, specifically understanding intricacies of change in 'small cultures' (Moosa 2013).

The most obvious is one of language, creating an unequal power dynamic between my Chinese colleague and myself. However, there were deeper cultural issues possibly at work, which revealed hidden inequalities. The micro-aggressive use of language in meetings may have been an outward demonstration of the term 'Foreign Expert'. Initially, it exposed my rudimentary grasp of Chinese and the fact that I needed people who could translate orally and in written form. This would be a demonstration of my right to such a title and the government rewards that went with it. The government-imposed use of a 'Foreign Expert' created a tension with the academia perspective of academic sovereignty. This was demonstrated through the introduction of new signage in Chinese, the appropriation of teaching space with no discussion and the remodelling of the teaching building with little UK management input.

Secondly, having understood the concept of 'Face' and 'Guanxi' from an academic perspective, I learnt that the lived application is very different and much more subtle. If briefed on government policy with regard to innovation and creativity prior to the first meeting in Entry 2, I would have been able to consider the action and patiently translate the action being taken and why (Nussbaum 1997) rather than putting myself in a position of not building a colleague's position. This is a hidden inequality, although a theoretical knowledge is good, understanding it from a lived perspective is painful and can have lasting consequences. From a cultural perspective, I did not deliver the University's expectation of *Guanxi*, in terms of bringing top-rated UK Universities to the College. It could be that the senior Chinese management team did interpret this as not showing Face to either the University or government. In other words I had not demonstrated gratitude for the position (Koh 2003).

Alternatively, was it actually more to do with being in the wrong place at the wrong time? Issues with Chinese academic sovereignty and Chinese control continue to be reported in the newspapers, and the tension between innovation and creativity and of academic control was being played out in the 'small culture' of the College. This is evidenced by the changing of signs, the more prominent use of Chinese in meetings and the changing use of classrooms with no discussion. These are signs of changing academic dominance in an environment based on UK academic culture. However, without a guide, someone to help untangle what is the norm for Chinese culture generally and what is specifically to do with the 'small culture' of this particular College and University does create its own inequalities in terms of how to respond to situations.

Ultimately, I think, from a personal perspective, that the biggest hidden inequality is in the title of Foreign Expert and the privileges and expectations that surround it. As an expatriate one does not necessarily see oneself as an expert, the main reasons are to learn from the inside about another culture, to have the opportunity of really experiencing that culture. Fang and Faure (2011) suggested that if you travel to China for two weeks, you feel as if you could write a book, if you go for six months, you feel you could write a journal article, if you stay for longer, you realise how little you know. Although there is much research on cultural intelligence and the ability to be culturally adaptive (Ang et al. 2006, 2007), it would seem this starts to develop when learning takes place in an arena that is culturally changing (Suransky and Alma 2018) and you then reflect on the experience as suggested by Ng and Earley (2006).

One of the fundamental resources that I have identified for an expatriate working abroad is the importance of a Home Country National (HCN) to help with building networks, understanding the context, understanding how to develop trust with colleagues and helping when there are limited resources (e.g. translating). The building of networks is important in the first instance when trying to gather information, access and make best use of resources available and with making sense overall of the situation (Liu and Shaffer 2005; Wang and Varma 2017). Expatriate support can help in spanning boundaries with other networks of expatriates and nationals to develop social networks (Liu and Shaffer 2005), but HCNs are essential in building internal networks. The tension here is the issues with disparity in pay and conditions between the expatriate and HCN and how the 'Expert' can reciprocate (Uhl-Bien 2000). I believe that probably the reciprocity may be in giving due respect and enhancing 'Face' in terms of the HCN's multicultural understanding and experience.

References

Alvesson, M., and H. Willmott. 2003. *Studying management critically*. London: Sage Publications.

Ang, S., L. Van Dyne, and C. Koh. 2006. Personality correlates of the four-factor model of cultural intelligence. *Group and Organization Management* 31: 100–123.

Ang, S., L. Van Dyne, C. Koh, K. Yee Ng, K. Templer, C. Tay, and N. Chandrasekar. 2007. Cultural intelligence: Its measurement and effects on cultural judgment and decision making, cultural adaptation and task performance. *Management and Organization Review* 3: 335–371.

Barthes, R. 1983. *The fashion system*. Berkeley: University of California Press.

Blum, S.D. 1997. Naming practices and the power of words in China. *Language in Society* 26: 357–379.

Breeze, R. 2007. How personal is this text? Researching writer and reader presence in student writing using Wordsmith Tools. *CORELL: Computer Resources for Language Learning* 1: 14–21.

Buzard, J. 2003. On auto-ethnographic authority. *The Yale Journal of Criticism* 16: 61–91.

Caligiuri, P., and J. Bonache. 2016. Evolving and enduring challenges in global mobility. *Journal of World Business* 51: 127–141.

Deem, R., K. Ho Mok, and L. Lucas. 2008. Transforming higher education in whose image? Exploring the concept of the 'world-class' university in Europe and Asia. *Higher Education Policy* 21: 83–97.

Denzin, N.K. 2000. Aesthetics and the practices of qualitative inquiry. *Qualitative Inquiry* 6: 256–265.

Derrida, J. 1976. *Of grammatology*. Baltimore: Johns Hopkins University Press.

Edwards, R. 2006. What's in a name? Chinese learners and the practice of adopting 'English' names. *Language, Culture and Curriculum* 19: 90–103.

Ellis, C.S., and A.P. Bochner. 2006. Analyzing analytic autoethnography: An autopsy. *Journal of Contemporary Ethnography* 35: 429–449.

Fang, T., and G. Faure. 2011. Chinese communication characteristics: A Yin Yang perspective. *International Journal of Intercultural Relations* 35: 320–333.

Foucault, M. 1977. *Discipline and punish*. Trans. Alan Sheridan. New York: Vintage, 1979.

Gant, V. 2017. 'Reflections on a birthday': An auto-ethnographic account of caring for a child with a learning disability. *Qualitative Social Work* 16: 734–741.

Humphreys, M. 2005. Getting personal: Reflexivity and autoethnographic vignettes. *Qualitative Inquiry* 11: 840–860.

Humphreys, M., and T.J. Watson. 2009. Ethnographic practices: From 'writing-up ethnographic research' to 'writing ethnography'. In *Organizational ethnography: Studying the complexities of everyday life*, ed. S. Ybema, D. Yanow, H. Wels, and F. Kamsteeg, 40–55. London: Sage Publications.

Hutchins, H.M., and H. Rainbolt. 2017. What triggers imposter phenomenon among academic faculty? A critical incident study exploring antecedents, coping, and development opportunities. *Human Resource Development International* 20: 194–214.

Hwang, K.-K. 1987. Face and favor: The Chinese power game. *American Journal of Sociology* 94: 944–974.

Johnson, P., and J. Duberley. 2003. Reflexivity in management research. *Journal of Management Studies* 40: 1279–1303.

Knights, D., and C.A. Clarke. 2014. It's a bittersweet symphony, this life: Fragile academic selves and insecure identities at work. *Organization Studies* 35: 335–357.

Koh, A. 2003. Global flows of foreign talent: Identity anxieties in Singapore's ethnoscape. *SOJOURN: Journal of Social Issues in Southeast Asia* 18: 230–256.

Li, M., S.C. Qiu, and Z. Liu. 2016. The Chinese way of response to hospitality service failure: The effects of face and guanxi. *International Journal of Hospitality Management* 57: 18–29.

Liu, X., and M. Shaffer. 2005. An investigation of expatriate adjustment and performance: A social capital perspective. *International Journal of Cross Cultural Management* 5: 235–254.

Mao, J., and Y. Shen. 2015. Cultural identity change in expatriates: A social network perspective. *Human Relations* 68: 1533–1556.

McIlveen, P. 2008. Autoethnography as a method for reflexive research and practice in vocational psychology. *Australian Journal of Career Development* 17: 13–20.

McNulty, Y., and C. Brewster. 2017. Theorizing the meaning(s) of 'expatriate': Establishing boundary conditions for business expatriates. *The International Journal of Human Resource Management* 28: 27–61.

Misiaszek, L.I. 2018. *China with 'foreign talent' characteristics: A 'guerrilla' auto-ethnography of performing 'foreign talentness' in a Chinese university*, Feeling academic in the neoliberal university. Cham: Palgrave Macmillan.

Moosa, D. 2013. Challenges to anonymity and representation in educational qualitative research in a small community: A reflection on my research journey. *Compare: A Journal of Comparative and International Education* 43: 483–495.

Ng, K.-Y., and P.C. Earley. 2006. Culture+ intelligence: Old constructs, new frontiers. *Group and Organization Management* 31: 4–19.

Nussbaum, M.C. 1997. Kant and stoic cosmopolitanism. *Journal of Political Philosophy* 5: 1–25.

Qin, Y. 2014. Continuity through change: Background knowledge and China's international strategy. *The Chinese Journal of International Politics* 7: 285–314.

Ramalu, S., R. Rose, J. Uli, and N. Kumar. 2012. Cultural intelligence and expatriate performance in global assignment: The mediating role of adjustment. *International Journal of Business and Society* 13: 1–19.

Schembri, Sh., and M.V. Boyle. 2013. Visual ethnography: Achieving rigorous and authentic interpretations. *Journal of Business Research* 66: 1251–1254.

Scollon, R., R.W. Scollon, and R.H. Jones. 2011. *Intercultural communication: A discourse approach.* London: Wiley.

Shaffer, M.A., D.A. Harrison, H. Gregersen, J. Black, and L. Ferzandi. 2006. You can take it with you: Individual differences and expatriate effectiveness. *Journal of Applied Psychology* 91 (1): 109.

Southgate, B. 2003. *Postmodernism in history: Fear or freedom?* London: Routledge.

Sumara, D.J., and R. Luce-Kapler. 1993. Action research as a writerly text: Locating co-labouring in collaboration. *Educational Action Research* 1: 387–395.

Suransky, C., and H. Alma. 2018. An agonistic model of dialogue. *Journal of Constructivist Psychology* 31: 22–38.

Tharenou, Ph., and N. Caulfield. 2010. Will I stay or will I go? Explaining repatriation by self-initiated expatriates. *Academy of Management Journal* 53: 1009–1028.

Thrift, N. 2008. *Non-representational theory: Space, politics, affect.* London: Routledge.

Tosh, J. 2013. *The pursuit of history.* London: Routledge.

Uhl-Bien, M., G.B. Graen, and T.A. Scandura. 2000. Implications of leader–member exchange (LMX) for strategic human resource management systems: Relationships as social capital for competitive advantage. In *Research in personnel and human resource management,* ed. G. Ferris. Greenwich: JAI Press.

Vickers, D. 2008. Beyond the hegemonic narrative – A study of managers. *Journal of Organizational Change Management* 21: 560–573.

Wang, C.-H., and A. Varma. 2017. Cultural distance and expatriate failure rates: The moderating role of expatriate management practices. *The International Journal of Human Resource Management* 12: 1–20.

Weick, K.E. 1995. *Sensemaking in organizations.* London: SAGE.

Wilkins, S. 2017. Ethical issues in transnational higher education: The case of international branch campuses. *Studies in Higher Education* 42: 1385–1400.

Wolcott, H.T. 2009. *Ethnography: A way of seeing.* 2nd ed. Oxford: AltaMira Press.

Xiao-dong, Y.U. 2004. Enhancing university students' creativity: Reflection and suggestions. *Journal of Higher Education* 1: 018.

Yuqi, Z. 2006. On the reform of English major curriculum design and creative talents' cultivation model. *Foreign Languages and Their Teaching* 8: 008.

Index

© The Author(s) 2019
S. Nachmias, V. Caven (eds.), *Inequality and Organizational Practice*, Palgrave Explorations in Workplace Stigma, https://doi.org/10.1007/978-3-030-11647-7

Printed by Printforce, the Netherlands